Orston

A NOTTINGHAMSHIRE VILLAGE THROUGH THE CENTURIES

Written by

Paul Barnes

Second Edition Published in Great Britain in 2008 by TUCANNbooks

First Published in Great Britain in 1995 by Barny Books

ISBN 978-1-873257-88-3

Produced by: TUCANNdesign&print, 19 High Street, Heighington, Lincoln LN4 1RG
Tel & Fax: 01522 790009 • www.tucann.co.uk

Dedication

In memory of old Orstonians.

The author

Paul Barnes, Ph.D., has lived for about half of his life in Orston. He has an M.A. in Local and Regional History and has published various articles on the industrial and agricultural history of Orston. See www.paulbarnes.org.uk

Thanks

The book benefits hugely from the humour and insights of Brian Gunn and Brian Harrison who have written chapters. Various other people have contributed sections of chapters for which I am very grateful and their names appear in the chapters where appropriate. A feature of the book is the photos. For these, an enormous thank you must go to John Billot for all his work and patience. I would also particularly like to thank Rosemary Ruck for her efforts on a 1603 document originally written in Latin. She spent many days transcribing and translating it, only for us to discover that it had little relevance to this book. Such is the lot of the local historian!

The publication of the second edition of this book was made possible by the enormous efforts of many villagers. I would particularly like to thank Jean Smeeton, Sue Barnes and Barry Gibson for their considerable help in various ways. Last, and certainly not least, the book and photographs could not have come to press without a lot of organisation. For this we have to thank Gill and Ian Smellie, together with the help of Anne Johnson and Fiona Winfield.

From L to R: Gill Smellie, John Billot and Paul Barnes

The cover photograph is of The Green, circa 1900

CONTENTS

1. In and around Orston 6

2. Orston house names 18

3. The development of the village through the study of maps 23

4. Origins 28

5. Early days 30

6. The River Smite 32

7. The manor and manor house 35

8. Open field farming 38

9. The manor court 44

10. The provision of a wife's livelihood 46

11. Enclosure of the open fields and afterwards 48

12. Inventories 51

13. The beginnings of modern day farming 53

14. Population 57

15. The Industrial Revolution in Orston - gypsum mining 60

16. Religion 65

17. St Mary's Church 70

18. A seventeenth century ecclesiastical financial scandal 76

19. Orston Hall 77

20. Conduct and morality: the Archdeaconry Court and the criminal courts 81

21. Local Governance and the Poor Law 83

22. Education 87

23. Family connections 94

24. Changing occupations and trades over the last 150 years.................. 99

25. Industry and business in the 20th century.................. 103

26. Leisure.................. 107

27. The Orston song – 1950s 117

28. Sport.................. 121

29. Social satire, 1880 – 'Grand Exhibition of Burds and Hanimals at Horston'.................. 128

30. Life in Orston in 1900 131

31. Orston between the wars.................. 136

32. Orston during the last war.................. 145

33. Post War Orston 150

34. Orston in 1978.................. 158

35. The Pageant: Forty years old and still going 160

36. Orston today.................. 170

Church Street and the Durham Ox, circa 1900, with Chapel Sreet in the background

CHAPTER 1
IN AND AROUND ORSTON

A stroll around the village provides you with a considerable insight into Orston's history. Let us start at the north end of High Street and the footpath to Thoroton. In the first field you will see broken pieces of rock mainly on the left hand side as you walk towards Thoroton. The old maps show this to be the site of the original manor house and its many outbuildings. It has been claimed, although there is no historical evidence, that the house was built with the stone from a castle previously on the site. Around 1840 the manor house was demolished and Manor Farm was built at the opposite end of the village in its place. What happened to the stone that does not lie in this field? Perhaps some of it was used to build the stone walls in High Street and even around the Church.

Passing down High Street, we approach the Church (this is discussed in Chapter 17) and, what was, the Vicarage (despite its strange architecture, this is not old, being a rebuild in 1849 of an earlier vicarage on the same site) on the left and the Rectory, that is now called Orston Hall on the right. The Church, including these buildings, was given to the Dean and Chapter of Lincoln. Lincoln, as rector, was entitled to ten per cent of all income of the village inhabitants. As Orston was an agricultural community, this was given as produce and stored in a Tithe Barn. This survives, and is the large farm building in the Hall grounds on High Street. The rector employed a vicar who lived opposite. His income would have been substantial and he usually employed a curate who lived in a more humble house elsewhere in the village. For most of their history, the manor house and rectory were not occupied by their owners but leased. Which of the two lessees was "squire" of the village? (The squire was simply the "top" man). The evidence for the seventeenth century onwards that I have suggests that it was the occupier of the rectory.

Esdaile's Rutland Monuments 1845

Orston

Orston, Nottinghamshire, is two miles and a half west of Bottesford; the name is probably Danish, from the Danish god Thor. Earl Manvers is lord of the manor, who is descended from the Dukes of Kingston. There is a celebrated spa in this parish, and land left by some benevolent person to keep it in repair. This water is said to intoxicate, by reason of the great quantity of air contained in it.

The church is very ancient; one monument in the chancel claims particular notice, it is of freestone, for a lady who is finely attired. On the right shoulder are the arms of the de Roos family, and on the left those of her husband no doubt. The manor of Orston belonged to Isabella de Roos, heiress of the House of Albini, in 1300; this must be for a daughter of a de Lord de Roos, who has had the manor as her fortune, and carried it into another family, and she has been buried there. The costume of the work of the canopy around the head is about the time of Henry IV. Tradition says there was a Castle where the late Manor House stood, which might be a family residence. In the Chancel floor is a large slab with a flowered cross in the middle, bearing the date 1400; against the wall is a handsome marble slab for J.F. Middlemore, Esq., who resided at the Hall; he was a Banker at Nottingham, and died after an illness of thirty hours. This parish is about equally divided between arable and pasture land. There is about 350 Inhabitants.

A village's main street would normally be called High Street. With the manor house at one end and the church, rectory and vicarage at the other, it must surely have been. Today, it is somewhat on the edge of the village suggesting a shift to the south and east. The main farming effort would have been in the open fields on the south and east; the meadow land, requiring less attention, was alongside the River Smite on the west. It seems reasonable to believe a tendency for the villagers to build their houses nearer to their work and away from the River Smite which was prone to flooding.

The Spa

Opposite the Vicarage and Orston Hall is a small wood known as the Plantation. The land here is lower as the result of being dug for clay and, until the 1950s, a small brick works was on the site at the back of the Chapel Street council houses. The adjoining field was called Brickyard Close in the 1793 Enclosure Award. It was usual for a village with its own supply of clay to make its own bricks.

Turning right at the bottom of High Street down Smite Lane, in the centre of the field on the right (Holme Field) is the village well. It was written into the deeds of this land that villagers had a right of passage across it to collect drinking water. Mrs Abrams (who has recently died) remembered carrying water from it using the traditional means: a yoke. The well is still there. You will see in the fields on both sides of the road the original course of the River Smite.

On the left side of the road is a wood in which there are two fish ponds used for the Hall. The field behind the wood is known as The Park. This may have ancient origins as the shape of the wood where it adjoins The Park is very similar to those surrounding medieval parks which appear throughout the country that were kept for the use of the King and his officers.

In front of the church is the present village green. It is so small that it goes almost without being noticed because of its size - as do many in the area. Nevertheless, in earlier times it was larger extending over the area known as the Plantation and down to the Pinfold on Chapel Street. There were two pinfolds, although they may not have been in use at the same time. One was on the west side of High Street near Orchard House. The other, which was demolished in the 1950s, was in Chapel Street at the end of the council houses.

There were two public houses in Orston until the early 20th century. What is now known as the Durham

Ox on Church Street was originally called the Royal Oak. It took that name when the original Durham Ox located at, what is now known as Church Side Farm on Launder Street, closed. Church Street was known as Norton Street in the 19th century.

At the bottom of Chapel Street opposite the chapel is a most intriguing earthwork feature. As this field has never been ploughed, it is possible to see that the land is levelled and around it there are clearly banks and some pathways. This may have been a water meadow. (A water meadow is a piece of land which is flooded early in the year so as to produce the earliest hay). If this were the case, the Smite, upstream towards Aslockton where the dyke known as Bon Moor Drain connects, would have been dammed to push water down the dyke to the meadow. (See the maps in Chapter 3). Water meadows are common in the West Country but are relatively rare in the East Midlands. Another possible explanation is that it was a further area associated with the brick works mentioned earlier.

Orston is famous for gypsum mining (see Chapter 15) and some of the diggings near to, or in the village, are ancient. These are mainly in the area between Church Street and Mill Lane. There the land is undulated. This area was common land and part of Lougbon Common where any inhabitant would have been able to dig up a piece of gypsum to make plaster. The more modern gypsum workings are on the south side of Loughbon and near the railway line down Pit Lane.

Half way along Loughbon at The Old Blacksmith's is (one of the few house names in Orston that correctly describes its past use), what was until recently, the village smithy. At the junction of Loughbon and Mill Lane and set back from the road is the one remaining dovecote. As with many farm buildings in Orston, it has been converted into a house. Dovecotes were built to house pigeons providing a little variation in the winter diet for their owners. The Lord of the Manor was usually the only one to own a dovecote but there was nothing to prevent others from having birds roosting in their barns. (This is the explanation for the rows of small holes in the gables of some old barns). There were other dovecotes in Orston but these have long since been demolished. One was at the bottom of the hill as part of Manor Farm, another was in Lombard Street and another near Orston Hall. It may be because of the relative weakness and absence of the Lord of the Manor that there were so many in Orston.

Turning left at the end of Loughbon, about half a mile down Mill Lane, on the highest piece of ground of course, is the site of the village windmill. (See Chapter25).

Just before the football and cricket ground (and what were the tennis courts) is the site of the spa. Reference to it is quite early (*1769, Description of England*)

> *At Orston is a mineral water which as it rises out of the spring, has a sweet chalybete, and a little roughish taste; but when it has stood for sometime it becomes harsh. With the addition of a little predominating salt of a calcareous nitre it will purge those of a Gross Habit of Body, and turn the throat and tongue of its Drinker perfectly Black. It is good in the Hypochrondiac Melancholy, Scurvy, want of Appetite, Costiveness, Stoppage of the urine, Obstruction of the Bowels, Ulcers in the Lungs, Indigestion, Pain in the Stomach, and to aid the Vaporous Debility of Ladies.*

However, there is no evidence to suggest that it was either famous or popular. With the opening up of the countryside by the railways in the mid-nineteenth century, many villages with railway access attempted to promote their spas in an attempt to encourage visitors. In an extensive and authoritative catalogue of them, which ran into two volumes, made at the height of this craze, A.B. Granville, in *Spas of England*, failed to give Orston a mention. Similarly, in the nineteenth century guides to the county of Nottinghamshire, it received minimal attention.

The right hand turn at the end of Loughbon leads to Lombard Street, an area of the village known as the City and Pit Lane. Halfway down Lombard Street on the right hand side just before Willow Cottage (formerly Berken) is an old narrow barn running at right angles to the road. This was a maltings, for a long time probably owned by the Maltby family living in Yew Tree Farm nearby. (See William Maltby's inventory in Chapter 12). It is interesting to speculate as to how good the beer that was brewed in Orston was; there is no evidence. It is well known that gypsum water provides particularly good beer and it is possible that, even though most beer was brewed locally until the nineteenth century, Orston beer may have been sold to villages nearby.

Lombard Street peters out into an unmade public road known as Pit Lane. It is interesting to think of how little more than one hundred years ago that this was the principal road to one of the largest gypsum mines and plaster manufacturers in the East Midlands. (See Chapter 15).

Rather than turning right to go down Lombard Street but taking the left fork up the hill there are two interesting buildings at the top. The first on the left is Manor Farm. The farm house is a particularly imposing building, no doubt built to be so as it was to replace the manor house, and to be seen from any point in the parish. The other is the new mill which has now been converted into houses. Built around 1920, it was a mechanised mill which made animal food and has been the single largest employer for most of this century. The daunting house next to it was that of the mill's owner, of course.

The layout of Orston today gives very little indication of how it was in the past, even the recent past. For example, in the late nineteenth century there was much terraced housing built for agricultural and gypsum workers, often referred to as Rows. Some of this was in Chapel Street near the Chapel and known as New Row. These have now been demolished and replaced by modern houses, now known as Chapel Garth. Although little now remains, terraced housing was also along The Row, hence the name, which is now merely a track off Lombard Street.

Between the modern houses and barn conversions and actually within others are many houses dating back to the nineteenth century and beyond. In fact most of the houses on Chapel Street, and many on Church Street, the south side of Loughbon and Lombard Street date from the mid nineteenth century, even though, of course, they have changed considerably. Those on Loughbon and Chapel Street were probably built on the sites of previous houses.

The Row, what is now Chapel Garth, circa 1950.

The changes are revealed by the brickwork. For example, in response to their owners' needs, the height of many was raised. The change in the colour of the brickwork gives this away. It is also interesting to see that some houses are built of very lightly coloured bricks. These bricks would have come from the brick and plaster works in either the centre of, or just outside, the village where the presence of gypsum lightened the colour of the brick.

Of course, at one time the houses would have been thatched. It is possible to tell from the gable ends of some of the houses, that this was so, e.g. 'The Gables' and 'Little Gables'. I suspect that with the increased supply of clay from the gypsum works in the second half of the nineteenth century, thatch was replaced by pantiles.

> *Orston, If we come from the hilltop we look down on its red roofs nestling in the trees. The low road, shaded by trees brings up to two bridges, spanning the River Smite and a brook. The prettiest corner is by the stone church.*
>
> *Nottinghamshire, by Arthur Mee, 1938*

In addition to the Church and the Hall, which are described later, there are seven listed buildings that would have been the homes of large farmers. These are:

The Woodlands – early 18th century and 20th century
The Chestnuts – late 17th century, mid 19th and late 19th century
The Gables – Hill Farm's farmhouse, late 17th century and early and mid 19th century
Scotney's Cottage, previously known as *Hamilton's Farmhouse* – late 17th century and late 19th century
Mulhouse, previously known as *The Ferns* – around 1785 and early and mid 19th century
Laburnum Cottage – circa 1800 and 20th century

Whilst the houses of yeomen are substantially built, the homes of peasants are not and are usually demolished. As a result, those dating from, say the 18th century, are rare and few are listed. In Orston there are none. However, Little Gables on the Row does provide an insight into what peasants' housing around 1800 looked like. Around that time, there was an initiative to build new houses for peasants on the outskirts of the village on common land. Orston is a classic example. A long row of houses was built on the Row (hence the name). Nothing now remains of these, other than Little Gables and Vale Cottage, but that has largely been rebuilt and extended. Next to these on Lombard Street, another row of houses was built. Sunrise Cottage and Muffins Gap remain but have been substantially rebuilt and extended to such an extent (especially the latter) as to bear no recognition to their original form.

It should not be thought that even Little Gables fully resembles what it was like originally. It was four small (minute by today's standards) one up - one down thatched houses. It was partly rebuilt in the late 1950s by the local conservative MP who lived there. Naturally, he required modern conveniences. (Margaret Thatcher was a friend and Enoch Powell stayed there). An outer layer of bricks was added (most would have been single brick if not mud) the ground floor lowered (19th century people were smaller) and it was, of course, rendered for a chocolate box effect.

Little Gables was originally four one-up, one-down terraced houses, part of The Row. The Row was built in 1800 for agricultural workers on common land and originally a row of about 16 one-up and-one down houses. In 1880 there were 45 people living here.

Outside Orston, are the industrial buildings, referred to as the Mushroom Farm (see Chapter 25) and, what were, two outlying farms, 'High Field Farm', whose name derives from the name of the open field in which it lies (see Chapter 8) and 'The Grange', meaning a farm on the outskirts of a parish. But more of house names in the next chapter.

The 'gingang' or 'ginny', at the head of Church Street and originally part of Dovecote Farm until recently demolished. This was a farm building that housed a wheel turned by an ox or horse which walked round and round to drive a threshing machine or chaff cutter. Until just before its demolition, most of the winding machinery was in place.

The Woodlands

Manor Farm, 1912.

Manfield House, now knownas The Gables, circa 1896.

Scotney's Cottage prior to restoration, circa 1988.

Old farmhouse on the site of White Acres, High Street, circa 1900.

The Chestnuts, Mill Lane

Tudor Cottage, Chapel Street, circa 1950

The Maltings, Lombard Street

View of Mill Lane from Staythorpe House, 1936, Mrs Edith Walker with her daughter Jean.

Dovecote at the foot of Orston hill, circa 1930

Churchside Farm, what was the Durham Ox, on Launder Street.

High Street, circa 1900.

What is now known as Poppy Cottage, Lombard Street, 1897, Frederick Walker with some of his children.

CHAPTER 2
ORSTON HOUSE NAMES

by Brian Harrison

At the junction of Mill Lane and Spa Lane stands Ridgeway so named for the ridges leading in two directions. Final Furlong is next. This could have some connection to horse racing. Laburnum Cottage is the first of many houses named after a tree that can be found in the garden. Waverley was named from the ridge and furrow in the adjacent fields. The Pebbles hints at the drive construction. Dovecote Cottage once had a cote for doves.

Looking down the length of Loughbon is The Chestnuts, our second tree related house. Wheelwrights Barn on the site of a workshop for a wheel man. Behind, is a house named Loughbon, a recent naming, not an inspired choice. Attached is Manor Farm Cottage once belonging to Manor Farm.

At the Lombard Street and Hill Road junction is Orston Village Hall, home of many diverse activities. The first house is Laneside beside the lane, QED. Scotneys' Cottage used to be owned by the Scotney family. Next door is Alnwick. Having bought the land, it had to have a title for registration purposes. The new owner, having connections with Alnwick, called it thus.

The first of four council-built houses, contains what remains of the stay at home Wakefields. Nos 2 and 3 follow before Landclose Cottage after the name of the field close to. By the footpath is Berken. *They* liked it so much, they used it twice. Last on the left is Long Acre named after the field of which it is part. A bit boring but it will do.

Retracing our footsteps: Poppy Cottage is nice. Muffins Gap had other names before this. The Oxford English Dictionary claims that a muffin is 'one who dangles after a young woman'. What more could one ask?

The Row boasts three houses. The first is Sunrise Cottage. This could not be better named. Vale Cottage is a cottage in the Vale. Little Gables - see later.

Back in Lombard Street: Plumtree Cottage (3rd tree) now has plum trees in the garden. 2007 saw a good crop of Victorias vanish into thin air. Scrumping is not dead. Kids it was not you! Brookford House formerly Derwent presumably de-rated to a brook with a Cortina. Ramswin Farm has had many functions in the past, riding stables, chicken farm, market garden, but how it got its name I don't fully know. Apparently, when it was a riding school, they won a riding event and Ramswin is the winners' initials. The Old Stables do well to promote equine rather than poultry. Willow Cottage (4th tree) does have such a tree. The Bottom Mill, once part of the Maule's empire (see Chapter 25), is due for conversion soon.

Yewtree Farm (5th tree) is currently undergoing a major refit and will come up with a few more dwellings. A fine specimen of a taxus is in the garden. South Oak Barn (6th tree) neither has an oak nor is south of one. Obviously, the estate agents know Orston tradition.

Beside the Walk is Yew Tree Farm Cottage, (7th tree) home of a local legend. I'm sure his name will be perpetuated in renaming this house Bernard's Cottage.

The arboreal theme continues with Orchard Cottage more fruity than others. Eastways faces the east and the road. Next door needs a lime tree planting to qualify as Linden House-later (8th tree). The Hollows was so named after a previous owner organised a competition in the Durham Ox to find a name. ('The White House' came second). Nice one.

Limehaus Deli must be one of the smallest shops in captivity. It is attached to The Willows (9th tree). There is an osier in the estate as you would expect. Fourways stands on the corner of Loughbon. I knew there were two, suspected there were three, but FOUR never.

The first house on Loughbon is Loughbon Cottage, once known as Loughbon Villa. It never was a villa, cottage is great. The Eaves is next. It definitely has lots of eaves. Staythorpe House was built for an émigré from Staythorpe 1820ish. On the site of the primitive chapel next to the old stink dyke stands The Brook. Before global warming, water appeared in this redundant sewer once or twice a year. At best it is a storm drain. Why choose this name when Brookhouse is the other side of the road?

The Old Blacksmith's was the workshop of the last blacksmith. Magson Cottage was built by Thos Magson for his family and tailor's business. A descendant still lives in Orston today. Next is Priory Lodge, I suspect it is not a priory or a lodge but it is not Dunroamin nor is it tree based.

The next building is one of about six that can claim to be the site of a post office. Beauvale housed the owner of the post office and Beauvale Stores. This house once contained a bakery. Adjoining is Mulhouse, one time home to a farm, a slaughterhouse, a saddlery, a brick and tile factory, and Two's Company until they moved to the Mushroom Farm. Next door is Mrs Taylor's. When her brother came to live with her, he had to give his new address. He gave the name by which it is known today, Taylor's Cottage. That sounds good to me. On the corner of Loughbon and Chapel Street is The White House, a former village shop and perhaps the home of the amorous youth in the village song. Behind the shop was a terrace of five but and ben houses. The first two were demolished to provide off-road parking and a small garden about 35 years ago. Hope Cottage is now the first, When all is lost we still have hope. Springtime Cottage: the name suggests violets, daffodils and erysimum. White Gates is the last of this trio. Alas, it has no longer has gates. A footpath, known as the Walk, boasts three houses no 1 and no 3 and no 6. Another but and ben row all numbered before Syringa Cottage. Again, this evokes vision of lilac and galanthus (the last one I promise) Next are six bungalows designated for senior citizens and other delinquents 1-6. Left into Chapel Garth; alas all of these are numbered. The other side of the road is The Rookery. They must have their share of these birds. We do! Tudor Park is another recent building. One assumes it is to replace the demolished Tudor Cottage. Park must be where to leave the car.

Towards the church, the houses on the left side are all council-built and only have numbers. The Green, known as Town Road in 1920, has The Old Cottage. Some of it is quite new; the four remaining houses are numbered 1-4 and phone box.

The Old Vicarage used to house an old vicar in the good old days. Where High Street meets Launder Street is the now completed Old Vicarage Coach House. Stables may be but not coaches, unless it was a very small coach.

Orston Hall is well documented elsewhere, Belvedere is beautiful to see. Mistletoe Cottage, Orston is a bit north for this tree-related parasite but it is recorded in the village. Orchard House is a house in a group of fruit trees (10th tree), Bramley House maintains the tree (11th tree) image. Little Orchard (12th tree) takes it over the top. Bay Tree House (13th tree) is more of a bush at the moment. Next is Alrene House - another made up name, I suspect. White Acres was not named after a snow storm but by the vicar before he could baptise a child born there. Green Acres: are they by any chance related? Another non-specific, The Cottage, to be added to the list. Carlin House gives its name to the company but its origins are lost in the mists of time. (Not even Paul Barnes knows whose grandparents gave it its name in the 30s. It was then called Ivy House).

Ahead to the right is Corner Field Barn. Could it be that it was a barn in a corner of a field? Elementary, my dear Watson. Next is Brandon House, formally Cherry Trees. It had no such trees anyway so go with Brandon House.

Clawson Lodge sits well in its own grounds. How it got that name, I do not know. The Ridings is tucked away behind the shrubs. Bob Wilkinson named it after his riding school. (See chapter 35) Also out of sight is Kerson, another made up name, the final syllable from each of the two names. This seems to be a popular method of getting an original name. The Bungalow is as others are. At right angles to the road is The Homestead. Quite right, I cannot argue with that. Behind the wall and its fine gates is The Brackens. I doubt there is much bracken within its boundaries. Maeldune is Anglo Saxon for what we know as Malvern or Church on the hill. The current residents hail from Malvern.

Ash View is next (14th tree). There must be an ash tree in sight. The Laurels (15th tree) is obvious, did Stan really live here? One of the only two birds is Robin Cottage. I hope he thrives. My last entry on High Street is Westray, witness to the dying embers of the sun each day.

The first on the left in Launder Street is Launder Cottage where the old washer woman sets the standard for the street. Enter Churchside Mews. Three out of keeping houses overfill this plot. The first is Churchside House, next is No 2 Churchside Mews, the third is Talisman House. Charmed I'm sure. Churchside Farm House the oldest bit of this complex and was the original Durham Ox. The other side of the road is Church Cottage. What else could it be? Beside this is the old school, now HQ for Carlin Construction. Back on the left is The White House. Where would we be without them?

Of the remaining two houses, the first is Matty's Cottage. That is great. Matty was a legend, the older he grew the more of a curmudgeonly figure he cast, his own man, beholden to no one. Adjacent to Matty's Cottage is End Cottage. That is what it is. Left into Church Street is Ballamoar House: a Manx word meaning big house. Alongside, are no's 2 & 3 council-built houses. Across the road is The Barn which tells you nothing. Winterbeck Cottage tells its own story, as does Dovecote Farm, twice. There are two Dovecote Farms. This might confuse a city dweller but not we simple country folk. Orston School is next before The Cottage, the only house without a letter box. The Durham Ox Inn is run by villagers for villagers, use it or lose it. Innominate House to the south of the Ox is overpowering. The Woodlands is my favourite house. Left into Loughbon is Church End. Dear reader, please draw your own conclusions as to why this house was called so.

Lyndhurst could refer to a village in Hampshire. Sycamore House (16th tree). Welcome back stalwart tree; we have missed you like we miss the tree. Sasare: one could make up anything about this and not be wrong, it is named after a gold mine in Africa. The Brook was mentioned earlier. Then follow three pairs of council-built houses now all in private ownership but most unnamed. Galibier Cottage – all frogs welcome. Left onto Mill Lane is Jasmine Lodge, a fragrant flower but a bitter fruit. Tinkers Moon demands explanation. The lady of the house read a book as a child called the Tinkers Moon and decided then to call

Matty Gladders and Mrs Webster, 1983

a suitable house by this name. She did; a hope realized.

Restarting at the railway line, the outer fringes of Orston for me, Highview was built by the army during WW2 as part of a search light unit, hence Highview. Hill House is a house on a hill. Highfields must take its name from its location as do many. The Limes, to the best of my knowledge, has no lime tree (17th tree) but it might have one soon. The Old Mill was converted into three dwellings numbered 1,2 and 3. Manor Farm House is the only house on Lordship at the moment. There could be a few more soon.

Hilltop starts off with Mill Lee, built in the shelter of the mill. From this point, some houses have numbers, some have names and some have both. No 1 then No 2 Orston View and so it has, Waysmeet close enough for me, Larkrise is next - suppose they do. Pipers Croft is stolen from the Wirral by the first owners. Franweir is next. I think I prefer No 6. Elmcrest is No 9 but 15 in the tree count. There's no elm and it's not the crest. Two more numbers then Hill Farm or not a farm but on a hill. Fields House, in a field, Folly House, Wrens Lodge Wrens, Lodge No 2 and 3 and Barn End and Stable Cottage all conspire to confuse those that do not know.

The last house fittingly belongs to the Smellies. The Gables with its Flemish style gable and a fine wisteria at the back sets this house apart from many. It is said that an offspring of a prior owner acquired a small unnamed row of houses in the City. These were converted into Little Gables, current home of Professor Paul Barnes. Is that a coincidence?

The house names in Orston are many and varied, predictable and unpredictable, obvious and obscure. There are some good ones and some appalling ones. The White House, The Bungalow, The Cottage need a prefix to set them apart from the rest. Made up names do not get my wholesale approval but they have their place. My award for best name goes to Matty's Cottage.

Yew Tree Farm circa 1950.

Staythorpe House in the 1930s

The Gables

Tudor Park, Chapel Street

CHAPTER 3
THE DEVELOPMENT OF THE VILLAGE THROUGH THE STUDY OF MAPS

The earliest map to show the layout of the village is Camden's map of 1637. It confirms High Street as the main thoroughfare (hence the name) with the Manor House at the north end and the Church (the centre of the village) at the south. High Street had another purpose; it connected with the important Belvoir-Haselford Ferry road and the road to Newark.

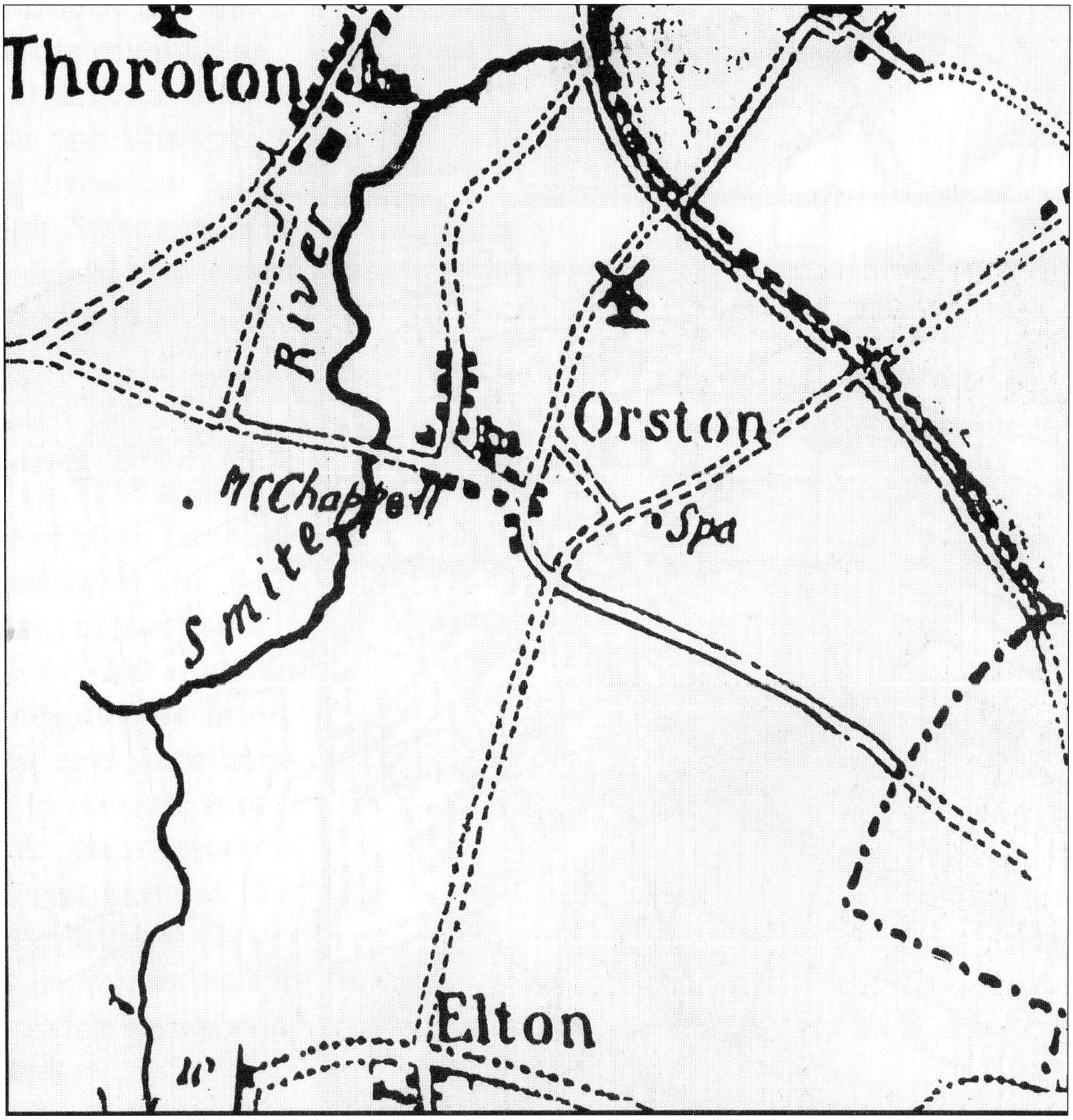

Camden, 1637

The next detailed map to be drawn up was for the Enclosure Award in 1793. It shows a number of developments, notably 'back lanes' which led to the open fields where inhabitants' gardens backed onto one another – now known as Chapel Street and Church Street.

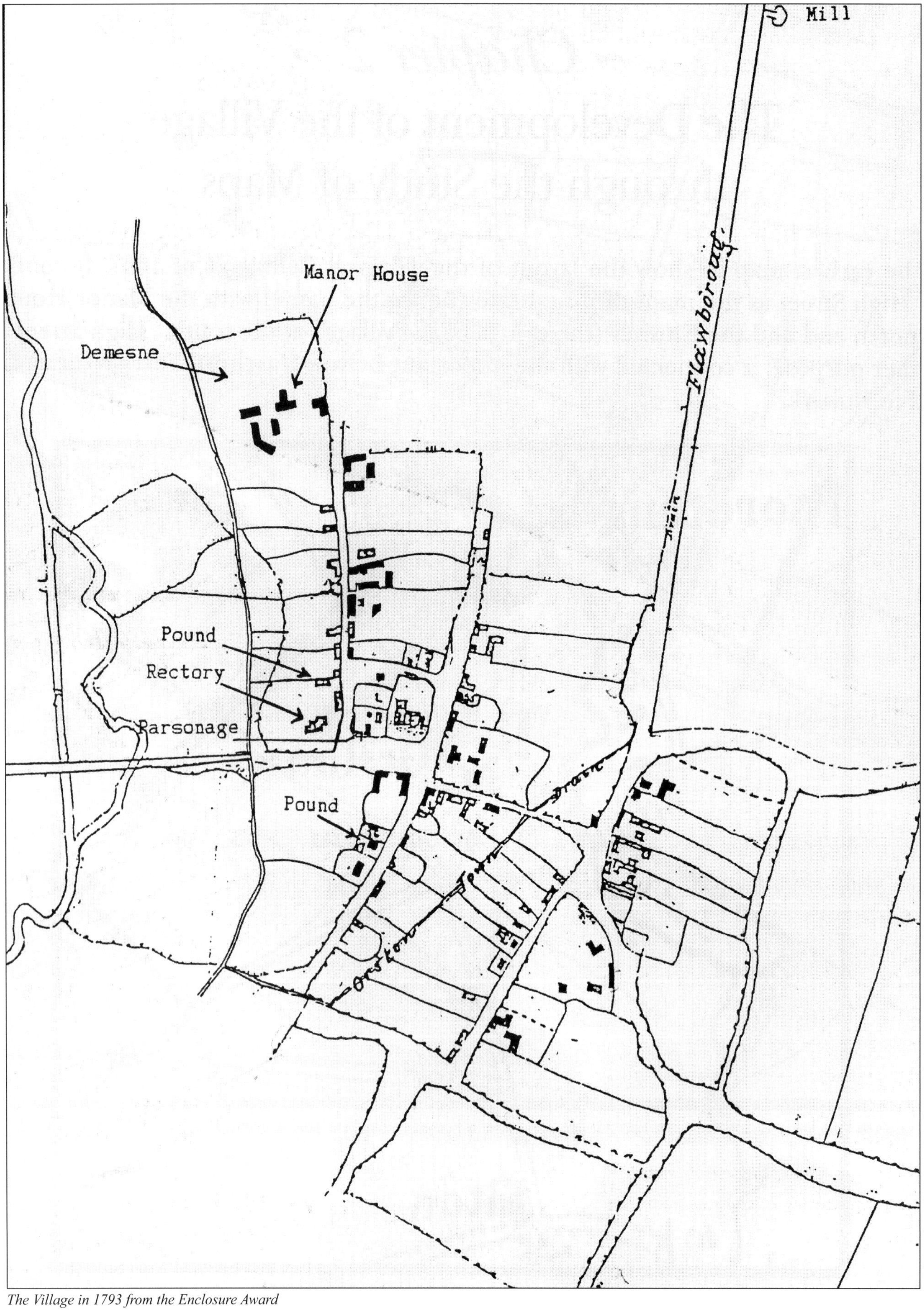

The Village in 1793 from the Enclosure Award

The purpose of the Enclosure Award was to divide up the open fields into smaller more manageable fields - as we know them today. As a result, it also determined which roads were to continue for that purpose. The continuation of High Street to Flawborough was relegated to becoming a bridle road, as was the road to Whatton, which incidentally did not feature in the Camden map of 1637. The Enclosure Award map also showed a continuation of the Row at the bottom of Lombard Street to join Elton road. No doubt this was a short cut to the open fields. The 1824 Ordnance Survey map shows one change; a road going from the north end of High Street to Mill Lane. No doubt this would have provided a short cut to the Mill.

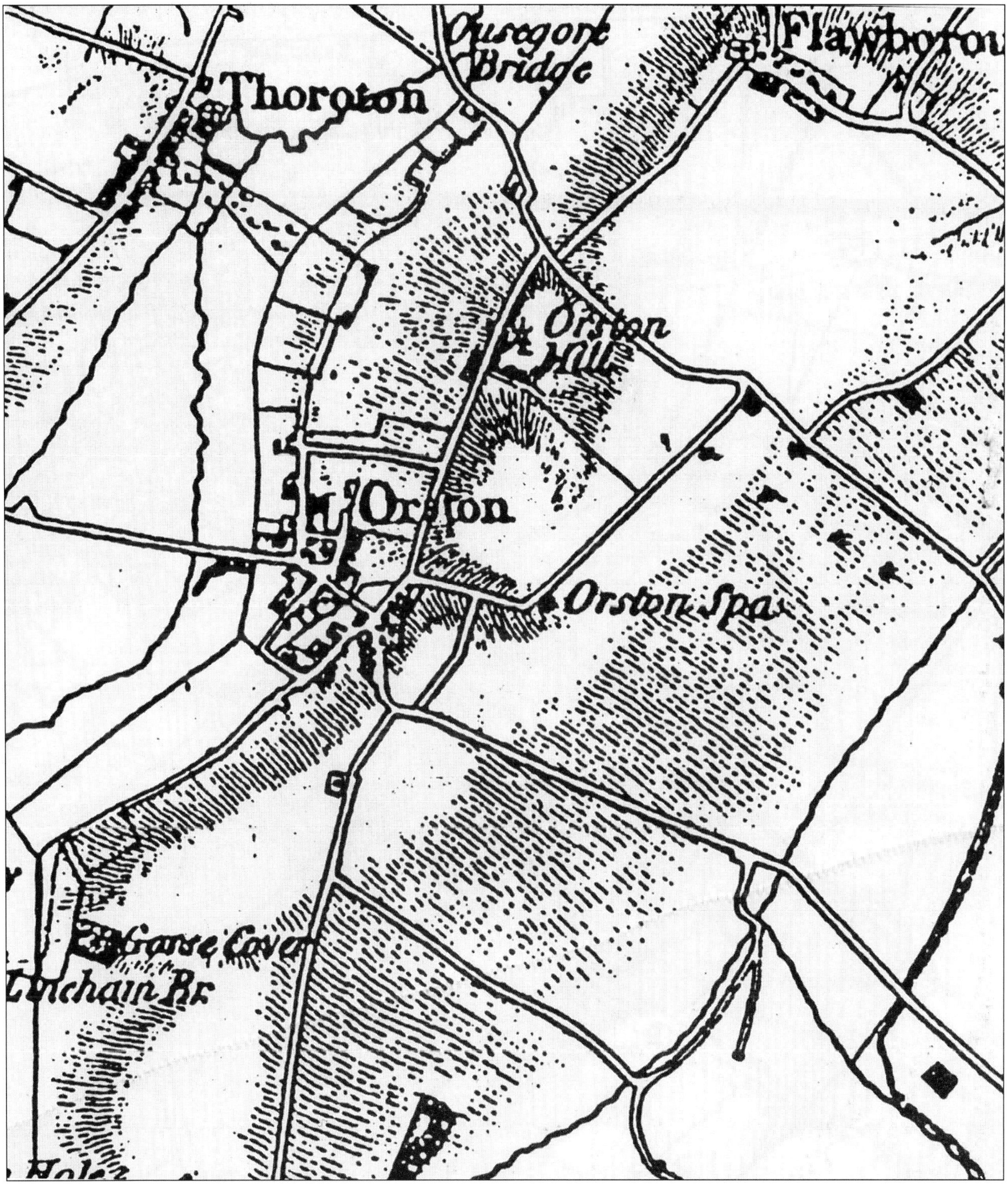

The Village, 1824

This map and that of Sanderson's in 1835 assert the importance of Moor Lane (its name coming from Bon Moor, the area through which it passes) as the road to Whatton, despite the intentions of the enclosure commissioners to relegate it to a bridle road. Sanderson is also of interest because it is the first map to show the actual layout as opposed to the 1793 map which shows what was intended.

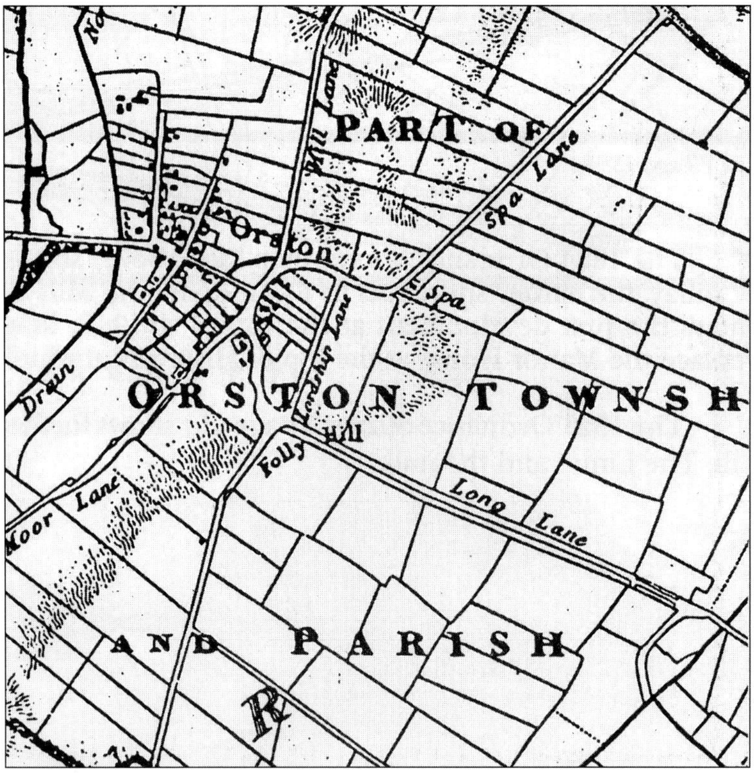

Sanderson, 1835

The Village 1884

The 1884 Ordnance Survey map shows a similar road structure to that of today. The earlier short cuts to Elton Road and Mill Lane have disappeared. It also shows the first development at the top of the hill, Manor Farm, replacing the manor House at the top of High Street which had been demolished. It is interesting that, until then the village was entirely located at the foot of the escarpment. The map also shows the establishment of the Orston brick and plaster works down Pit Lane.

The 1921 Ordnance Survey show further development at the top of the hill, The Limes and The Mill.

(below) The Village, 1884

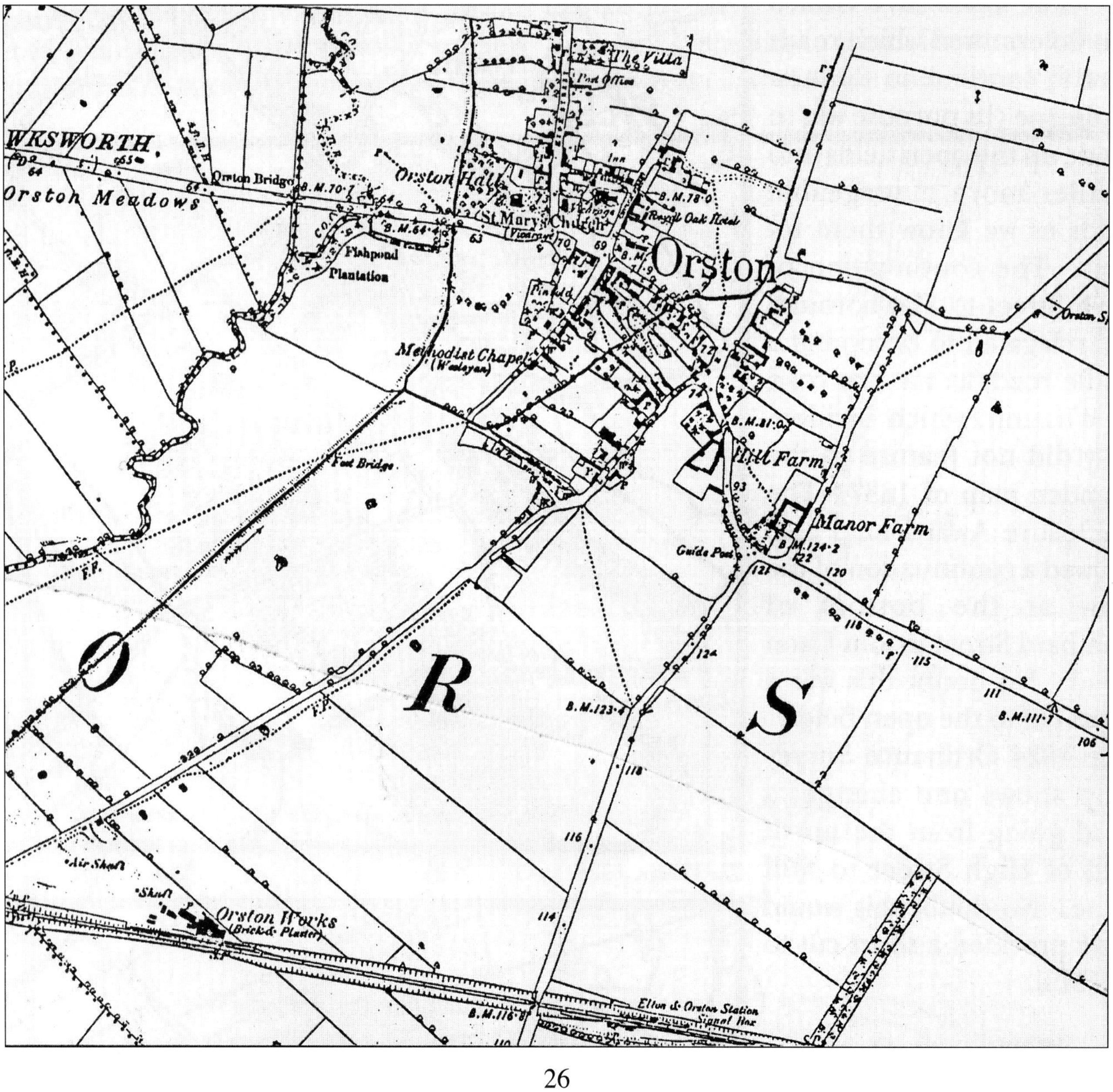

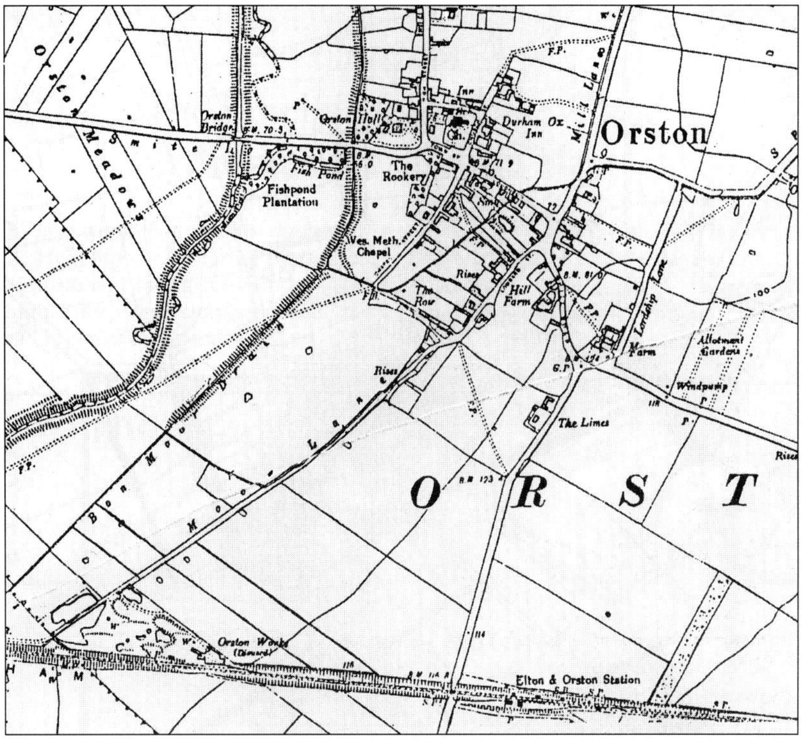

The Village, 1921

The final map, 1979, is marked to show the hedges prior to enclosure in 1793. The enclosure Award of 1793 transformed the countryside by replacing 3 open fields by much smaller ones separated by hedges which continue to this day.

The village, 1979. The hedges marked in bold are pre-enclosure, i.e. pre 1793. See Chapters 8 and 11

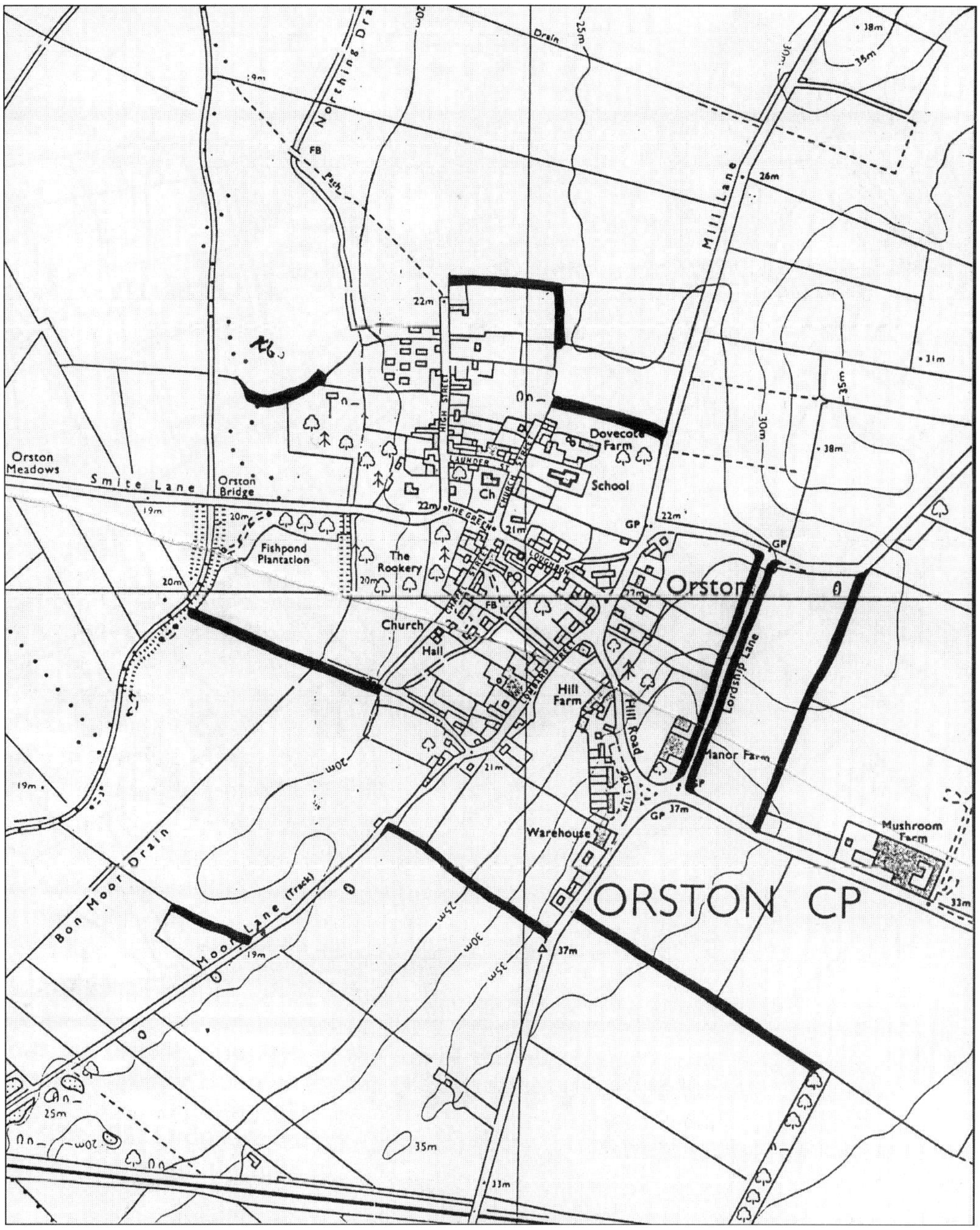

The Village, 1979. The hedges marked in bold are pre-enclosure, i.e. pre-1793. See Chapter 11.

CHAPTER 4
ORIGINS

Orston is situated at the foot of a narrow limestone escarpment, referred to by geologists as 'Blue Lias', which runs irregularly across the low ground on the edge of the Trent valley through Bunny Hill to beyond Newark in the north. This ridge also contains the villages of Cotham, Flawborough, Kilvington, Staunton, Granby, Elton, Sutton, Barnstone and Langar. What makes these different is that they are all situated on the ridge, whereas the original Orston was located at the foot.

There has probably been a settlement on the site since at least 1,000 BC. Settlers called Nordics came down from the Belvoir hills and cleared the water meadows linked up by an old road to Nottingham, Gainsborough and Newark. They had sheep, pigs, goats and cows. They made cheese and salted bacon. By the first century AD, there was a Roman station at Margidunum, between Bingham and East Bridgford. After the Roman evacuation, the English soon appeared, coming along the Fosse Way and the Vale of Belvoir. Orston would then grow into a typical village: a green in the middle with a church, a smithy and houses and barns grouped around.

According to "Place names of Nottinghamshire", the name Orston originates from the Old English Ordrices tun which means "the farmstead of Ordric". Ordric was the leader of the small settlement. Some early references to the settlement are Oschintone, 1086 (*the Domesday Book*), Orskinton, 1242, Orston, 1284, Horston, 1428 and Horson, c. 1500. The initial 'H' may represent an attempt at connecting the name with horse and the pronunciation at the time.

At the time of the death of Edward the Confessor (1053) sixty "vills" in Nottinghamshire were grouped together into five great manors which, with their dependencies formed "sokes". (A vill was a division of a parish, such as a township, manor or tithing. A soke was a term used in Danelaw counties to describe a jurisdiction over a number of estates and villages). The five were Dunham, Bothamsall, Mansfield, Arnold and Orston. All except Bothamsall belonged to Edward and all five sokes became the possession of William the Conqueror. As sokes date to the Danelaw formed in this area in 877, it may be inferred that not only was Orston in existence then but it was sufficiently large and important as to be the head of the soke. The other villages comprising the soke were Scarrington, Staunton, Thoroton, Screveton and Aslockton. Tenants of the sokeland would come to Orston court at prescribed times to pay the royal rents, seek justice in disputes and make the communal agricultural arrangements. In the list of royal sokes Orston figures last but the order has no financial significance (which would indicate size) as the king's income from Dunham and Orston were approximately equal and more than double that of Bothamsall and Arnold.

The entry in the Domesday Book, 1086, for Orston was

> *In Oschintone King Edward had 3 carucates of land (assessed) to the geld. (There is) land for 10 ploughs. There the king has 3 ploughs and 3 sochmen on (de) 1 carucate of this land and 19 villeins and 11 bordars having 14 ploughs. There (is) a church and 2 priests having 1 plough and 1 ox, and 180 acres of meadow. In King Edward's time it was worth 30 pounds (£) by tale; now (it is worth) 20 pounds.*

The Domesday Book was a country-wide survey implemented by William the Conquerer in order to see how best to tax his vills based on their agricultural wealth. Geld was an Old English term for taxation based on land-holding. Most of the details for each entry, therefore, relate to how a vill should be assessed. The principal measure of arable land was the carucate which was the amount of land which could be ploughed in a year using one plough with an eight-ox team. It, therefore, varied with the soil quality between about 60 and 180 acres. In the case of Orston clay it would be on the low side! A ploughland is equivalent. The later references to ploughs in the entry relate to the number of plough teams. "£30 by tale" refers to a rent received rather than to an estimate of potential revenue. A comparison with some other vills shows the size and importance of Orston. It was, therefore, larger than most other villages in the area: larger than Radcliffe and second only to Bingham.

	Carucate	*Bovates*	*Plough lands*	*Teams*
Whatton	2	4	9	12
Shelford	5	3	9	10
Bingham	4	17	6	17.5
Staunton	2	1.2	6	8
Radcliffe	3	0	6	10
Scarrington	2	0	3	7.5
Orston	3	0	10	17

(a bovate was one eighth of a carucate)

A sochman was a free tenant. A villein was an unfree tenant after the Norman Conquest. He held his land subject to a range of agricultural services and fines. He was above the status of a slave but annexed to the Lord of the Manor. A bordar cottager had one of the lowest ranks. He had some land for subsistence but he was required to give agricultural and other services to the Lord free or for a small sum. Thirty-three people are mentioned in the Domesday Book: with their families, they would have amounted to a population of between 150 and 175 people.

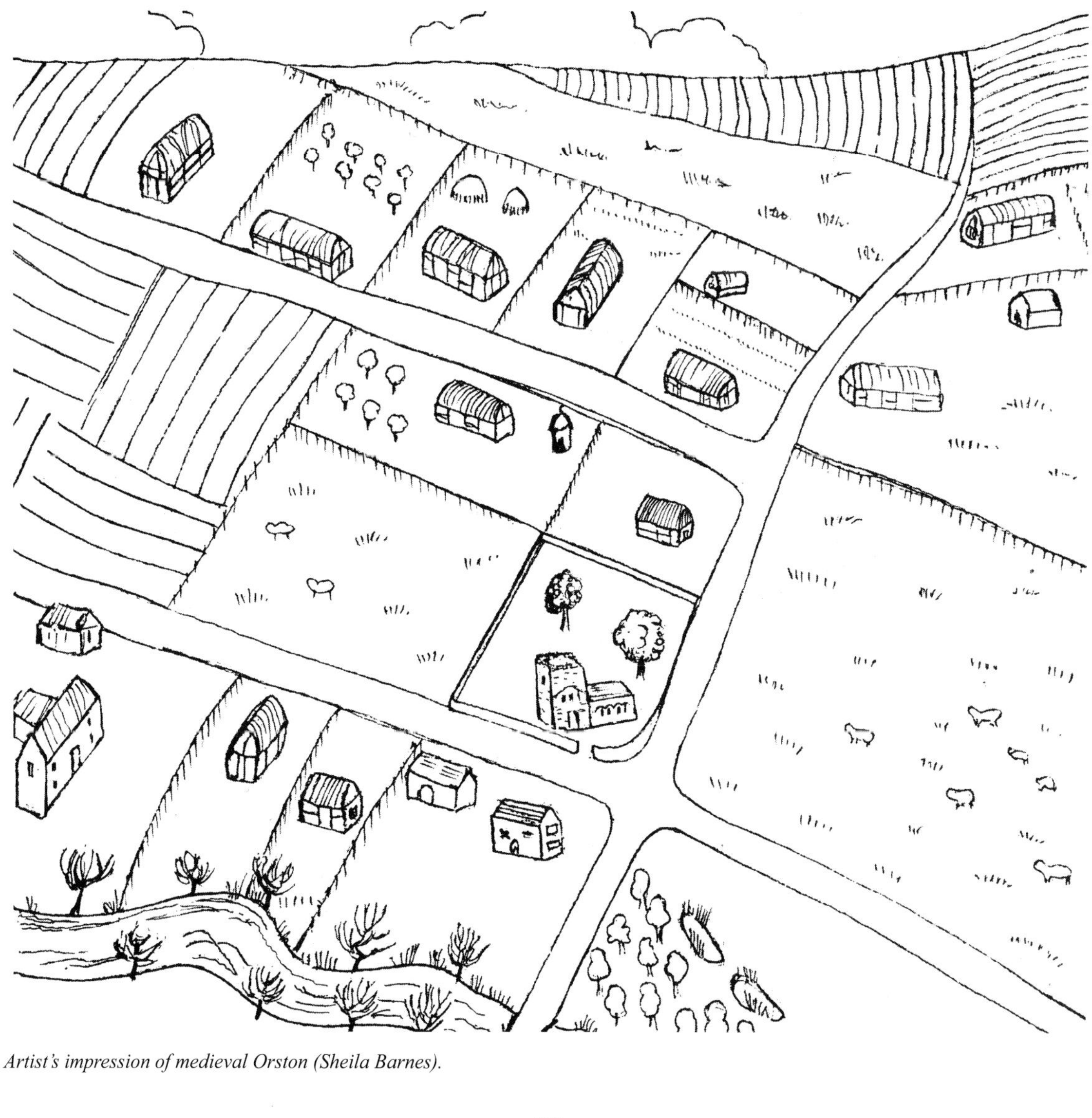

Artist's impression of medieval Orston (Sheila Barnes).

CHAPTER 5
EARLY DAYS

EARLY LAW AND DISORDER.

In 1280 John Coke of Orston, suspected of theft, fled with others and was proclaimed an outlaw. Four of them were in frankpledge to their lords (i.e. their lords were responsible for ensuring that they attend court to answer the charge). For not producing them for trial, these were adjudged to be in the mercy of the court.

Royal pardons were at that time often extended to outlaws in return for military service and in 1339 Alexander de Brighton, who had been accused of killing John of Orston, was pardoned subject to that condition and that he should stand trial if called to do so.

Later in the century an Orston man was pardoned for causing the death of a man in "a chance medley" but disorders were rife at that time and in the following century outlawry abounded everywhere. In 1375 a commission was appointed touching *'all extortions, conspiracies, and other grievances and excesses perpetrated'* at Orston and Warsop.

EARLY WARS

In 1346 John Bozen and his men from Orston fought at Crecy on the banks of the Somme, an important battle in the Hundred Years War where the longbowmen of Edward III beat the French knights.

The final record of the eighteenth century tells that Orston, Scarrington and Thoroton together had to pay £23. 11.0. for failure to provide their men for the army fighting France.

EARLY POLITICS

On the eve of the parliamentary election of 1593 a letter from Orston to the Countess of Rutland informed her that all the freeholders had been interviewed and had promised to vote for the earl's nominee. Within a few days sent *'36s. in reward to the towne of Orston to be bestoed upon the poor there and towards the mayntaynynge of the hye ways'.*

St Mary's Church with watercarrier, lady with pram and little girl in foreground, circa 1910.

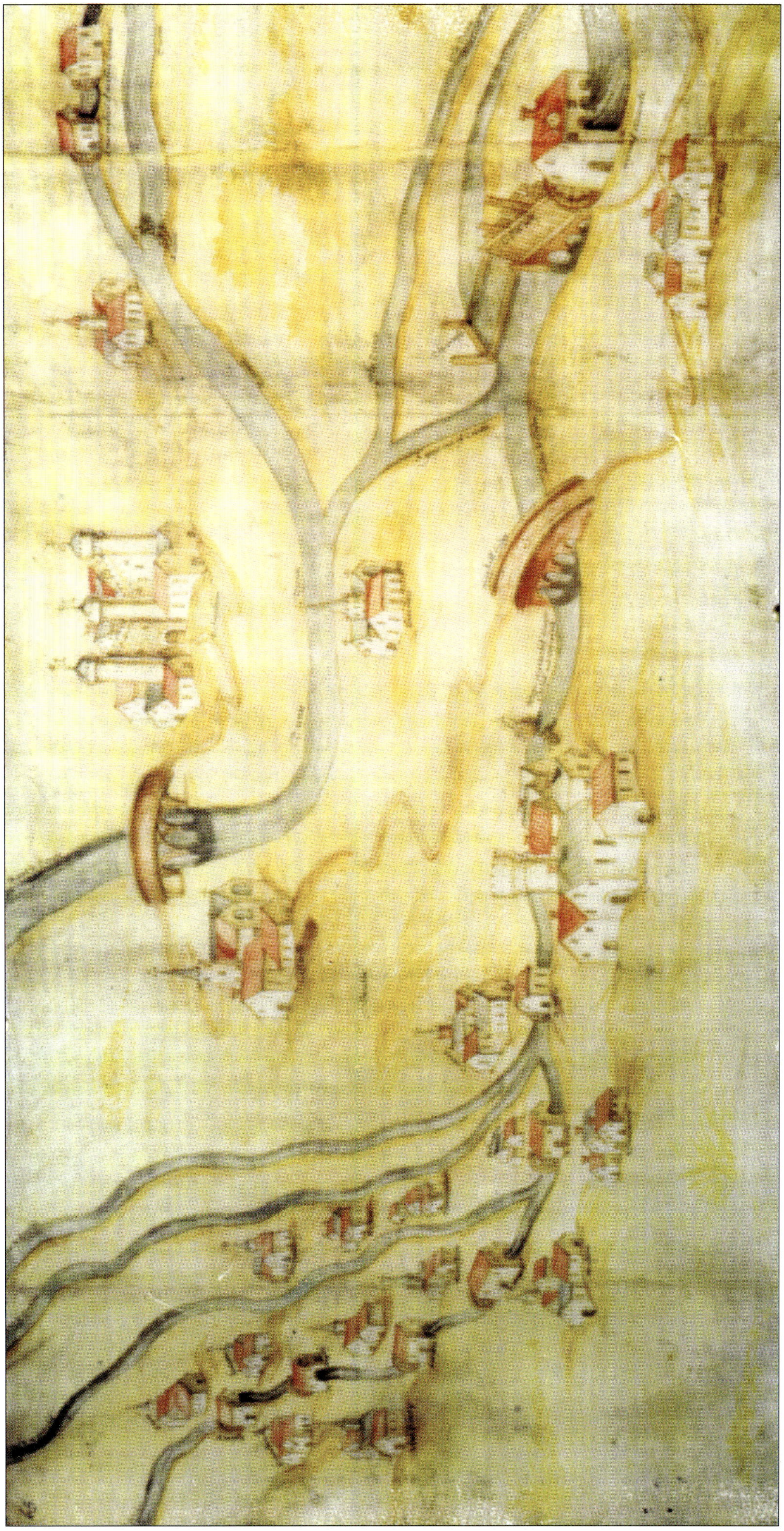

A map of the River Trent and its tributaries 'in Henry VIII's time' showing Orston (see back cover) and the surrounding villages.

CHAPTER 6
THE RIVER SMITE

The Patent Rolls of 1328 show that a commission was appointed to deal with the floods which submerged the low lands and meadows of the Vale of Belvoir. The Devon and Smite were silted up and had overflowed, the inundation being particularly bad between Orston and Thoroton. The commissioners then ascribed the immediate cause of flooding to the mill which held up water at Hawton and the lack of a ditch across Syerston meadow.

No doubt a remedy was found but things were soon bad again and new commissioners were appointed from time to time. In 1342 for instance the channels of these streams were again reported to be choked up by sand, gravel and growing trees. A commission was appointed under the crown on the following terms

> *'Whereas the waters of Deven, Smyte and Kersyk (presumably Car Dyke), and certain dykes and places through which divers waters in the Vale of Belvoir, in the wapentakes of Bingham and Newark, between the towns of Flintham and Orston, run down to the said water of Deven and on to the water of Trent, are now so much narrowe and obstructed by sand shingle, and plantation of trees, that on that account and on default of trenches which ought to be made there for draining and saving the low lands and meadows, many inundations daily occur and whereas the bridges and causeys (a pavement or raised footpath) of Wendelsford, Horscroft and Langbrig and others in those parts are so broken that in winter it is only possible to approach and cross them with much difficulty and danger, they (the members of the commission) are to survey the waters, dykes, places, and the destructions in these, the bridges, causeys and their breaches, to make new trenches were necessary, provided that compensation to those on whose soil these are made, by those whose lands will benefit by such trenches'.*

The commission was also asked to ascertain by whose default the damages had occurred and they were instructed to take the necessary steps to prevent it from recurring. The burden would largely fall upon the villeins and other lowly labourers who were bound to the manors upon which they lived and who paid by their labour in these and other ways to their lords for the privilege of being able to maintain a miserable and precarious existence.

In 1350 another inquiry into flooding of the district was instituted. It found that between Orston and Thoroton, the land was inundated and that the water of the Smite could not escape because it was held up at a mill at Hawton and for the lack of a ditch across Syerston meadow. The stream was so choked up with sand, shingle and trees that its course was narrowed. The Horscroft and other bridges and causeys were decayed and useless. This was an old grievance and continued for centuries to come until the Vale was intersected by dykes and ditches and the Smite was kept free from encumbrances.

The situation was largely resolved during the reign of Henry IV (1422-1461) when the village and its environs were flooded through obstructions in the Smite. As a result numerous dykes were cut at the expense of those who would benefit.

In 1605 each Orston householder was fined one shilling for not keeping the channel of the Smite free and causing floods.

In 1633 the inhabitants of Orston and Thoroton were presented *'for want of a Bridge over the River of Smyte in a place called Hoscoe als Horscroft bridge* [nowadays called Oscar Bridge or Waterloo] *being now a fford between the Lordships of the said two Townes in the highway leading to fflintham and divers other places of this County to the market Towne of Grantham'*. The presentment goes on to say that there *'hath been noe bridge at all for 40 years last past, yet it is confessed that before that time and within memory there was a bridge for carriages, and being of noe use for that purpose but a great hinderance to the passage of the water in that river was decayed and taken away'*.

The Court ordered that the inhabitants of Orston and Thoroton make a new bridge; but on the 6th October 1634, the inhabitants of the parishes brought into Court *'a copy of an order or law of Sewers made on 3rd June last past by seaven Commissioners for that part of the County under their hands and seals laying down divers reasons therein seeming to this Court sufficient'*. The reasons were *'That a bridge for carriages is needles and unususeful in regard to the ffoard the is ebb well stoned and gravelled and at all times much better and surer way, then the way at either end thereof, especially on that side near Thorraton, wch way lying in a low and levell ground a great distance from the river and oft overflowen cannot be made passable for carriages at all times But when they come to the said ffoard they may more safely pass over: And if a bridge for carriages should be set up to that height wch the level of the ground would beare it would stop the passage of the water to the overflowing of the highway and make it much worse than it was'*.

The Court of Sewers however *'thought it needful that a bridge for horsemen, beasts and footmen should be set up more above that ffoard in a place by them appointed to a convenient height and widness wch might serve at all times* (when there could be any use for a Bridge) *for all passengers if there were care also had to raise a banke from thence in the low ground for horses beasts and footmen, and to keep the cartways in good repair'*.

For that the inhabitants petitioned and an Order was made that *'they make and keep in repair the horse bridge and bank referred to in the Order of the Commissioners of Sewers and to diligently repair the ways for carriages on either side of the river and that the Order for the making of a carriage bridge be not enforced'*. The horse bridge was evidently constructed and in 1686 the inhabitants of the two parishes were indicted for non-repair of it.

The Smite has been straightened and, of course, in recent times deepened. The enclosure award of 1793 shows that a channel had been already cut to straighten the Smite nearest to the village and Smite Lane no doubt to prevent flooding and silting. The old course must have been blocked off some time later. The Smite towards Whatton was straightened during the following century. A new bridge was constructed over the Smite on Smite Lane in 1883.

Smite Bridge, circa 1985 L to R: Vickie Wakefield, Donna Roberts, Michelle Wakefield.

River Smite, 1928.

Thoroton Bridge, 1927.

CHAPTER 7
THE MANOR AND MANOR HOUSE

Soon after his conquest of England and the commissioning of the Domesday Book, William I (1066-1087) devised a new system of government which centred on the basic tenurial unit of the 'manor'. The Lord of the Manor owned the land and the peasants had a duty to serve him. The duties and responsibilities of all were codified and the manorial court was instituted to enforce them. Slowly actual service to the Lord in return for land (knights' service, sergeanty etc) was replaced by monetary payments.

The manor of Orston belonged to the Crown until Richard I (1189-1199) bestowed it on William de Albini to hold by feudal military service. According to the terms of the grant, the Albinis were to keep *'in demesne 32 oxgangs of land, every oxgang, or bovate containing 16 acres of arable and 2 acres of meadow: every oxgange being worth 12s. per acre, and further 68 oxgangs in free socage'*. The term demesne refers to the land which formed the main farm of the Lord of the Manor. The villein tenants, as part of their obligations, had to regularly work on the demesne lands. Free socage refers to free tenure without obligation of military service. Thus, based on an oxgang/bovate of 16 acres and the manor comprising 1800 acres, we may conclude that about one third of the land was part of the demesne (580 acres), one ninth being meadow, and two thirds was common land (1220 acres), although it is likely that much of this common land would have been woodland.

During the reign of Richard I, his brother John, the Earl of Mortain, was given an allowance of £13 a year out of Orston. Later, he had to pay £100 to take possession of 'Oskintone'. The manor seems to have been taken from the Albini family by Robert de Orston as in 1200 he was sued by Petronella, an Albini, for her share. In a hot dispute, the lady seized the manor and Robert appealed to the law for its recovery. The pleadings were contradictory and the outcome of the case is unknown. The third William de Albini, who was also Lord of Belvoir, was one of the barons who compelled King John to sign the Magna Carta in 1215. When King John sallied out of Nottingham Castle in 1215 on a revengeful expedition, marking his course by a trail of sword and fire, Orston was unlikely to have been spared! William died in 1241 leaving a daughter, Isabel who married Robert, Lord Roos, ten years later.

In the Wars of the Roses (1455-1471) Lord Roos was on the losing side. Fighting for the Lancastrians in 1464, he was taken captive and beheaded. Orston and his other estates became obscure. According to the Patent Rolls, the manor of Orston was granted by King Edward IV in 1467 to the Earl of Worcester and Phillipa, his sister, widow of the executed Thomas Roos. The manor seems to have remained in the family of Roos until 1508 when Edmond died without issue and it passed to his sister who married Sir Robert Manners. Their grandchild was created Earl of Rutland. Upon the death of the Earl of Rutland in 1632, the manor passed to his daughter who was the wife of the Duke of Buckingham. It was quickly sold to the first Duke of Kingston who unfortunately was a Royalist. Parliament bestowed his forfeited estates on William Pierpont of Thoresby, the earl's second son and a friend of Cromwell. Robert Pierrepont (1584-1643) was made Viscount Newark in 1627 and the first Earl of Kington upon Hull in 1628. The fifth earl, Evelyn Pierrepont, was made Marquess of Dorchester in 1706 and the first Duke of Kingston in 1715. The last Duke of Kingston died in 1773 leaving Orston and his other properties to his bigamous duchess and upon her death in 1788 the manor descended to his nephew, Charles, who took the name of Pierrepont instead of Medows, with whose posterity it continued into the 20th century.

Although Orston was a single manor (some parishes had more than one), the lord of the manor was not always the largest landowner by any means. This was the case with Orston from the mid eighteenth century onwards. (See Chapter 10 for an account of this).

Only a little is known about the Manor House and the demesne. The house stood in the field known as Brewsters at the north end of High street. Its shape is clearly shown on the enclosure award and a more detailed map made at that time (shown the end of this chapter). Obviously, the Lord of the Manor did not live there; his residence was at Belvoir, Holme Pierrepont or Thoresby Hall. He may have visited it and even stayed overnight when presiding over the manorial court which met about four times a year. For most of the time the Manor House and demesne appear to have been let. For example, in 1694 Widdow Brown and in 1788 Francis Vincent (a large farmer with land also in other parishes) were tenants of the house and nearby grass closes.

Evidence concerning the Manor House was discovered in 1952. The record in the *Numismatic Chronicle*, 1952 states:

> ORSTON TREASURE TROVE
> *1413 coins: Edward VI 6, Mary 42, Mary or Elizabeth 6, Elizabeth 643, James I 218, Charles I 498.*
>
> *On 6 February 1952, a tractor was ploughing Brewster's Field in the parish of Orston, Nottinghamshire. The field in question was under the plough for only the fourth time in living memory. A plan preserved with the Parish Award of 1796 suggests that buildings once occupied part at least of the ground, and one of the reasons why the field had remained permanent pasture was the presence just under the surface of large blocks of stone. These were described at the inquest as "needing two men to lift and carry away". At a depth of six inches the plough turned up the 1,413 coins. There was no trace of a container, and the men reported that the coins simply "lay in a heap". This may suggest that they had been buried in a sack or wrapped in a cloak.*
>
> *It is very noticeable that the Elizabethan and James I silver, though heavily circulated, was generally of very fair weight, whilst the Charles I silver was severely mutilated by clipping. This was especially true of Tower Mint coins struck after the King had taken the field. The approximate date of the hoard is fixed by a single coin from the degenerate dies of the post-1643 coinage, and it is surmised that the burial was occasioned by Rupert's surprise march on Newark in 1644. The complete absence of coins from the King's provincial mints may suggest that the hoard represents the family savings, accumulated over many years, of a local roundhead sympathizer rather than a cavalier in touch with the royal armies. In either case, it points to the completeness of parliamentary control of the area before Robert's relief of the royal forces shut up in Newark.*

Around 1840 the Manor House was demolished. Manor Farm at the top of the hill was built to replace it. No doubt it too was let. When the Manvers Estate was sold in 1911, the farm, occupied by Thomas Clayworth, and its 152 acres were sold for £3,150. Most of the land lay between Bottesford Lane and Flawborough Road along Lordship Lane, hence the name.

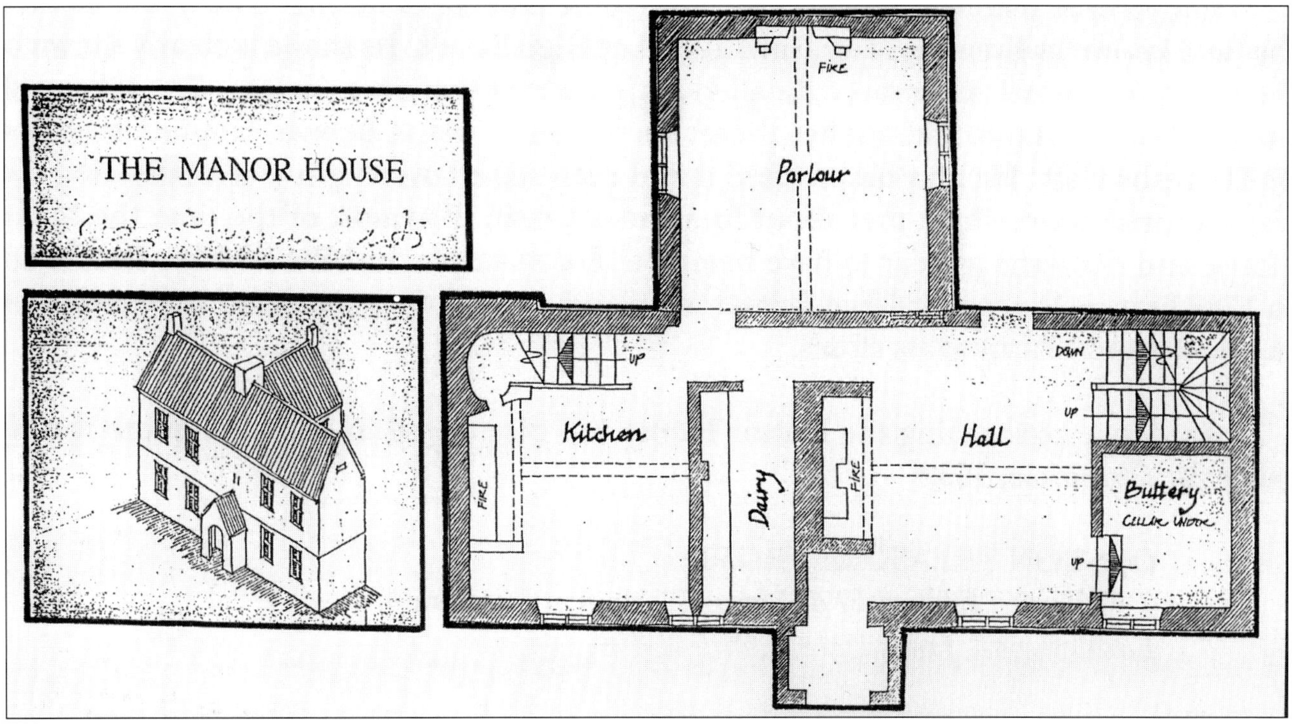

The Manor House – what it possibly looked like

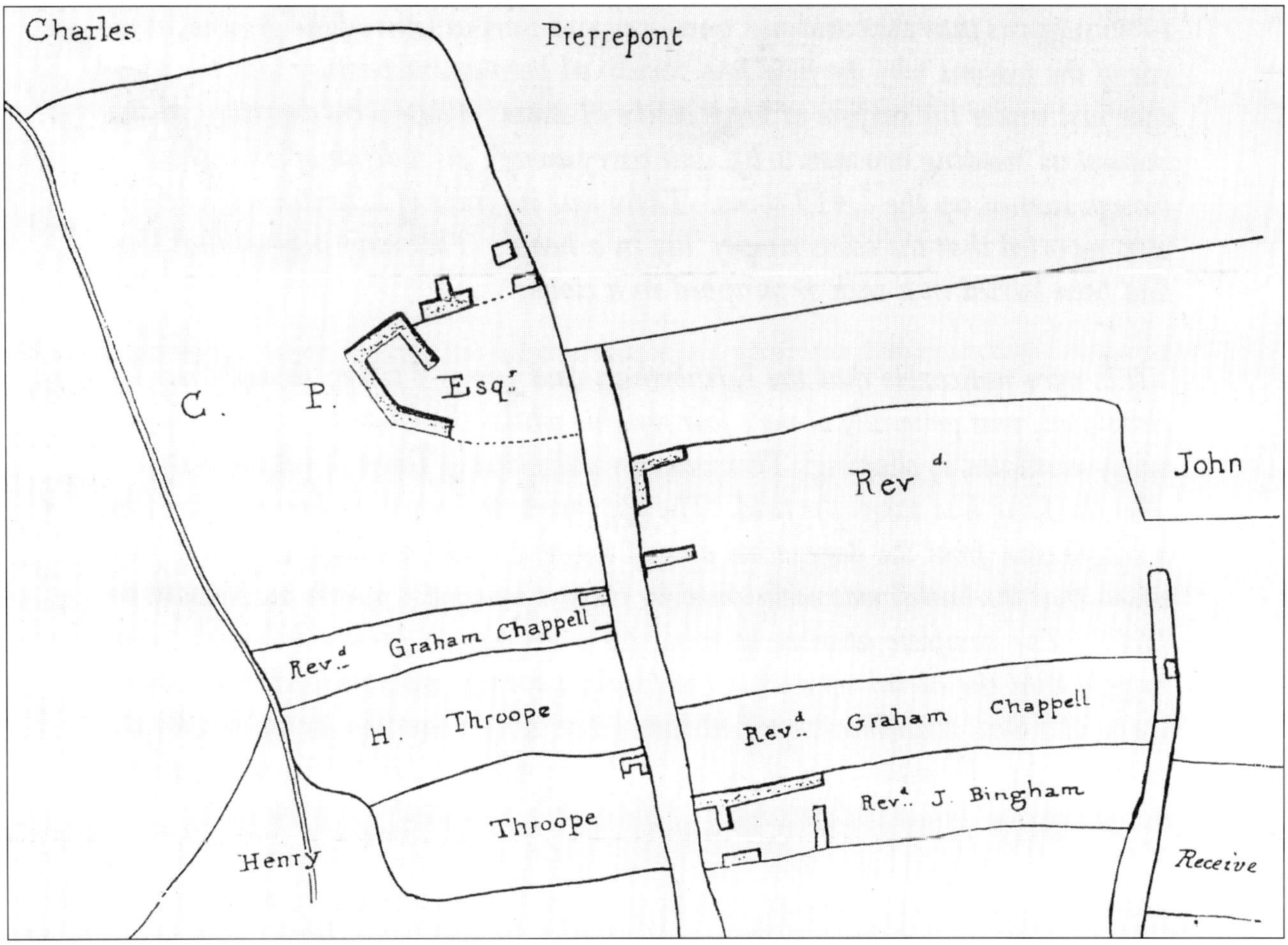

The Manor House and demesne, 1793.

CHAPTER 8
OPEN FIELD FARMING

Open field farming existed from time immemorial until enclosure in 1793. Essentially, it was a communal system in which almost everyone had some land in the open fields and access to grazing land on the commons. It depended on co-operation and agreement in which the community as a whole agreed on the crops to be grown and where the animals may graze. The conventions and rules governing these were fixed by the Court Leet, part of the Manor Court.

Orston had four open fields. These were known for most of the time as the Mill Field, Ozier Field, High Field and Little Field. See the map which shows their location around 1790. An estate survey of 1690 did not mention the Little Field, instead Cowman Field, previously known as Coleman Field, perhaps meaning Common Field. The 1633 Glebe Terrier did not refer to the High Field, instead Beckfields (probably because it was a long way from the village), so probably that was its former name. For a short period around 1650 there may have been five open fields: Ozier, Mill, High, Coleman and Orston. The latter two were probably part of what was High Field, as they were located near to it and in 1730 it was by far the largest field. This was probably a short-lived attempt to equalise the size of the open fields.

The Four Yearly Rotation of Crops at Orston

Year	***Winter-sown Corn***	***Winter/Spring***	***Spring-sown Barley****	***Fallow***
One	Ozier	Little	High	Mill
Two	Mill	Ozier	Little	High
Three	High	Mill	Ozier	Little
Four	Little	High	Mill	Ozier

* or peas/beans.

A four field system was slightly unusual where three was the most common in the Vale of Belvoir. The crops were typical. The fields were referred to in the Manor Court Rolls as 'The Corn Field', 'the Barley Field' and 'The Pease Field'. 'Pease' included both beans and peas. An equal acreage was devoted to wheat, barley and peas/beans. One field lay fallow. The inventories for Orston residents support this and suggest that an equal acreage was devoted to each and that other crops, e.g. oats, were not grown, although there is evidence that some rye, which was used in bread, was grown which was quite rare for Nottinghamshire (see Chapter 12). Wheat would be the winter crop, sown in the autumn, and barley would be sown in the spring. Peas and beans could be grown either as winter or spring crops. They may have even been sown in January or February, as on the demesne of William de Roos at Bottesford, which would have eased the pressure of work during the seasons. It is also likely that there would have been some cropping by furlong, or within a field, depending on the need for a particular crop and the fact that at Orston the acreage of the common fields was not equal. For instance, wheat and barley may have been grown in one field.

The open fields were divided up into sections known as furlongs. These in turn were divided up into strips known as 'lands' forming what we now know of as ridge and furrow. Traditionally, the length of a strip was that amount a plough team could plough without having to rest. The size of a land was that amount that could be ploughed by them in a day. The number of lands making up a furlong was determined by the lie of the land where the furrows always led downhill in order to drain the land.

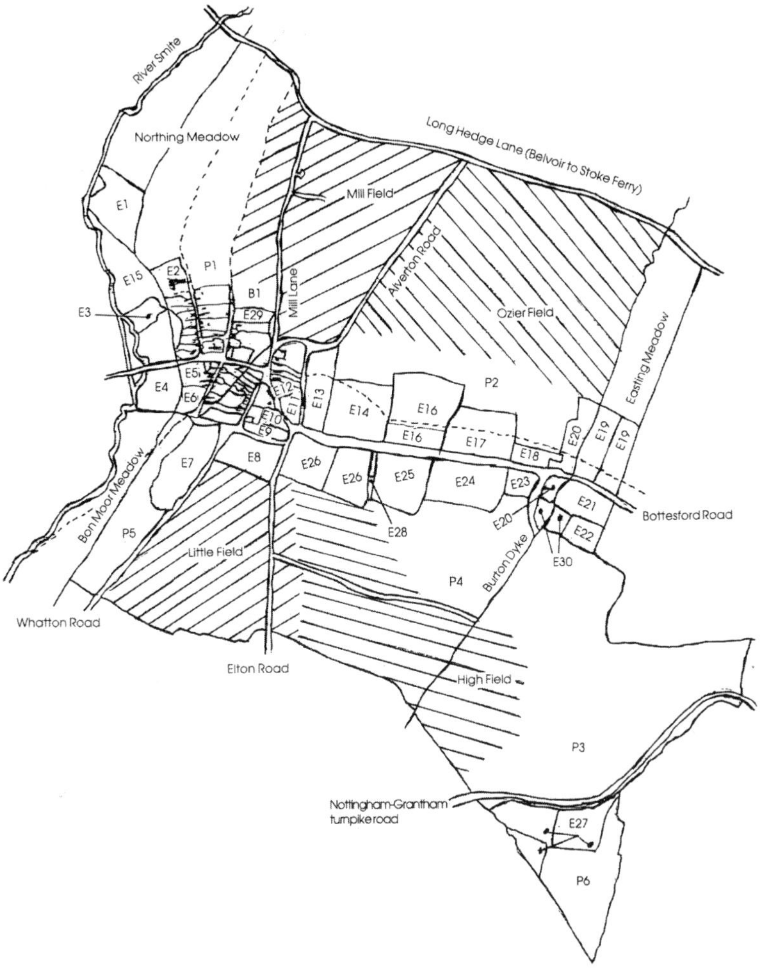

Enclosures
E1 Thoroton Folly Meadow
E2 The Manor House and Homestead
E3 Penny Farthing Piece
E4 Park Close
E5 Brick Yard Close
E6 Bell Holme
E7 Beanlands
E8 Land Close
E9 Five Leys
E10 not known
E11 Lordship Close
E12 not known
E13 Cow Close
E14 Great Dry Close
E15 Sutton Holme Close
E16 Middle Dry Closes
E17 Marriot Close
E18 not known
E19 Easting Closes
E20 -do-
E21 -do-
E22 -do-
E23 Little Dry Close
E24 Nether Dry Close
E25 Armer Close
E26 Long Closes
E27 Deepdale Closes
E28 Nether Long Close
E29 The Two Close
E30 Gunstones (Tethering grass. Lammas Land)

Pasture
P1 Nothing Leys (tethering grass. Lammas land)
P2 Burton Dyke Pasture ('old pasture')
P3 New Pasture
P4 Warhill Pasture ('old pasture')
P5 Bon Moor Pasture ('old pasture', Midsummer land)
P6 Deepdale ('new pasture')

Other
B1 Brick Yard

The layout of the open fields – circa 1790

Unfortunately, a map of the furrows of Orston does not exist although some of their names are known. See the table on the page 44.

The main issue in the maintenance of the open fields was access to the lands. In Orston access was across what were known as 'styes' and 'green furrows'. Styes were pathways or openings equivalent to what were known elsewhere as 'sykes'. Green furrows were narrow pathways between lands. However, because they were unmarked, it was always possible that these furrows could be encroached upon or simply ploughed up by farmers of adjacent lands, especially if a farmer happened to have those on both sides a green furrow. A by-law of the Court Leet in 1723 illustrates this. *'If any body Have plowed up any furrows ye shall lay them down as broad as the common furrows is upon ye same furlong before Lammas* (1 August until 1753) *next'*. A by-law was a decision of the Court Leet. As they were not fenced off, passage along a green furrow was likely to cause damage to the crops and, whilst they were growing, was restricted. A by-law in 1659 stated that *'no one shall ride down any corn field furer within the field of Orston till harvest begin except one hors or beast'*. Because the green furrows were narrow, they were mown and animals were not usually permitted to graze. A by-law in 1753 stated *'We agree to mow all the furrows in the Corn fields before Old Lammas Day on pain of one shilling a furrow for every default to be paid to the Lord of the said Mannor'*.

There was also the problem of ensuring that the furrows drained the land. Their clearance was known locally as 'gripping'. The responsibility for this was laid down by the Court Leet. For example, in 1641 it was provided that every *'inhabitant having land shall grip the sunside of his furrows of the three corn fields belonging to Orston aforsayd where and as oft as neyd shall require before Candlemas day* (2 February) *next ensuing'*. Other by-laws usually stated that gripping should be done by Plough Monday (the first Monday in January) and on one occasion, in 1721, on St Andrews Day (30 November).

The critical issue in the open field system was not the arable land but access to grazing land and the movement of animals between different types of grassland in order to make the best use of it. The limiting factor in mixed farming regions at that time was the amount of pasture and whether there was sufficient hay and grass to feed an animal, especially through winter. If there was not a valuable animal would have to be killed. At Orston, as elsewhere, in addition to the commons, pasture was in the form of meadow land, the best being near the river. Usually the meadows would be closed until Lammas so that grass could be grown for haymaking.

Other grazing was in 'leys', which were pieces of temporarily enclosed pasture in the open fields, and permanent enclosures outside the open fields, known as closes. In addition, Orston created what was called Lammas land which could be grazed by tethered animals until 1 August, and Midsummer Land which was probably only grazed between May-day and the end of June, giving just sufficient time for a July crop of hay. For the location of some of these, see the map of the open fields.

Once the harvest of a furlong had been completed, it was 'broken' and horses and cattle could be tethered to eat the stubble. It was a matter of how they could remain. By-laws were regularly made or amended to allow grazing until St Thomas's day (21 December). For example, in 1775 it was agreed *'that the wheat field be laid* ('laid' bare of animals) *and that no sort of cattle come into it from this day* (21 December). *That all the fields be driven* (the animals be driven off) *on Plough Monday'*. There were distinct advantages of certain smaller animals such as sheep grazing on a fallow, or newly sown, field. There were distinct advantages of certain small animals, such as sheep, being allowed to continue to graze on newly sown land. They clean it by eating the weeds, adding a small amount of manure and trample over it helping to lay a good seed bed. This was recognised, for example on St Thomas's Day 1759 it was agreed *'to Drive all the fields of grat guds large animals this day'* and in 1721 it was agreed that sheep could stay in the fields after sowing when, *'nether Horse Beast or Swine shall come into the wheat fields of Orston or Thoroton after the wheat is sown'*.

Until then, grazing would have been limited to the common pasture and areas within the open fields, which, for one reason or another, were unfit for tillage. In many other places these were called 'sykes' but in Orston they were known as 'styes'. After harvest the styes were usually thrown open for common grazing. Before then free grazing on them was not possible as the animals would stray into the open fields. They had to be tethered until 'wheat be gotten in' or Lammas. In some years the tethering of animals was barred altogether in certain styes; for example, in Warwell stye because of excessively wet weather.

Villagers were allowed to graze their animals on the commons, Bon Moor (either side of Pit Lane) and Loughbon (between Mill Lane and Church Street) and the outer regions towards Bottesford around Burton dyke and Deepdale or Debdale. See the map. However, grazing was strictly limited to the 'stint'. The stinting arrangements fixed the number of animals allowed to graze per oxgang (about 16 acres) of land an inhabitant held. For example, in 1655 the Court Leet fixed the stint at 2 beasts and 10 sheep per oxgang for each inhabitant and 1.5 beast and 5 sheep for an ancient cottager.

There is evidence of problems in English agriculture between 1730 and 1760 that had been brought about by changes that had first occurred during the previous century and known as the Agricultural Revolution. These included innovations such as new crops and floated water meadows. The former, notably turnips and legumes such as sainfoin and clover, had actually been available from as early as the 16th century, but their use had not been fully recognised. These combined to increase agricultural productivity in light loam districts such as East Anglia as they helped to relieve the problem of too little fodder with which to over-winter a large stock of farm animals. The economic effects of increased productivity spread throughout the country at a time of static population and falling grain prices.

Locally, farmers were faced with difficulties. Around Orston, they could not pay their rents and the Duke of Kingston, as with other landlords, had no option but to help them out. The Manor Court rolls record heirs being fined for not taking up lands they had inherited. Agriculture needed to adapt. One answer was to move from arable farming to pasture. These changes began to occur in Orston from about 1730. A sign of this was a reduced stint. Farmers sought to keep more animals but stock became so numerous that the permanent grassland was exhausted well before the meadows were opened. The stint, which refers to the numbers of animals a household was allowed to graze, was converted in 1705 from two beasts and ten sheep per oxgang of land held for a householder and one and a half beasts and five sheep for an ancient cottager to eight sheep and four sheep respectively, irrespective of land held.

To accommodate more animals, it was necessary to create more permanent pasture. In 1730 part of the Ozier Field was taken out of arable production and turned over to permanent pasture. There had been other attempts; as early as 1719 it was agreed that *'the Hall Dike & Colchered Close nook Layes by layd to the Pasture'*, but this was a relatively small area. The next major change probably followed in 1753, or just before, when the 'New Pasture' was created out of part of the High Field. A by-law of 1730 states *'We agree that the sheep shall go eight for an oxgang & four for a cottage in ye Ozier Field'*. This is the first reference in the manor court rolls to grazing there. Thus, although there is no indication of how much was put to permanent grazing, it may be inferred as a significant amount and a significant change of use of, what was, arable land.

The estate survey of 1788 clarified the new arrangements. The old Pasture, *'known by the names of Worrel Pasture Burton dike Pasture and Bonmoor Pasture'* was to be stocked at one beast to the oxgang. Debdale and the New Pasture were to be stocked *'with young beast at 1 ½ acre to a gate'*, a 'gate' or 'gait' being the number of animals that could be pasture in proportion to the amount of arable held.

There were other methods of converting old arable land to permanent pasture and making the remaining arable farming more efficient (the increased manure available would also have raised productivity). In many parishes this mainly involved the 'gathering' of lands. Here strips in the open fields which had hitherto been randomly distributed were rationalised and consolidated into blocks. These groups of strips were then enclosed in some way, probably temporarily, as they do not appear as existing enclosures on the enclosure award map. The 1742 survey referred to 10 arable lands in 'Hard Wong' and 15 grass leys in 'Square Wong'.

It is not clear how much arable land was converted to permanent pasture. The whereabouts of the original boundaries of the open fields are not known and there are no topographical indications of their outer boundaries. There is no hint in the by-law which adds part of the Ozier field to the common pasture as to the acreage involved, although some arable land remained. More information does exist about the New Pasture and shows that it was a large area, the outer part of the High Field. A survey in 1788 also states that 'Debdale and the new Pasture make one Pasture' and the enclosure map shows the area of New Pasture 'much of the area on the eastern side of Warhill Drain' and Debdale (the most remote area near Bottesford). Possibly, this was the easiest land to convert because it was so far from the village.

Ridge-and-furrow still existing today, together with photographic evident of lost ridge-and-furrow, and hedges dating from enclosure in the mill and little fields along the escarpment, indicate that arable land here was also turned to pasture. How much land was turned to pasture? The Enclosure Act provides a formula for the allotment of tithes which may be used to compute the likely proportions of arable and pasture land. It suggests that around 1550 acres were pasture (86%) and 400 acres were arable (14%) by the time of enclosure. (My calculations are presented in *Transactions of the Thoroton Society of Nottinghamshire*, 101, 1997, pp. 125-132. Unfortunately, there are no earlier figures against which these may be compared.

To sum up, the open field system of farming which had served agricultural communities for centuries was unable to cope with the new requirements of the Agricultural Revolution. More pasture land had to be created out of the arable open fields. Even though, this was the purpose of Enclosure, in Orston, as no doubt elsewhere, it was already occurring in various ways well before 1793 and on a large scale.

Aerial photo, 1950

Furlongs and Wongs*

1633 Glebe Terrier	*Terriers and other manuscripts 1642-1702*	*1650 Glebe Terrier*	*1788 Estate Survey*
Mill Field Northland Northern Staplehill Little Cliff Barlands **Ozier Field** Crothorne Gate Half Acres Longlands Eastend **Coleman Field** Longlands **Beckfields** Headlands Burklands Oandale Hill **Mill Field**	Barlands Staplehill Longlands Reds Norlands Clineseale **Ozier Field** Crothgat/ Crothongat Netherbut Wed furroeoes Longlands Crowthorngate Easting Staning Butt **Coleman Field** Half Acre Loung landes Rondles Barlands Redes Middle More Hill **Beckfields** Warwell Nether Headland Staning Ston Pitte Beckands/ Beckende Oundle Sandlands **High Field** Half Acre Worell Ondill/Aundell/ Aundle Little indike Kandnige Burlands/ Burtlands Borthandes Debdale Headlands Holme	**Mill Field** North Barlands Staple Hill Handells Cliff Dales Little Cliff **Ozier Field** Cranthorne Gate Green Butt Orston Field Netherbutt Easting Half Acre Long Lands **Coleman Field** Coleman Hill **High Field** Standing Warwell Halands Ann Dale Lyome Sandale Burtlands	**Mill Field** Headland Barlands Cross Red New Millhill Old Millhill West End Chevesdale Bowling Green wong Spa Wong **Ozier Field** Half Acre Bottom Acres The Butts Top of the Butts Half Acre wong Grissel wong **Little Field** Hill Side Headland Half Acre **High Field** Over Headland Half Acre Horndale Hill Little Dyke Branston wong Home Butts Over Bosoms wong

** All are furlongs unless stated to be wongs. Wongs are parts of the open fields temporarily enclosed and grassed. Headlands are strips of land at the end of a ploughed furlong upon which the plough turned. It was then ploughed at right angles. Butts were pieces of land in the open fields which, because of its irregular shape, were shorter than the usual strips.*

CHAPTER 9
THE MANOR COURT

The manor court was the main administrative unit of the manor. It comprised the Court Leet, which handled agricultural matters, and the Court Baron, which dealt with policing the community and resolving disputes. Fines went to the Lord of the Manor and provided him with a substantial additional income. In practice, as at Orston, the business of the two courts was combined. The business for Orston and Thoroton was at times also combined but at other times transacted separately.

All inhabitants over the age of twelve were required to attend and, if not, they were liable to a fine. The Court probably met in the hall of the manor house and would either be presided over by the Lord himself or, more likely, his steward. The decisions by the court were recorded by the clerk in the court roll and provide a comprehensive account of life and the management of the open field system. The court rolls for Orston from 1641 to the end of the Court in 1793 have survived, together with a few earlier ones and are kept in the British Museum. Here is the first.

The Court Leet and Baron 27 April 1641

1. We refer the suters to the court roules
2. We present the Inhabitants of Orston for not housing Artiliry xjs
3. We likewise present the inhabitants of Orston for there Buttes not to be in good repare
4. We present the Inhabitants of Thoroton for not housing Artiliry xjs
5. We present Thomas Branson for breaking the size of alle xjs
6. We present Janet Lambe for the Like xjs
7. We present Thomas Grey for bruing of Alle without Lisence
8. We make a paine att this Court that every inhabitant of Orston shall shoure his part of Lufburne Comon whoso against his owne ground betwixt Richard Challand his yard and the Smyth sufficiently before Maundy Thursday in default of who shall offend xiis
9. It that noe inhabitant shall tether any kind of chattell in the wheat feeld styes or furrows till the wheat begotton in paine for every default iii - iiis except in wed furrowes & the hade att grissell wong
10. We present James Bell & William Clarke the younger for suspitcious walking in the nights vis
11. It That noe inhabitants shall tether noe horses or any kind of other chattel within any part of Stale meadow on paine for every default till they be in court
12. We present francis - for making ablud upon Janet Goodbourne wife of Nicholas Goodbourne
13. We present Thomas Wright John Huggett Henry Peake to be overseers for our fields this year following

Henry Flower
Thomas Wright
John Cliffe

Items 2 and 3 may relate to the inhabitants' relationship to the two sides in Civil War which started the following year.

The officers of the court were:
The Steward - the chief agent of the Lord of the Manor for the management of the manor. He usually presided over the courts and kept the records.
The Bailiffe - the professional supervisor of the manor, appointed from outside by the Lord of the Manor.

The Constable - an officer of the court with a wide range of responsibilities. They included i) the supervision of the watch and ward, ii) the upkeep of the stocks, iii) the inspection of alehouses, iv) the apprehension and detention of suspected criminals and the arrest of escaped prisoners, v) the suppression of riots and unlawful assemblies.
The Overseers for the fields
The Thirdborough - the petty constable of a township or manor.
The Pindar - the officer in charge of the pinfold or pound into which stray animals were put.
The Mole Catcher
The Reeve - elected by fellow tenants to organise the daily business of the manor. He was often their spokesman in negotiations with the Lord of the Manor or his representative. In return he received special grazing rights and remission of rent and feudal dues. He was, where no officer was appointed, in charge of the agricultural policy of the manor as well as being responsible for livestock.

Until 1661 the Court met four times each year, usually in January, April and October and on the feast of St Thomas the Apostle (21 December), although it was suspended during the period 1644-1650 because of the Civil War. After 1770 the Court did not meet so regularly and its importance began to decline as, no doubt did the power and patronage of the Lord of the Manor. From 1723, not only was there some inconsistency as to whom fines were paid 9to the lord of the manor, the relevant officer of the court, such as the constable for the non-repair of a fence, or as sometimes half each, but they also became much more spasmodic and gradually died out. Instead, the main concern of the Court was the implementation of new farming practices and the fixing of new arrangements based on general consent. Thus, the role of the court changed from the administration of agriculture primarily by the lord of the manor through his bailiff to becoming a record of agreements by the farming inhabitants as they moved towards a new agricultural system.

Harvesting in Nottinghamshire, 1635

CHAPTER 10
THE PROVISION OF A WIFE'S LIVELIHOOD

Most wills are dull documents. However, the will by Matthew Jackson, yeoman, who died in 1672 provides an interesting insight into the working of the open field system. It shows that there was a four field system. Traditionally, everyone would have an equal amount of land in each open field. This may not necessarily be physically the same land depending upon custom. In some townships, probably not Orston, lands (strips in the open fields) were allotted randomly each year so as to divide out the good and bad land fairly.

> *"I give & bequeath to Ellen my wife four acres of land that is to say in every field of Orston aforesaid one acre in every field after the rate of the fields during her natural life. Item I give & bequeath to my son in law Wm Wright & Margaret his wife my daughter twenty pounds thus provided that the said Wm Wright shall plowe & lead manure for the said four acres of land twelve loades of manure of one acre every yeare during the natural life of Ellen my said wife & to leade home her corne when it is ready during her life. And when the said Wm Wright receivieth the said twenty pounds to give to my said wife a Bond for sufficient ordering of the said land or - the said twenty pounds to be paid ......*
>
> *I give & bequeath unto Ellen my said wife the four acres of land half acre of meadow ground which I bought of Wm Beane so longe as she shall keep her self in my name ......".*

Haymaking in Nottinghamshire, 1635.

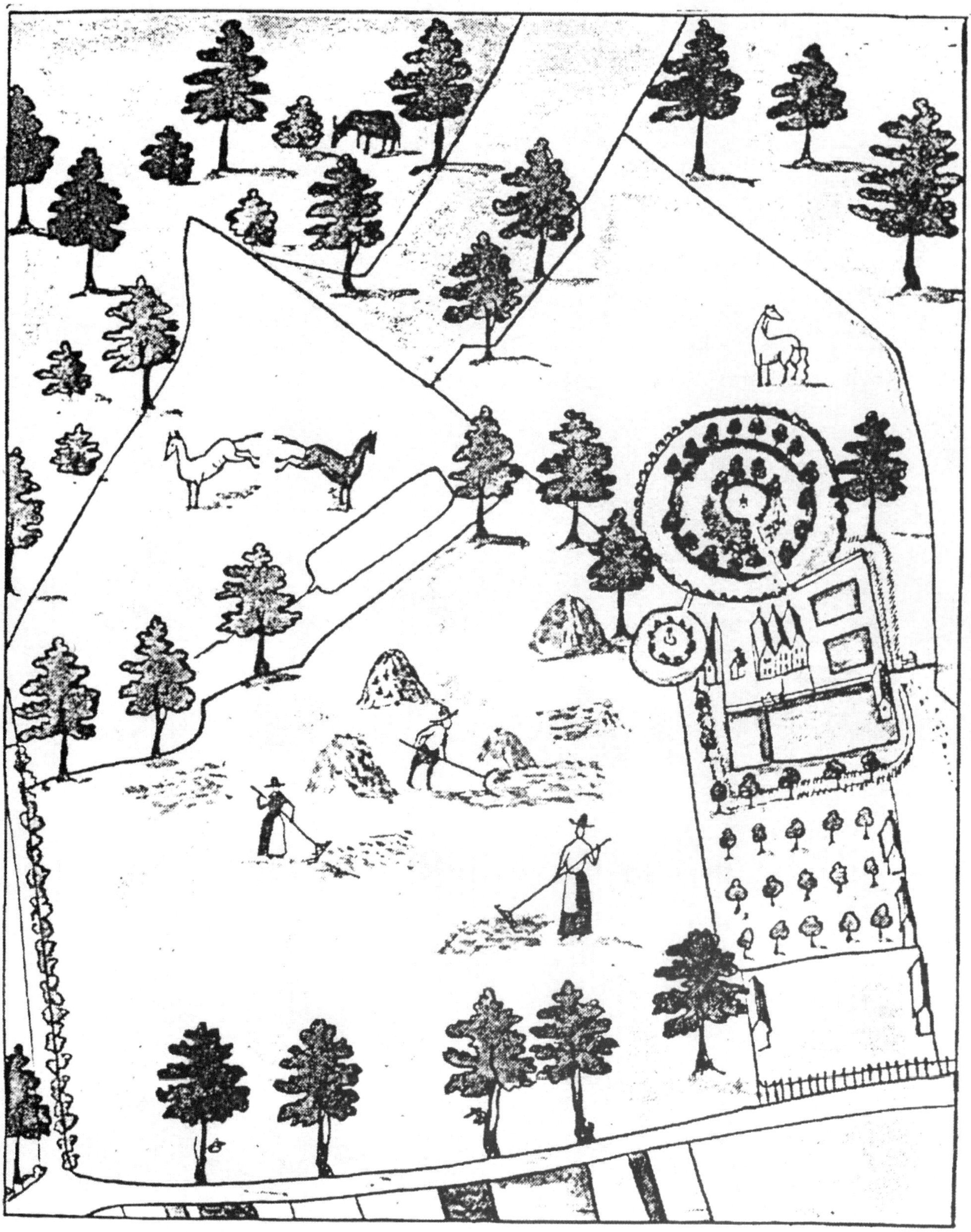

Haymaking in Nottinghamshire, 1635.

CHAPTER 11
ENCLOSURE OF THE OPEN FIELDS AND AFTERWARDS

Although it had begun much earlier, the ancient practice of open field farming was officially ended by the enclosure award in an act of parliament in 1793. It stated that there were about 2,200 acres in the townships of Orston and Thoroton. For Orston, which comprised of about 1,800 acres, the award was for 1,568 acres. The reason for the disparity was the existence of 'ancient enclosures', areas which were already hedged off and separately owned and therefore did not need to be included in the allocation of the open fields between the various claimants. These enclosures dated back to at least 1650 when a Glebe terrier noted that '*There are several enclosures (about 23 or 24 in number) containing betwixt two and three Hundred acres'*. However, in the Domesday of Inclosure of 1517 there is no reference to any inclosures at Orston so their creation must lie between these two dates. The recipients of the allotments are listed in the table.

Principal Recipients of Allotments in the 1793 Enclosure Award

	Acres
Dean and Chapter of Lincoln and the Rev Graham Chappell, the lessee.	296
Rev James Bingham	290
Rev Charles Wylde	120
Thomas Marshall	109
The Kington Estate (the Lord of the Manor)	103
Rev J.R. Litchford	98
William Marshall	92
The vicar, Rev E. Robson	68
Rev John Edwards	60
Rev Graham Chappell	26
14 others	306
Total	1568

The petition for Parliamentary enclosure of Orston was made by Charles Pierrepont, the owner of the Kingston estate, the other large landowners 'and others'. The grounds were that *'the Lands and grounds in the said Open Fields lie intermixed and dispersed, and they, together with the Commons and Waste Grounds, in their present Situation, are incapable of Improvement'*. The petition to enclose did not involve controversy and was not opposed. The reason for this was probably that, as described in Chapter 8, the enclosure of provisionally allocated land had already begun in anticipation of the actions of the enclosure commissioners. A footnote to an estate survey of 1788 says, *'This is now inclosing and the particulars to be sent as soon as sent out'*. Further, probably the most detrimental aspects of the open field system had already been overcome so that the enclosure award, when it arrived, was not such a radical change as may have been supposed.

Another factor that helped the change was the disposal between 1757 and 1788 of much of his land by the head of the Pierrepont family, who was the lord of the manor. By 1793 he was no longer the largest single landowner but the fifth. This came about by the sale of a large piece of land to the Duke of Portland, who in fact then became the largest single landowner. Also small pieces of land were probably also sold off to local inhabitants. The Enclosure Award for Orston is unusual for the large number of inhabitants receiving allocations.

Ownership of Land by the Kingston Estate

Year of Survey	*Acres*	*Tenants*
1690	737	29
1694	737	21
1742	645	21
1757	unknown	21
1788	218	1
1793	182½	1

Between 1694 and 1742 the number of tenant farmers remained roughly constant at around 30 but by 1793 this number had fallen considerably as many had either bought their land or were awarded it.

The number of farms continued to fall as the large estates broke up over the next hundred years or so. Part of the estate of the Dean and Chapter of Lincoln, including what is now known as Orston Hall, were sold in 1809. At the time of enclosure one of the largest landowners was Rev James Bingham, vicar of Epperstone. His estate was divided up and sold in 1853. The estate of the Pierrepont family, the head of which was still the lord of the manor and Lord Manvers, had finally dwindled to a mere 152 acres in 1911 when it was sold by auction in 1911, probably for estate duty reasons.

There were between 10 and 12 separate farms in Orston between 1832 and 1925. Five of them had more than 150 acres. This number did not significantly change until the 1960s.

Ridge and furrow, Mill Lane.

Approximate Farm Sizes based on Land Tax Returns -1793

	Acres		*Acres*
Thomas Bean	429	Francis Vincent	189
John Green	18	Henry Throop	7.5
William Green	4.5	Widdow Maltby	72
J. Kettleborrow	12	William Maltby	91.5
Richard Dewey	4.5	William Leake	4.5
John Bean	58	William Wilson	3.5
Widdow Harvey	48	William Hand	15
Samuel Throne	25	William Marshall	71
William Samson	10	Widdow Plumb	72.5
James Barrows	48	Thomas Maltby	62
J. Chettle	41	William Woodward	38
Thomas Wickham	47	Richard Kirk	1
Robert Chambers	10.5	Thomas Marshall	57.5
Thomas Cox	1	John Pepper	6
J. Bagguley	52.5	Thomas Linford	7
J. Cheetham	14	**Average**	**49**

Aerial photo of the village centre, circa 1995.

CHAPTER 12
INVENTORIES

Probate inventories were required by the ecclesiastical courts in the sixteenth to the eighteenth century for wealthy individuals in order to protect the executors from excessive claims and disputes. They would be drawn up by neighbours after the funeral. Inventories only exist for men as women were not considered as owners. They provide an interesting insight into possessions and the way in which people lived. Some inventories survive for Orston. Two of them are shown here. When reading the crops you should note the time of year.

Henry Wiseman - April 7 1722

Purse and apparel	*20.*	*0.*	*0.*
All - in the house	*5.*	*0.*	*0.*
All the brass & pewter & linnen in the kitching & Drink house	*13.*	*10.*	*0.*
Goods in the parlor	*4.*	*10.*	*0.*
In the other parlor & dairy	*4.*	*0.*	*0.*
In the chamber over the parlor	*1.*	*10.*	*0.*
In the chamber over the house	*7.*	*0.*	*0.*
In the little chamber	*3.*	*0.*	*0.*
In the chamber over the kitchen	*8.*	*0.*	*0.*
Things in the -	*3.*	*10.*	*0.*
Horses	*60.*	*0.*	*0.*
Sheep	*25.*	*0.*	*0.*
Beasts & calves	*59.*	*0.*	*0.*
Young calves	*2.*	*0.*	*0.*
Swine	*6.*	*10.*	*0.*
Corne in the corne	*20.*	*0.*	*0.*
Hay	*25.*	*0.*	*0.*
Grasses in the stables materials & other things	*7.*	*10.*	*0.*
Wagons & Carts & other materials	*25.*	*0.*	*0.*
The growing crop of corne	*102.*	*0.*	*0.*
Things seen & unseen		*10.*	*0.*
	397.	*10.*	*0.*

William Maltby -17 November 1718

Purse & apparrel	4. 0. 0.
Plate and linen	20. 0. 0.
In the pantry Brasse and pewte	6. 0. 0.
In the brewhouse the copper & brewing vessels	5. 0. 0.
In the house table & chairs & his irons	2. 6. 0.
In the best parlour & chamber one bed - and tables	17. 0. 0.
In the old parlour one bed and bedding & glass chairs and drawers	5. 0. 0.
In the chamber above it one bed and - and boxes	4. 0. 0.
The chamber over the house one bed and cheste & one -	2. 0. 0.
In the other chamber	1. 0. 0.
In the Garral Cheeses	1. 0. 0.
In the - chamber two beds & bedding	1. 0. 0.
In the Celler Barrells and Drink	1. 10. 0.
In the Corn Chamber Corn	10. 0.
Coals & - wood & Oakwood	4. 0. 0.
In the Dairy & Buttery	1. 0. 0.
Horses Mares & foles	110. 0. 0.
Cows & young beasts	63. 0. 0.
Pasture sheep and fallow sheep	124. 0. 0.
Corn at home wheat barley & pease	106. 0. 0.
Wheat upon the ground	35. 0. 0.
Barly clotts and pease ground	42. 0. 0.
Hay at home & abroad	40. 0. 0.
fouling & poules	1. 10. 0.
for carriages and gear	28. 0. 0.
malt	15. 0. 0.
- & mangers	2. 10. 0.
ploughs & harrows	1. 0. 0.
swine & troughs	5. 10. 0.
-	6. 0. 0.
2 hovells	2. 0. 0.
things seen & unseen	10. 0.
	704. 15. 0.

CHAPTER 13
THE BEGINNINGS OF MODERN DAY FARMING.

by Brian Gunn.

Between the wars, farmers found a way of surviving the world-wide depression: 'Dog and Stick farming', all grass and minimal expense. The penny pinching showed in pastures slowly being covered by bushes and ant-hills and buildings crumbling into picturesque decay. To some eyes green heaven, to others neglected hell.

However, thanks to the Milk Marketing Board, a regular income. Formerly, farmers individually made deals with dairies, settling for all kinds of prices with buyers who were unreliable payers. Now all milk was sold to the MMB at a uniform price and the cheque came without fail every month.

In the 1940s, dairy farming was the mainstay of agriculture in Orston. There were five herds in the village. At Hill Farm was the gentlemanly Walter Baguley with the biggest herd. At the end of High Street were Ted Caunt and John Maule, known as the Company. Next to the school was Wilfred Gunn; on Launder Street, Edgar Lovegrove and near the Green, where Newton's business is now was Wilmot Walker, who had lost part of a finger in WW1.

Traditional arable farmers rather looked down on the dairymen. 'When he finished with his mother's tit, he went on to a cow's' was a common remark. There was often pique in this as the malodorous dairyman, always shod in caked Wellingtons, his person and clothes stinking of cows, was the only man in farming making money.

The reliance on the dairy herd made the village filthy. The cows in the summer marched through the village four times daily between the farmsteads and their grazings, discharging great quantities of what we nowadays call slurry and treading the unpaved areas into strangely corrugated mud. Citizens who only know the manicured Orston we live in today can hardly imagine the squalor of the streets of yesteryear.

The Baguley herd produced a single but deep embankment across Station Road at the top end of today's hill top. The Gunn herd crossed Mill lane usually with side trips to the Cricket field which was grazed during the war. Lovegroves used every street in the village to reach their various grazings. The Company walked theirs the length of High Street. No neatly kept patches of lawn then, not a wisp of grass. Regularly marching cows created a corrugated walkway in the clay, with a daily topping.

The star turn was the Walker herd. He had dogs trained to chase his cows out of his yard to minimise cleaning. They unloaded out on the street at the Green corner and the swamp permanently extended from pavement to pavement. The inescapable smell hung over the whole village.

The Wartime chapter recounts how 'Dog and Stick' was outlawed and the land brought back into full production. The extra labour needed was provided by land-girls, prisoners of war and the many extra hands needed at harvest time came from the army and airforce camps and schoolchildren. Some experiments, potatoes, sugar beet and flax were found unsuitable for Orston's heavy, sticky land. However, cereals grew well and the replacement of horses by tractors and the combine harvester enabled the regular farm staff to cope with the rushes of seed-time and harvest.

All political parties agreed that it was not in the national interest for agriculture to sink back into decay and the financial guarantees introduced during the war have been maintained ever since.

Ten years after the war, all nine farms in the village were mixed, with at least one livestock enterprise as well as the cereal acreage. The five dairy herds remained, plus sheep, pigs and poultry. But the momentum of change was unstoppable – corn was king!

This changed the landscape. Large machinery functions better in big fields and bogs down less away from the hedgerows. The wartime airfield and the huge clearance at Flawborough Farms showed the way and, wherever practical, hedges were grubbed up.

It changed the pattern of mixed farming. With enough equipment to grow corn on half the holding, a farmer can have the whole farm under the plough and the manifest success of the all-arable man cast doubt on the value of subsidiary livestock enterprises. So the sheep, the beef, the pigs and the poultry disappeared. One by one, the dairy herds closed down. The last survivor was Leslie Lovegrove who closed down in 1994. Throughout the 60s, 70s, 80s and into the 90s, corn growing flourished in Orston. New varieties, better machinery, storage and chemicals and the introduction of oilseed rape as a convenient break crop all helped. Farms have amalgamated and the workforce has dwindled to a tiny handful.

In 1973, Britain finally joined the European Union and our farming fell under the political control of the Common Agricultural Policy. When this was formulated in the 1950s, the main objective was to maximise production and so reduce Europe's reliance on the outside world for food. Technical advances and a guaranteed market were the chosen tools. Output per hectare, as well as in total, soared in Europe, as it did in Britain and Orston. By the early 1990s, overproduction had become a serious problem and the surplus 'mountains' an embarrassment.

There was also popular distaste for the new 'prairie' farming. Not just nostalgia for an imagined pretty yesteryear but real concern for endangered wildlife and anger at the waste of public money.

In 1993, by order of Brussels, farmers began to be paid to act as a kind of gardener of the countryside. Stewardship of the land became the objective rather than all-out production. Under the controversial 'set-aside' provisions, farmers were paid a dole to leave a part of their arable land out of production for a year, each plot being brought back into the rotation the following year to keep the land usable. Many hedgerows were replanted and hedge cutting banned for four months in the year to allow birds a peaceful nesting season. The use of poisonous chemicals near watercourses was not allowed. A broad band of land left uncultivated around the arable fields as a wildlife refuge was rewarded from Europe as was tree planting.

One new livestock development is Sheardown's free-range poultry enterprise near Flawborough. There are more laying hens there than in the whole of Orston in former days. Grassland is used by the many horses now kept for pleasure in Orston – more than a hundred at the last count.

During 2007, the situation changed. Adverse weather conditions (arguably the result of global warming) and millions of third world people, newly prosperous, wanted to eat like Americans. The grain mountains have been eaten and there is a shortage of wheat. No more set-aside: that land is being brought back into production. Farming in Orston in 2008 is changing again, as it always has and always will – in response to supply and demand.

Aerial view of Yew Tree Farm, circa 1950.

Mr Ball and daughter, 1902, who lived in Scotney's Cottage. Mr Ball was a farm labourer at Hill Farm.

(above) Manor Farm stackyard, 1912.

Lodge Farm.

Dovecote Farmhouse. Circa 1985.

(above) Ted Caunt's farm on High Street (now known as Cornerfield Barn) circa 1950

White Acres, circa 1960.

(below) Steam plough engine, 1920, ridden by Mr J. Draper (L) and Mr James Wakefield (R).

CHAPTER 14
POPULATION

From 1642 onwards there is sufficient information to be able to estimate the population of Orston quite accurately. Prior to then there is the Domesday Book which indicates that the population was between 150 and 175 suggesting a large village, certainly above average, existed at that time. Other aspects of the Domesday entry (see the chapter on Origins) suggest that Orston was not only prosperous but the principal village of the area.

From 1801 official census information exists. From 1642 to 1801 it is possible to estimate the population using independent surveys and the parish registers of births and deaths. The rest of this chapter will be split between these two periods.

1642-1801
There are a number of surveys that occurred during the period but only a few are of help in estimating the total population. The Hearth Tax return for 1674 lists a total of 47 households of which 4 are discharged. As it only counts the number of households with hearths and it gives no indication of how many lived in each, any population estimate can be only very approximate but national averages may also be used. It will be seen from this that the rectory (now known as Orston Hall) occupied by Constance Kerchevall was the largest house. Ezekiell Diglane was the vicar and lived in the vicarage on the site of the present Old Vicarage. The 1664 return is spoiled so that the total households is not known.

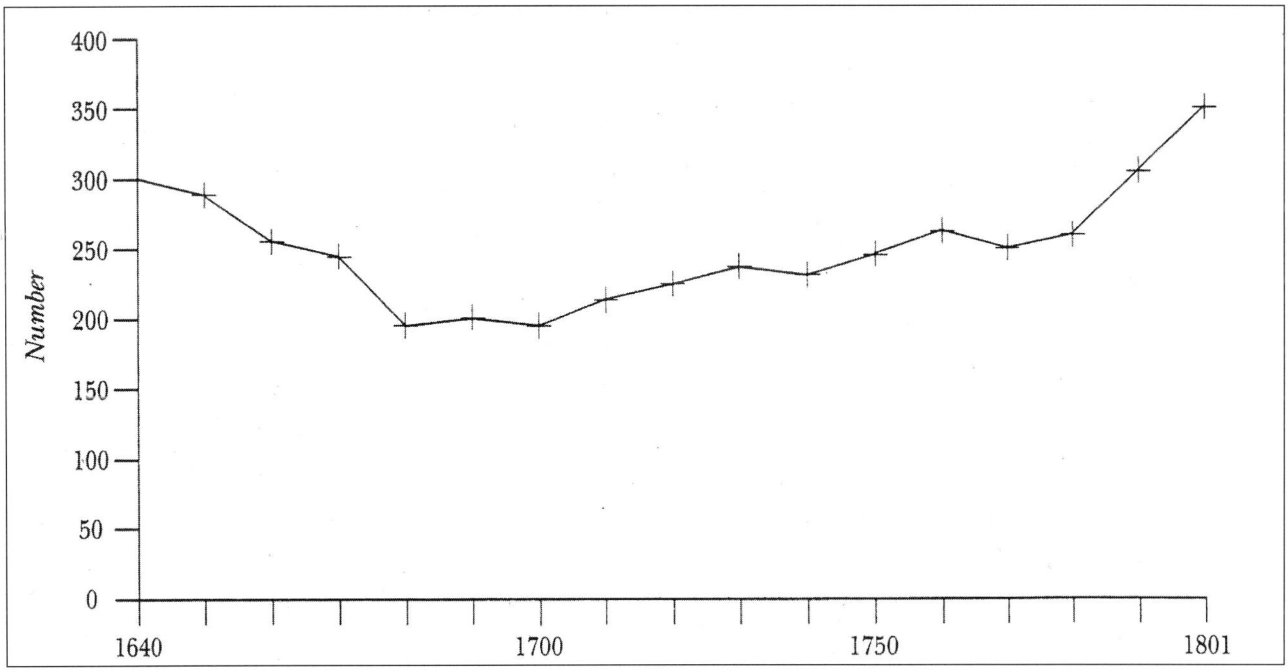

Ten-yearly population estimates, 1640-1801.

The parish registers do not show population numbers but they may be used to calculate movements between dates. Ten yearly estimates have been made. At the beginning of the period the population was about 300 and at the end it was 351. It appears that, even though there was emigration out of the village of about 2 per year, with the exception of the 1680-1720 period when there was slight immigration into the village of two per decade during 1680-1700 and one per decade during 1700-1720, from 1700 onwards there was a slowly rising population. The reasons for this are clear: from 1710 the mortality rate was lower and from 1730 the birth rate was higher.

These trends are similar to, and in line with, those revealed for Nottinghamshire villages and the country as a whole. For the period 1642-1676 the declining population was repeated throughout the country where there was a 20 percent fall which was attributed to reduced fertility as a result of uncertainty (a reduced birth rate), rising mortality and continued migration to the towns. Migration to the towns continued into, and throughout, the eighteenth century, both in Nottinghamshire and elsewhere. However, the improving birth and mortality rates more than compensated for this which is consistent with the steadily increasing population for Orston.

The table below compares Orston with average populations for Nottinghamshire villages. It shows that, whilst migration to the new towns was the main factor in population changes, Orston remained above the average size and this difference actually increased.

Nottinghamshire Agricultural and industrial Population Changes (average population)

	1674	***1743***	***1764***	***1801***
Industrial village	230	340	462	908
Agricultural village	166	187	199	276
Orston	200	220	253	351

Nottinghamshire Population Changes 1642-1676

	1642	**1676**	**% change**
Bingham Hundred	5784	4376	-24
Orston	300	200	-33

1801-2001

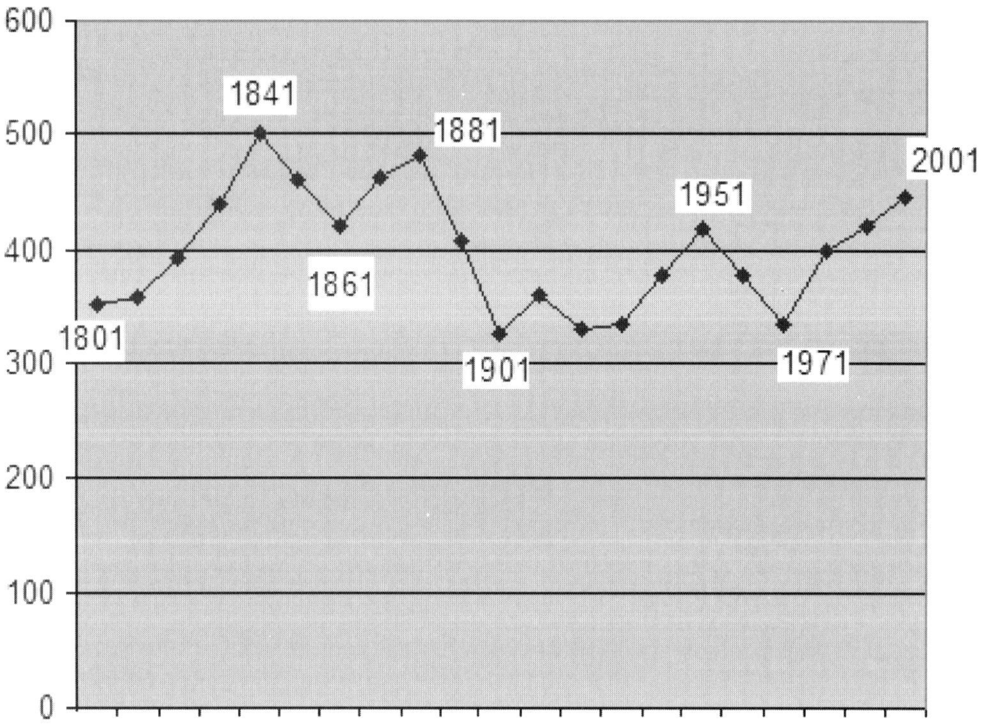

Ten-yearly population statistics 1801-2001

The graph shows the decline of Orston as an agricultural village during the nineteenth century as the movement to the towns and cities increased with the industrial revolution. The growth between 1831 and 1841 was probably due to the introduction of hosiery manufacture and the increase over the 1861-1881 period was undoubtedly due to gypsum working.

The maintenance of Orston's population during the twentieth century must be seen in terms of the expansion elsewhere. Whilst there may have been little change during the first half of the twentieth century, the decline of agricultural employment was largely offset by the increase in commuters, mainly to Nottingham.

Nottinghamshire Population Changes 1801-2001

	Nottinghamshire	**Nottingham**	**Bingham**	**Orston**
1801	140,350	28,801	1,082	351
1901	514,628	239,743	1,604	326
Increase	267%	732%	48%	-7%
2001	748,510	266,988	8,655	445
Increase	45%	11%	540%	36%

Hearth Tax Return – 1664

		Hugh Lambe	i	William Maultby	i	Richard Clarke	i
Constance Kerchevall	6	William Wiseman	i	Hugh Hixon	i	William Clarke	i
Ezkiell Diglane	2	Thomas Wiseman	i	John Challand	i	Henry Rignett	i
Henry Norman	3	Henry Wiseman	i	Thomas Wallis	i	Widow Storey	i
Matthew Jackson	i	John Kettlebarne	i	George Wright	i	Roger Burchby	i
Henry Bampton	i	John Archer	i	William Pell	i	Margarett Taylor	i
Thomas Ludlay	i	Thomas Patchett	i	John Salmon	i	Richard Green	i
Robert Smith	i	Henry Challand	i	Francis Smith	i	William Rest	i
Robert Newsome	i	William Storer	i	Robert Green	i	Anne Simpson	i
Edward Green	i	Thomas Storer	i	Robert Challand	i	Roger Dennis	i
William Claytor	i	Widow Litherland	i	Eliz Ashton	i	John Harnis	i
William Smith	i	Richard Stafford	i	Ro… ..ke…	I	Nicholas Goodbarne	i
Edward Burton	i	Thomas Marshall	i			Robert Haley	i
Robert Braunston	i	Widow Huggett	i	*Hole here several entries missing*		Susan Attenborow	i
William Hall	i	Thomas Charity	i			John Key	i
John Smith	i	Griffin Wright	i	**NOT CHARGEABLE**		William Challand	i
Anthony Wright	i	Richard Huskinson	i	Robert Wickham	I	James Edenborow	i
Richard Challand	i	Henry Huggett	i	John Lame	I	William Smith	i
John Braunston	i	Thomas Harvey	i	Widow Kettlebarne	I	Richard Ellis	i
George Flower	i	William Ragsdale	i	Henry Breedon	I	Joseph Clifton	i
Widow Blumfield	i	John Maultby	i	Ellen Rest	I	Alice Robinson	i
Richard Marshall	i	William Beane	i	Widow Dore	I	Alice Kenerker	i
Peter Ragby	i	Thomas Wright	i	William bell	I	Katherine Fisher	i
							30

Hearth Tax Return – 1674

John Jalland	2	Griffin Wright	1	Henry Norman	3	Mr John Kerchevall	6
Hugh Higgens	2	Thomas Charity	2	William Dawson	2	Mr Digling	3
William Wright	2	Widow Higgin	2	George Wright	1	Henry Flower	1
William Maultby	2	Widow Jackson	1	George Marshall	2	John Branson	1
Thomas Maultby, sen	2	Edward Pears	1	Nicholas Man	2		71
William Maultby	2	Robert Seywell (Empty)	2	Thomas Browne	2	**DISCHARGED BY LEGAL CERTIFICATE**	
William Rest	1	Henry Wiseman	1	Matthew Jackson	1	Widow Breedon	1
Robert Wicome	1	Thomas Wiseman	1	Henry Bampton	1	Richard Greene	1
Thomas Wright	1	Widow Storey	1	Widow Higgin	2	Roger Brichby	1
Henry Higgen	1	Henry Scrimshaw	1	William Smith	1	Widow Mantle	2
John Greene	2	Hugh Lambe	2	Edward Barton	1		
William Clarke	2	Anthony Wright	2	Thomas Linford	1		
Henry Jalland	1	John Smith	2	Robert Branson	1		

CHAPTER 15
THE INDUSTRIAL REVOLUTION IN ORSTON - GYPSUM MINING

Although there are gypsum quarries in the area, it is hard to imagine that Orston was once primarily a mining village. In fact, in earlier centuries Orston was probably the most important village in the East Midlands for gypsum. According to the Nottinghamshire volume of the *Victoria History of the Counties of England,* the gypsum at Orston was 'the finest in the Kingdom'. Also under the undergrowth in the Girl Guides' land near the Nottingham to Grantham railway line lie the remains of the 'manufactory', a typically ambitious project of the Industrial Revolution, a plan of which survives in the Nottingham Archives Office. According to the *Newark Advertiser* (2/8/1865) it was the most modern and most efficient in Europe in 1865 and it has been estimated that from 1868-71 the Orston manufactory produced about 8 per cent of the nation's gypsum products. A photograph of the 'manufactory' also survives.

At that time, its main use was as plaster of Paris which according to its colour and purity, was used as a base for a variety of wall, ceiling and pottery products and other specialised plasters and patent cements. Raw ground gypsum was also used for various other purposes in agriculture and as a filler and whitener.

The digging for gypsum in Orston dates back much earlier than to the Industrial Revolution and probably to medieval times. Orston may have been a supplier to the medieval alabaster carvers of Nottingham famous for their relief carvings of panels of biblical subjects. It is likely that some of the effigies in Bottesford Church were carved out of Orston gypsum. The earliest documentary evidence is an account in 1541 for a payment by the Duke of Rutland. 'Nicholas Northe of Orston was paid 8s.4d. for digging 20 tons of plaster' (i.e. gypsum for plaster). It has been argued that an even earlier document refers to Orston. In the Collyweston accounts for 1502 payment was *'made to William Upton of the Vale of Bever for 62 tonne of plaster of Paris'* at 3s.0d. per ton, with carriage, stated to be 22 miles.

The most likely area for the casual digging of gypsum in Orston is in Loughbon Common, the area immediately north of Loughbon around the school field (hence the undulations in the ground from digging) and in the 'bell pits' scattered along Moor Lane.

The change from the casual digging of gypsum around Orston to the setting up of an integrated business involving both a quarry and a 'manufactory' dates to July 1860 when The Royal Plaster Works (so named because the owner of the land was also proprietor of the inn, the Royal Oak) were built in the centre of the village and worked by Messrs Willis & Co. of London. The pit still exists behind the houses on the south side of Loughbon together with some of the original buildings (now incorporated into what is known as Mulhouse) and ovens. The terraced houses on Chapel Street were originally miners' cottages.

In 1864, the Royal Plaster Works failed and was taken over by William Jacobs, already a well-known gypsum quarrier and manufacturer at Beacon Hill, Newark. He was soon joined by James Carter, an auctioneer and stock and share broker from Nottingham, who recognised the opportunity to raise the necessary money by means of forming a limited liability company which was all the rage at that time. Carter and Jacobs commissioned the digging of a large pit and the building of a factory on the land Carter owned just outside the village near the new railway line in part of what is now the Guide Camp. This land was probably already worked for gypsum on a small scale and the quality of the stone known to be good. Building of the works began in 1864 and took about two years.

Unfortunately the offer of shares to the general public by Newark's first limited liability company, the Vale of Belvoir and Newark Plaster, Cement and Mineral Co. Ltd, in 1865 to raise the additional money needed was unsuccessful. The claims made in the prospectus were probably too grand to be believed, a common fault with prospectuses at that time. However, Carter and Jacobs together with William Newton, a prominent Newark solicitor, were committed to the venture and the grand opening on 3 April 1866 went ahead nevertheless.

> *'This took the form of a dinner to which a number of the principal inhabitants of the place, the workmen in the employ of the firm and several friends sat down ... The whole village was astir and the bells rung a merry peal in honour of the occasion .... The cloth having been drawn, Mr Jacobs, proposed the health of his partner, Mr James Carter of Nottingham, with that of the company's solicitor, Mr W.Newton of Newark ... The health of several friends present was given and responded to and a very pleasant evening was spent; the company remaining to a late hour. Prior to the dinner visitors were conducted over the works, which were in full operation, the steam engine of 35 horse-power driving the stones used in grinding the gypsum. The capacious ovens are arranged in the most convenient position for the reception of the plaster with the least amount of labour possible. The grinding is carried on in close proximity, and a siding from the Great Northern Railway runs close to the works, so that the plaster is placed on the trucks from the building in which it is manufactured. The saving in cost of labour and cartage must therefore be immense. The first truck of plaster was sent away in the early part of February last, for the eminent firm of C.J. Hilton and Co. the extensive cement manufacturers, Upper Thames Street, London. W.C.Anderson, Esq. (one of the firm), had previously visited these works, and was well satisfied with their extent and construction, and the superior quality of the deposit of gypsum, that he gave an order for 1,200 tons to be delivered within twelve months. Brick making is carried on upon the premises, and one builder has given an order for about a million'.* (Newark Advertiser 11/4/1866).

The excitement did not last. Even though Carter and Jacobs were helped by William Newton and Hardy & Co., Grantham bankers, the business went under in 1873. Some of the partners in Hardy & Co. bought it at the liquidator's auction and continued to run it until 1897 when it was sold to the general manager, Richard Almond. The change in ownership in 1897 coincided with a change in the way gypsum was dug. Hitherto it had largely been mined underground. From about this date this ceased and open-cast mining began. The two large lakes on either side of the Whatton bridle road today are the result. The first pond on the left hand side walking from Orston is much deeper and was used as part of the system for pumping water out of the underground mine. The works were closed around 1914.

The digging for gypsum and clay, for bricks, tiles, land drains, drain pipes etc. are closely linked. Clay would be dug out in large quantities in getting to the gypsum. It made sense that it should be utilised especially as large baking ovens were available from heating the gypsum. Clay was mostly worked during the summer months leaving the winter for gypsum.

Gypsum is no longer dug in Orston.

Part of the Royal Plaster works, circa 1990, now part of Mulhouse

The village of Orston is on the borders of Nottinghamshire, 9 miles south of Newark, out of the way to anywhere and everywhere, and before the discovery of these gypsum beds *a terra incognita*, which wagged on like o'her places do, no less celebrated for Crow yards, cats, mice, and sparrows. Certainly there is something to be seen at Orston. Its church yard is planted with chesnut trees, presenting an *ensemble* quite pleasing to the eye; with an old-fashioned church which has stood for seven centuries, and which we shall be glad to hear of the Vale of Belvoir and Newark Plaster Company restoring. There is likewise a roadside inn, whereat, if you can't get bitter beer and other liquid amenities of civilized life, you can get a glimpse of Orston peasant life, which the local sons of toil evidently regard as being made up of beer and tobacco. And then there is a Chalybeate spa, the water of which is said to be truly appetizing, although the flavour thereof is like to that of stale ink, and the odour stygeab. The great river Smite runs close by, and abounds in sticke bats, water cresses, and minnows; and the Elton Station on the Ambergate line is a mile away. The advent of this railroad has opened out a new era in the history of Orston, as without this means for transit close at hand, its gypsum beds might have lain at rest for ever. In a small paddock in the centre of the village, the excavations for gypsum have been carried on by Messrs. Jacob and Carter for some months.

(above) An extract from 'A visit by a "Times" correspondent to the Newark and vale of Belvoir Plaster Works at Orston', Newark Advertiser, 2nd August, 1865.

The Plaster Works circa 1930 just before demolition

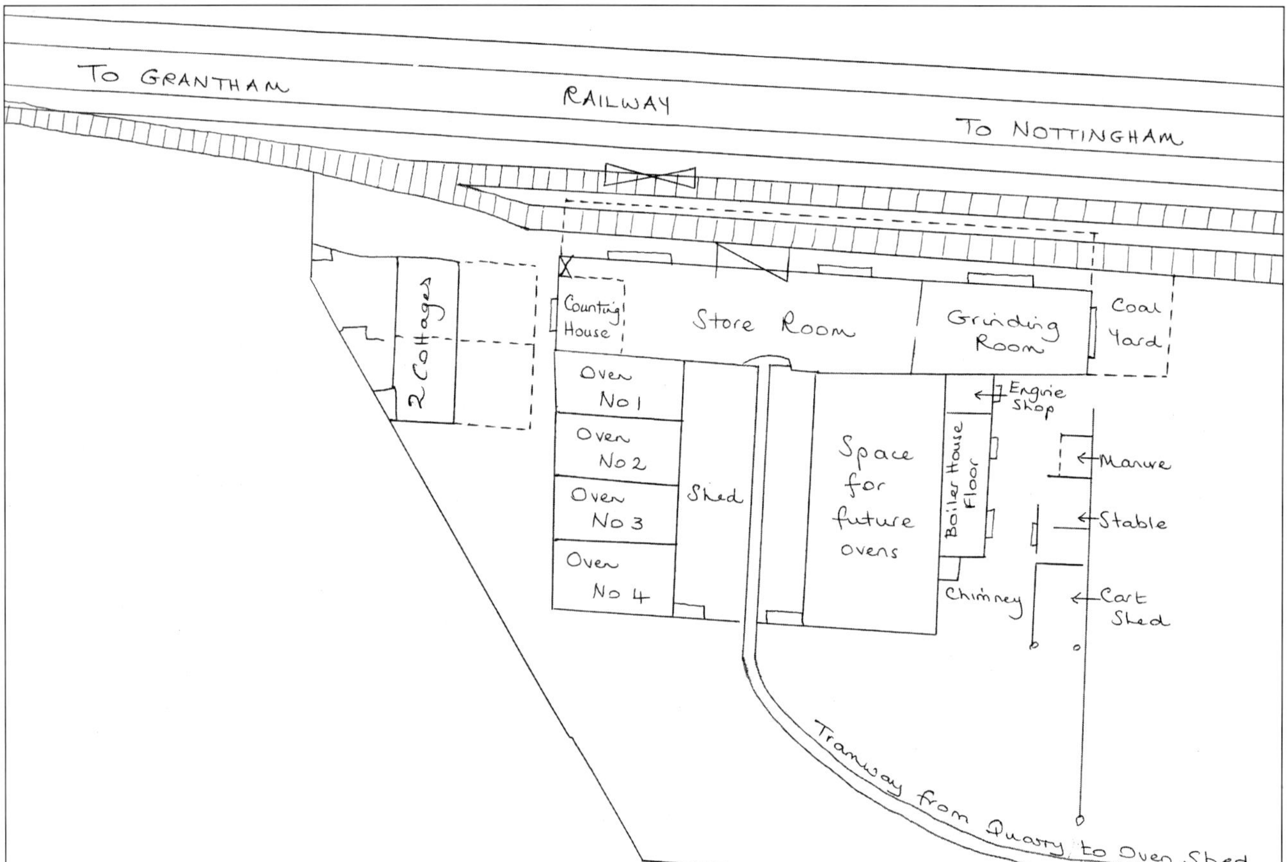

Plan of the 'manufactory'.

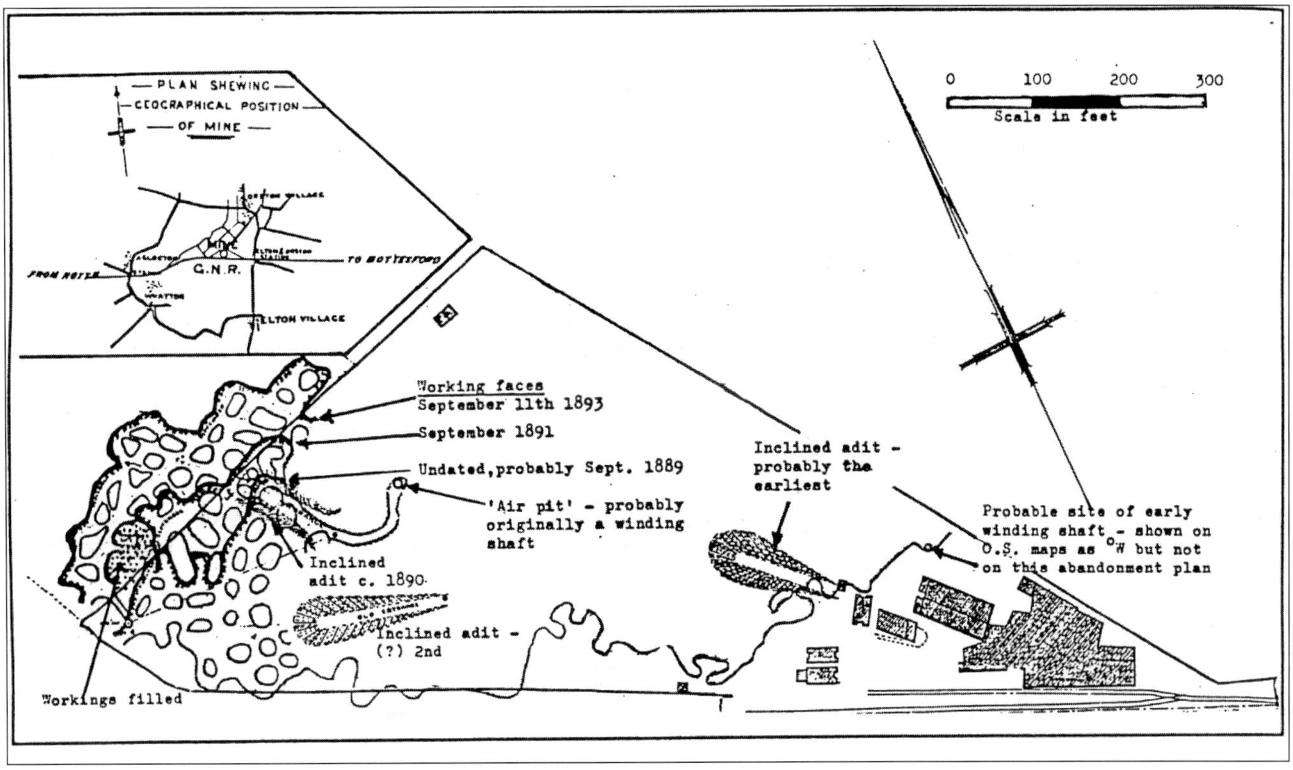

Abandonment plan, 1894

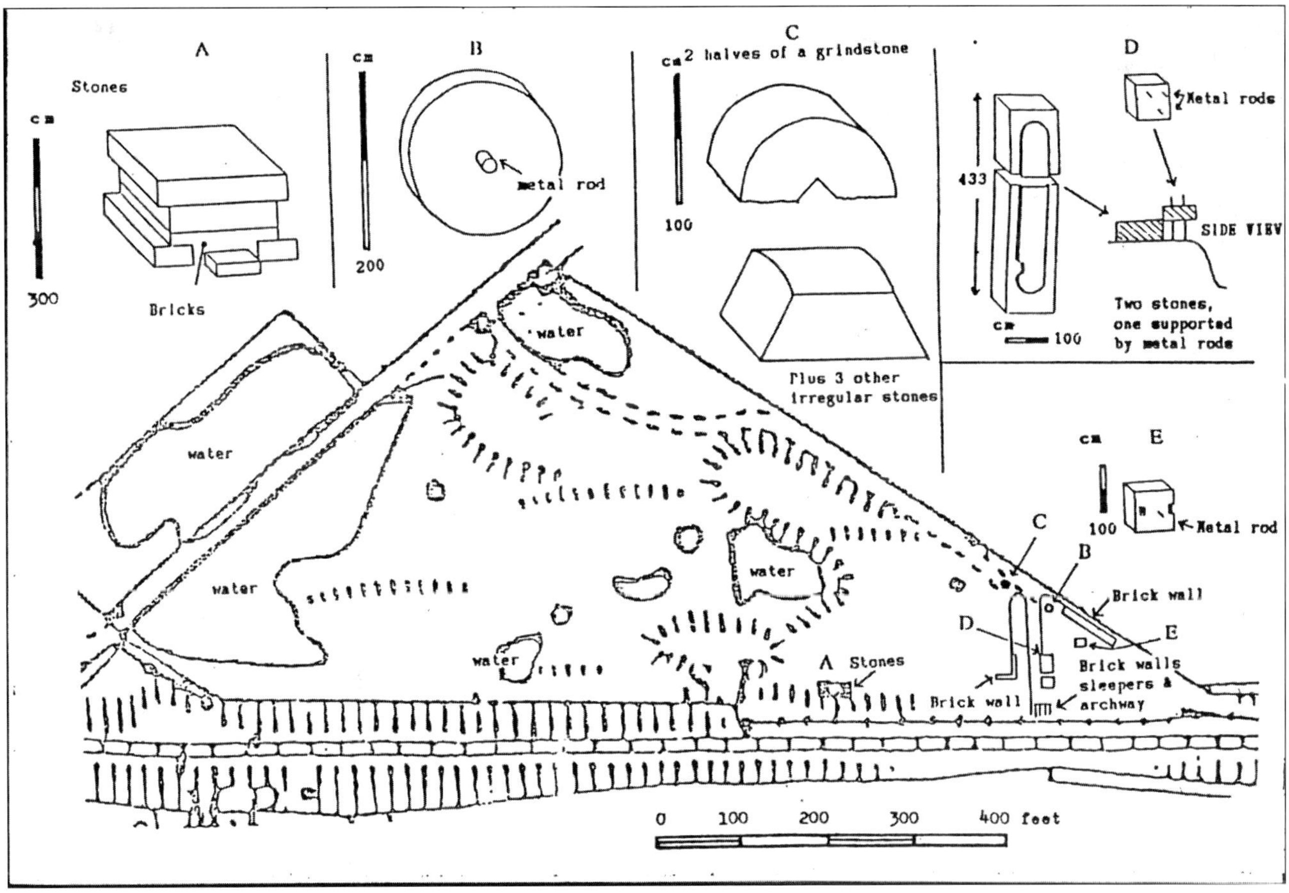

Remains of the manufactory today

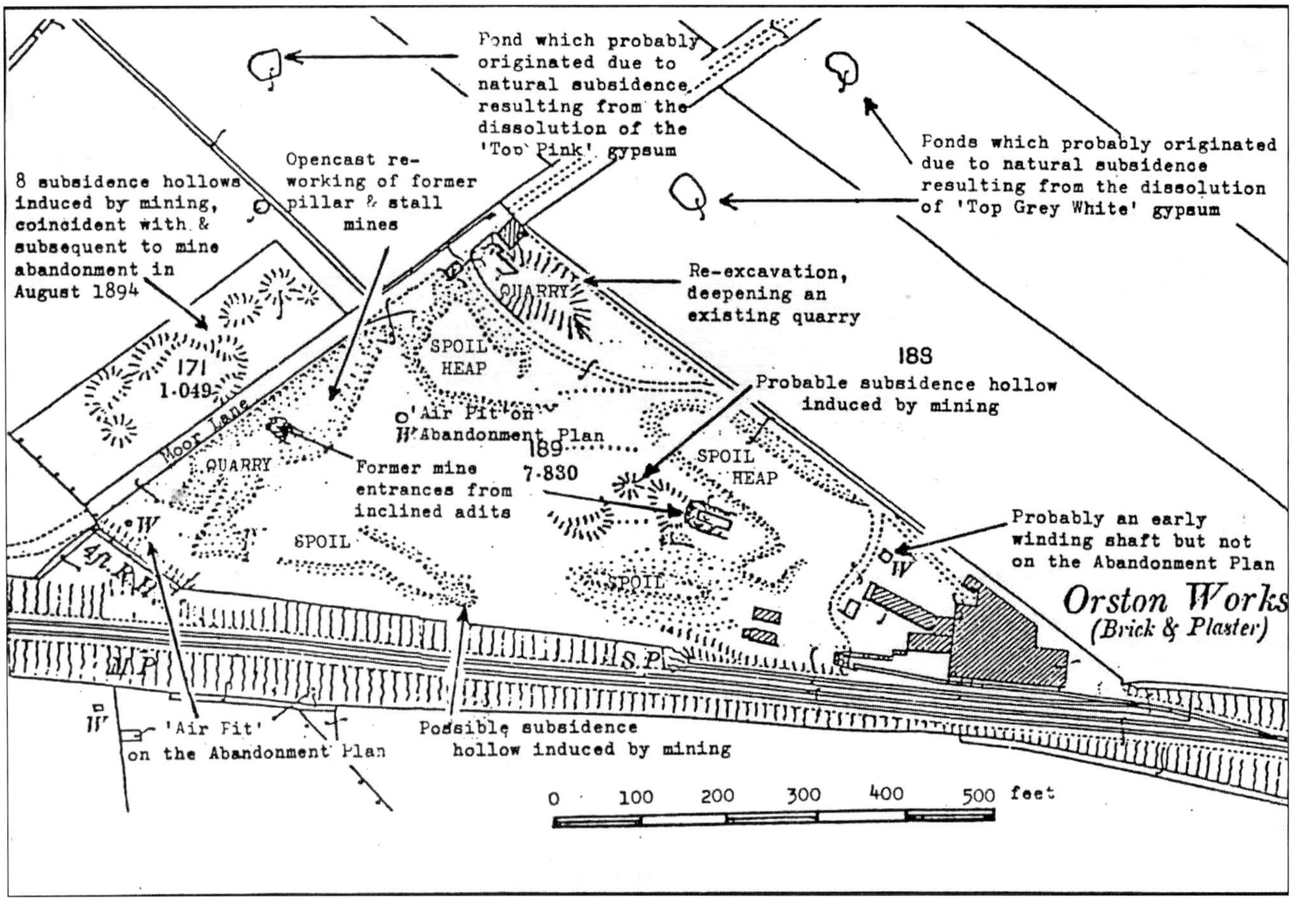

Annotated 1900 O.S. map of the land and works

PLASTER OF PARIS WORKS.

FREEHOLD LAND AND HOUSES,

ORSTON, NOTTINGHAMSHIRE,

Near Elton Station, Great Northern Railway.

MR. W. WOOD

Will Sell by Auction

On MONDAY, AUGUST 16, 1869,

At the "ROYAL OAK," Orston, at 5 for 6 o'clock, p.m.,

THE VALUABLE

FREEHOLD PROPERTY,

Now known as the ROYAL PLASTER WORKS,

Comprising nearly an acre of land, partly worked; seven-roomed dwelling-house fronting Loughbon Street; stabling, coach-house, ovens, engine-house, and mill, with 14-horse engine by Worssam; 21-ft. boiler, mill machinery, and out-door plant, embracing every requisite for carrying on the trade; all in working order, having quite recently undergone thorough repair. If not disposed of in one lot, will be divided, and offered as follows:—

LOT 1.—The seven-roomed dwelling-house, yard, stable, and coach-house, with 12ft. 6in. right of way from Loughbon Street, say front 17ft. 6in. by 82ft.

LOT 2.—The piece of land adjoining, with the five ovens and substantial roofing, two smoke shafts as standing, five pair of oven doors, furnace doors, bars, braces, and girders; with 12ft. 6in. right of way from Loughbon Street. Front of this building 59 ft. by 21ft. 6in.

LOT 3.—The piece of land adjoining lot 2, with 12ft. 6in. right of way from Loughbon Street, with erection of engine-house, mill, and tall smoke shaft as standing, including furnace doors, bars, &c. Say, front 33ft. 10in. by 51ft. 6in.

LOT 4.—The eligible piece of land adjoining last lot, and running therefrom to the dyke by land in occupation of Thomas Winfield, on the south 158ft., thence by the dyke on the east 155ft., to land of Mr. J. Marshall, and by the same on the north 148 ft.

Auction notice of the Royal Plaster Works, located on Loughbon. Note the Sale of terraced houses in Chapel Street.

The excitement did not last. Even though Carter and Jacobs were helped by William Newton, a prominent Newark solicitor, and Hardy & Co, Grantham bankers, the business went under in 1873. Some of the partners in Hardy and Co bought it at the liquidator's auction but it continued to lose money until 1897 when it was sold to the general manager, Richard Almond. The change in ownership in 1897 coincided with a change in the way gypsum was dug. Hitherto it had largely been mined underground. From about this date this ceased and open-cast mining began. The two large lakes on either side of the Whatton bridle road today are the result. The works were closed around 1914.

Sale notice for the Royal Plaster Works in the centre of the village

CHAPTER 16
RELIGION

The section of this chapter relating to Methodism and the Methodist Chapel is based on notes prepared, just before his death, by Philip Chambers and a description of the building by Elizabeth Smeeton.

On 5 December 1093 King William Rufus (William II) gave the churches of Mansfield, Ashbourn, Chesterfield and Orston to the cathedral at Lincoln and the gift of the living (the post of vicar) of Orston has been with the Dean and Chapter of Lincoln until modern times. (The appropriation of a rectory to a foundation outside the county is quite unusual, there are sixteen others in the whole of the Nottinghamshire). It is interesting to note that the gift of Orston was *'for my soul and the soul of my father and my mother'*. Until 1093 William was an atheist and when ecclesiastical vacancies occurred he kept them vacant. He then fell ill and became worried about his soul and felt the need to perform some good acts. The gift of Orston was made on the day after an even greater gesture - the filling of the vacant position of Archbishop of Canterbury. It is likely that the church at that time was a wooden structure and that the earliest parts of the present structure date from soon after 1093. The famous masons from the Guild of St Mary at Lincoln would have been sent to replace the pre-conquest building with more imposing structures.

For most of its history, St Mary's has had its own vicar appointed by the rector. However, he was not always resident in Orston. For example, from 1804 to 1817 Edward Robson was licensed to reside in London where he served as a curate at Whitechapel. In 1743 Thomas Wakefield declared himself *'too infirm in health'* to live in the parish but he provided a curate to whom he gave £35 a year and some surplice fees. Even if the vicar did reside in the village, he may not have taken church services and performed pastoral duties but employed a curate to do them.

One of the oldest references to the church is the Taxation Roll of Pope Nicholas IV in 1291 which gives the clear annual value of the church of Horston, which was appropriated to the Collegiate Church of Lincoln, at £60, the pension of the Vicar of Horston being valued at £10. These values, seen comparatively, suggest a substantial and rich church and community; for example, Ratcliffe on Soar was £46.13s.4d., Bingham £53.6s.8d. and Mansfield £26.13s.4d.

Probably the greatest event in the history of Christianity in England was, of course, the breaking away from Rome in 1534 and the establishment of the Church of England. But this did not see the end of Catholicism at the local level. Many preferred the 'old religion'. Protestantism was seen as nouveau, gentlemen preferred Catholicism and it had a massive underground resistance by the gentry. Rome also sent over highly trained priests as missionaries. The authorities eventually responded by making it treason from 1581 for a person to be reconciled to Catholicism and parishioners were fined up to £20 per month for missing church on four or more successive Sundays. The Vale of Belvoir was described as an *'.... oasis of papists in a vast desert of protestantism'*. Orston registered a number of church absentees including William Maultby, senior, and William Maultby, junior, who were fined for not attending church for a month. Papists were known as recusants and their names were recorded on the Recusant Rolls. These included for Orston Ann, wife of Anthony Ffearborne, gentleman (1606-25); John Hammerton, gentleman and wife (1607-10) and Helen Child (1604).

The next major involvement of religion with politics occurred during the Civil War when some clergy even gave up their livings to fight (for example, John Featley of Langar who left his twenty one children

St Mary's Church harvest festival, pre-electric lighting, circa 1930.

behind). The two sides were theologically divided, the Cromwellian side representing the new puritanical movement. During Cromwellian rule clergy were expected to have acceptable puritan sympathies. Many found this difficult to sustain and were ousted from their livings, notably Lawson (Eakring), Luddington (East Retford) and Rustat (Widmerpool). Ezekiell Diglane, Vicar of Orston, was sufficiently old and philosophical about such matters by this time (he was ordained in 1627) and, like the Vicar of Bray, was unaffected by a change in beliefs. After the restoration, appointments to clerical positions and approval of the continuation of existing ones were again politically influenced and based on a clergyman's sympathies and training. Again Diglane, unlike some of his neighbouring incumbents, was unaffected.

Even if popular religion and beliefs in Orston were not affected by puritanism, they were affected later by non-conformity movements. The Compton Census of 1676 states that there were 200 communicants in Orston and three non-communicants. Archbishop Herrings' Visitation Return for 1743 states that there were *'three score or upwards?* [families] *One is a dissenter'*. It does not say why.

The most significant movement in Orston was Quakerism during the second half of the seventeenth century. Nottinghamshire was one of the first counties to receive Quakerism (1646) along with Leicestershire and Derbyshire. Fox, the founder of the movement, visited the area around Orston and stayed in the Vale of Belvoir. From an early date, Quakers were actively persecuted by the State and the established church. William and Mary Maultby (see Chapter 21) fell foul of the authorities on a number of occasions and some of their family eventually emigrated to Pennsylvania to join a Quaker community.

The churchwardens' accounts for 1689 also provide an interesting illustration of the tension of these times. They contain an entry of 3s. spent during the previous year *'when the Bishops were set at liberty'*. This money had been spent on ale and tobacco for the bell-ringers, whose pealing of the bells indicated local delight at the acquittal of seven bishops who had refused to obey the illegal command of James II to order the reading in all churches of the Declaration of Indulgence which he had issued for the toleration of all non-conformists including Roman Catholics.

The Baptists had little impact. In 1812 Alderman Barber of Nottingham set out on a crusade for funds for the erection of a Baptist chapel in the city. At Orston he obtained £14.3.6d. mainly from the Marshalls, who were wealthy farmers, and the Wickhams. Although there is one in Bottesford, there has never been an attempt to build a Baptist chapel in Orston.

Until he became disaffected by it, John Wesley was a frequent visitor to Nottinghamshire. His nearest venture to Orston was probably to Bingham in 1770 of which he wrote *'I really admired the exquisite stupidity of the people. They gaped and stared, while I was speaking of death and judgment, as if they had never heard of such things before. And they were not helped by two surly, ill-mannered clergymen, who seemed to be just as wise as themselves'*. Perhaps he should have preached on love and humility.

Methodism as a separate church, began soon after John Wesley's death in 1791. Prior to having a building for the purpose, the early Methodists worshipped together in one another's houses or outbuildings. The first Wesleyan chapel in Nottinghamshire, in East Leake, was built in 1798. The first Methodist Chapel in Orston was built in 1805.The chapel today, which stands on the site of the original chapel, dates from 1848. The plaque on its wall describes it as a Wesleyan chapel. The chapel was extended in 1869 when the vestry was erected after a small portion of land was given for the purpose by Christopher Staveley.

The early Methodist church quickly divided into separate church bodies. Primitive Methodism was formed in 1811 and in 1870 established its own chapel in Orston, next to the dyke, on Loughbon. It is possible that, during this period, Methodism became more popular than the Church of England. The two Methodist chapels, combined, had more services: the Wesleyans having two Sunday services and one on a Tuesday evening, the Primitives also having two Sunday services and one on a Friday evening whereas the Church of England had two Sunday services and a third every alternate Sunday.

Perhaps the most interesting religious event during the nineteenth century for the local historian is the 1851 religious census, a thorough survey of church capacities and attendances. It showed St Mary's to have 300 seats, 120 free places and 180 others, and the Wesleyan Methodist Chapel to have 161 seats, 75 free spaces and 86 others. On the day of the census, 20 March 1851, 120 people attended the morning service at the church. There were no other services that day. At the Wesleyan Chapel there was no morning service, 75 attended the afternoon service and 64 in the evening.

Orston Methodist Chapel

What percentage of parishioners attended? As some individuals probably attended more than one service, the total number of attendees was not simply the total attendances. It has to be adjusted. The authoritative study of these statistics is based on the assumption that the total attendees were those who attended the best attended service plus one third of the less well attended services. On this basis, the average attendance for Nottinghamshire for the Church of England was 15.39% and for Wesleyan Methodists 6.46%. For Orston the statistics are, for the Church of England 26% and for Wesleyan Methodists 19%! Generally, the census was done very fairly and honestly, those returns which gave suspiciously high estimates were very much in the minority. Many clergymen and ministers took pains to point out special conditions which affected attendance; for example, in the northern part of the county, the evening service coincided with a thunderstorm. We can only conclude that, for Orston, either the village at that time was highly devout, or both the Church of England and Methodist returns were exaggerated.

In 1932, Primitive Methodists, Wesleyan Methodists, and various others rejoined to form the Methodist Conference. Probably soon afterwards, the Primitive Methodist Chapel was closed down. It was then used for various purposes, notably as a garage for haulage vehicles until eventually it was demolished in 1995, or thereabouts. A modern house, "The Brook", stands there today. The Wesleyan Chapel at the bottom of Chapel Street remains

Elizabeth Smeeton, a schoolgirl of 12 at the time but later to acquire a degree in archaeology, described the building as it was in 1978. '*The walls of the chapel are built of brick, the roof is made of slate, the guttering is metal painted black. There are five windows in the chapel, shaped like this:*

Over the door there are traces of an arch which has been bricked in. It was probably a sixth window. On the roof there is a brick chimney which is supported by an iron rod which is fastened onto the roof. On the ridge of the roof there is a squat wooden chimney which was probably the first one.

In the olden days people used more decoration on buildings than we do today because on the chapel there are 2 sorts of grating. The old fashioned sort is pretty.

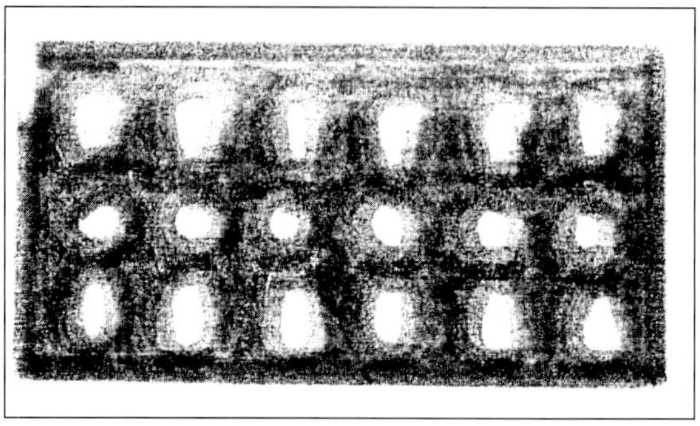

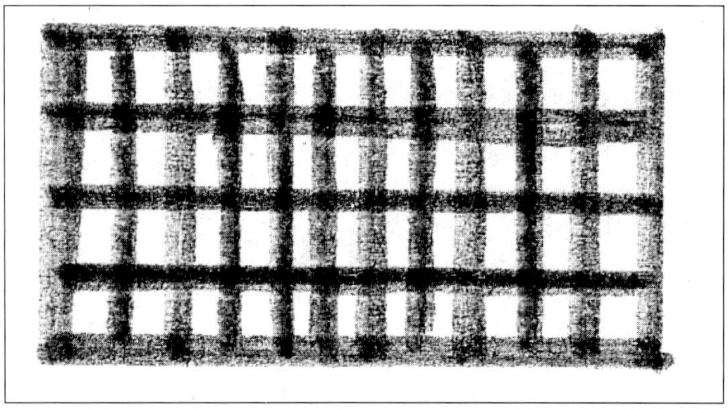

The modern sort is just a plain pattern.

The window is shaped like this.

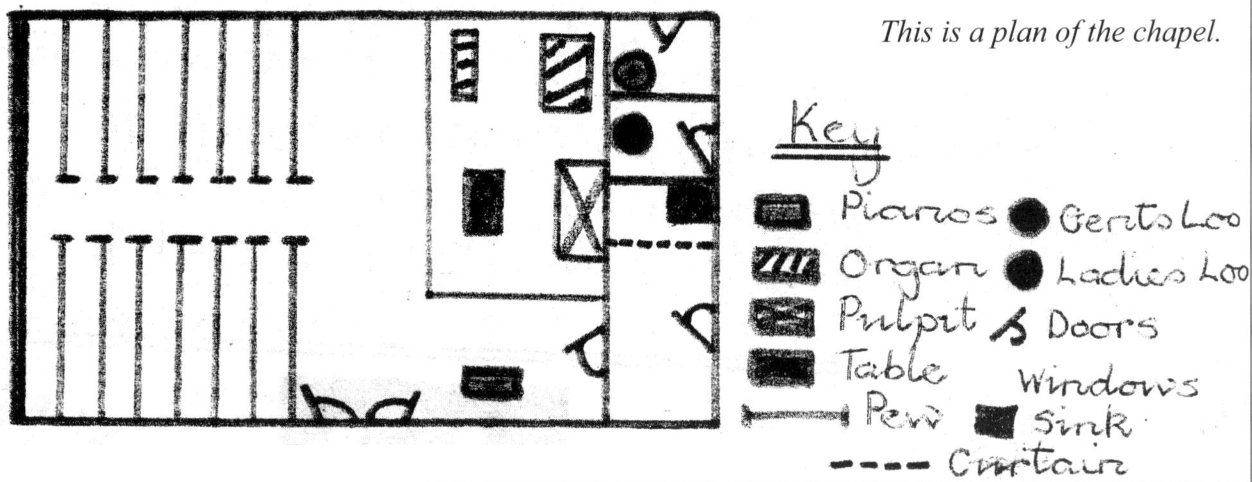

This is a plan of the chapel.

Philip Chambers remembers that '*The chapel was heated with a coke-burning stove called "tortoise" which sometimes got red hot. The old windows were replaced by three leaded lights in the 1980s donated by different families. Their names are at the bottom of the windows'.* The earliest organ he could remember was an American one which used suction rather than blowing. This was replaced by an electronic organ which did not last long as it was too expensive. This was replaced by a small pipe organ from a church in Stragglethorpe. It eventually went to Flintham chapel. The most recent organ has been here since about 1970. The hymn books were given by the Chambers family in memory of Gwen, Philip's first wife. The communion table and rail were given by the Maule family in memory of William Maule, a generous benefactor of the chapel.

Philip Chambers remembers Methodism in the first half of the twentieth century. He recalls his grandfather walking from Long Bennington to preach in the Primitive Methodist chapel. Most preachers had to walk to their 'appointments', sometimes ten miles there and ten miles back. The Newark Methodist Circuit, of which Orston was part, had a 'wagonette' to collect the preachers and take them to their appointments

One of the most important events in the year which continued well into the 1960s was the Sunday School Anniversary Day. Special songs and recitations were given by the children from a raised platform. Everyone had a new dress or suit for that day. Relatives used to come from long distances to hear and see the children. Since the death of Philip Chambers, Donald and John Maule, attendances at the chapel steadily have declined.

Orston School 1950

CHAPTER 17
ST. MARY'S CHURCH

By Mr Harry Gill (previously published in The Transactions of the Thoroton Society)

At first sight this church does not arrest the attention of the antiquary owing to the modernised exterior, but when well seen into it is found to be full of interest. The south porch is obviously and entirely new (1888) and the remainder of the south front has been renewed in parts again and again.

The necessity for these frequent reparations is attributable to the geological formation of the site. The whole of the Vale of Belvoir was at one time a lake, the clay bed whereof shrinks and swells with every change of temperature, and this plays havoc with the foundations; witness the billowy effect seen in the floor of this church – which is on one level throughout its entire length; and in the wavy lines of a horizontal scroll-moulding which runs beneath the window-sills in the north aisle.

The antiquity of the building is apparent upon entering. The spreading arches of the pier-arcades, the beauty and variety of the window tracery, and the sense of size and spaciousness, all proclaim that when in its pristine condition this church was important and beautiful.

No written records of the earlier building epochs are extant, but history may be read from the stones. The pier-arcades are the most ancient part of the work now visible, albeit they have been altered from their original condition in order to conform with the later additions.

To all who are familiar with mediaeval architecture the alternating cylindrical and octagonal piers standing upon 'water-holding' base mouldings and capped with right-angle head mouldings, the semi-circular arches in two recessed orders, having plain double chamfers to the south arcade and keeled bowtells to the north arcade, speak of the 'Transition' period between the Norman and the Early English style of architecture and are thus eloquent of the closing years of the 12th century (Henry II).

The (Thoroton) Society paid a visit to another church, almost identical with this so far as the pier-arcades are concerned, at Edwinstowe. Although some distance apart there is reason why the churches of St Mary at Orston and St Mary at Edwinstowe are so much akin.

In Domesday, the manor of Orston and the manor of Mansfield (whereof Edwinstowe was Berewick) were both held by the King. In 1093, King William Rufus gave both these churches with their emoluments to the Bishop of Lincoln. It is therefore a fair assumption that not very long after the date of the gift of the famous masons from the Guild of St Mary at Lincoln would be set to work to replace the pre-conquest buildings with more imposing structures, the remains whereof are before us today. The stonework of the interior still retains its original character, although it has been dressed over in parts renewed again and again.

In spite of these reparations, mason-marks and incised inscriptions in 'black letter' may be found on piers but these doubtless date from the 14th century reconstruction, to be mentioned in detail later.

The chancel is a little later and wider than the nave. It dates from the middle of the 13th century (Henry III). The plan conforms with the idea then prevailing, of a double square. The windows – three single lancets on either side and a triple lancet at the east end – are elegant examples of their kind, graceful in shape and pleasing in their proportions. Their hood mouldings have, for the most, characteristic 'mask' terminals, but here and there a fully developed carved head appears to have emerged from the embryonic state. A beautiful two-light window, to the west of the priest's door, was made for the accommodation of an acolyte, whose duty it was to ring the sacring bell at a shuttered opening which took the place of the lower panes of the window.

There is evidence that the original aisles were much narrower than we see them now, so that, if we wish to trace the development of the church in chronological sequence, the enlargement of the south aisle to its present width (18ft) must be first considered. This extension was necessary in order to obtain a side chapel. A piscine in the south wall, with stone credence, still remains to indicate the position of the altar. I think the inception of this chapel was due to a benefactress whose effigy we shall shortly have occasion to notice.

It is clear from the style of it that this chapel was built toward the end of the reign of Edward I, or early in the reign of Edward II. The tracery of the windows, especially the one eastward of the south porch, is exotic. Nothing like it has been seen in this neighbourhood before. I made a drawing of it in 1874, ere yet the hand of the 'restorer' had been laid upon it, which shows that the design of it is still unaltered, and I know that some of the ancient stonework is retained in its composition.

The end windows of this aisle are 15th century, substations, but the obvious discrepancy between the jamb mouldings and the tracery heads suggest that when in their original condition these windows would resemble the others.

I venture a suggestion that the wonderful work in the newly founded college chapel at Merton (1274-1308) most probably inspired someone to emulation in this south aisle. We cannot determine who it was, but we may cherish supposition. Was Anselmus de Stokyng, the send vicar here of whom we have any record (1292-1321) an alumnus of Merton? Was he impressed, not so much by the theology at Merton as by the architecture of his college chapel, and thus led direct to a reproduction in miniature here, or did the master-mason of the Lincoln Guild of Craftsmen hail from Merton? Not unlikely, for, apart from the priesthood, there was no vocation in that day more attractive than to a learned man of peace than architecture.

The north aisle was brought to equal width with the south aisle at a somewhat late scale and in a clumsy design. These facts point to a late 14th century date, say the closing years of the reign of Edward III. The plague-stricken year would thus intervene between erection of the south aisle and the north aisle. This suggestion gains support from the processional doorway on the north side (now blocked), a feature which came into general use at the time of the 'Black Death' (1349).

A fine stone effigy now lies on the floor at the east end of the north aisle, whence it was removed from the sill of the north-west window, and before that it lay in the chancel.

My enquiries have led me to think that the effigy was not originally set up in this church at all, but that it was brought here from the monastic church of St Mary at Newstead (Stamford) at the time of the suppression, just as other early effigies of the great families of de Roos and Manners were removed from the Priory Church of Croxton to Bottesford church.

The effigy carries no inscription, but in the style of dress, the diminutive angels which smooth the pillow, and the details of the canopy proclaim it to be the workmanship of the early 14th century. Traces of lineage however, are borne on two small shields; one, above the right shoulder, bears three water bougets for de Roos, Lords of Belvoir and of the manor of Orston in the late 13th and 14th century.

These arms were originally borne by the great family of Trusbut of Wartre in Holderness, hence '*Troois boutz d'eau'* was indicative of their name and estates. When the sole heiress of Trusbut was married to a de Roos, he took himself their arms – *gules three water bougets or*. The shields above the left shoulder bears two chevrons within a bordure which I read to be D'Albini, the predecessors of de Roos, in the Lordship of Belvoir in the 12th and 13th centuries – *argent two chevrons within a bordure gules.*

The followers of D'Albini, who lived on adjacent manors, and who were called upon to attend their lord in times of need, were distinguished by coat armour only slightly different from their superior lord. For instance, the Stauntons of Staunton, who held their lands by '*tenture of castle guard'*, bore the same ordinaries sable with the bordure engrailed. They lived within sight of the castle of Belvoir, and were under obligation to repair thither with their retainers whenever standard flew from the summit of the Keep.

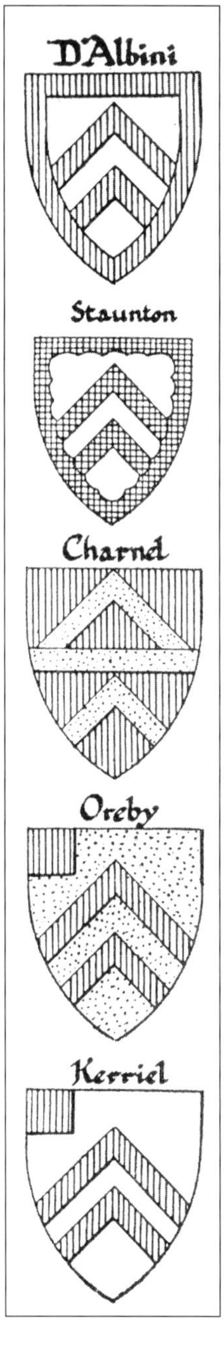

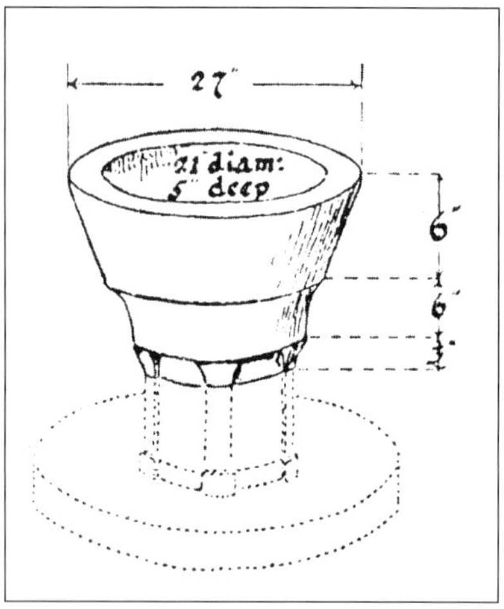

The Charnels of Muston *bore gules a fesse or between two vhevrons.*

The Orveys of Abb Kettleby – *or two chevrons and a canton gules.*

The Kerriels of Croxton *argent two chevrons and a canton gules.*

Authorities differ slightly in the rendering of these arms, but I have followed our own historian Dr Thoroton.

In the absence of tinctures it is not surprising that guesses have been made as to the identity of the second shield of the monument. My reading of the heraldry inclines me to think that the monument records the last D'Albini, who became the Lady de Roos by marriage. The manor of Orston was held by the Crown until King Richard I granted it to William de Albini who held in succession died leaving his daughter Isabella sole heiress. She married Robert de Roos and conveyed the estates to him.

The figure is represented with a heart or a reliquary between upraised hands. This is intended to indicate that the heart of the individual was given to God, or as a token that a vow to Holy church has been duly fulfilled. We know that Isabella's grandfather had built and endowed a Hospital at Bridge of Wass, between Offington and Stamford. Her father had confirmed the gift, and she herself must have been a benefactress, for she was buried '*... in the church attached to the Hospital of St. Mary of Newstead. AD 1301'*.

'The priory of Austin Canons, dedicated to Mary, the Blessed Virgin Mary, by Stamford, Lincs' or *'Newstede by Uffingham,'* as it was alternatively styled has now almost gone out of recollection. If this effigy was brought to the home at Orston at the spoliation, as I have suggested, it is the only link which remains.

Before quitting the north aisle, the two western bays of the roof whereof should be noticed. The attached principals, the beams studded with 'nail-heaf' enrichments, and the carved pendentas, go to make a fine specimen of 14th century carpentry. The nave once had a roof in correspondence if we may judge by the water tabling at the west end of the aisle; the present nave roof was put on late in the 15th century when the clerestory was added.

The sturdy seats in the north aisle illustrated the church benches of generations ago.

At the eastern end of the north aisle a blocked-up doorway which once led to the rood-loft is still in evidence. A small fragment of oak tracery from the rood-screen- a relic of by-gone days – is displayed near the south respond of the chancel arch. It was found embedded in a lath and plaster partition which separated the chancel from the nave during the latitudinarian period.

The plain circular bowl of a 'Transitional' font, although not in use is still being, and may yet be restored. It was probably thrown out of the church during the Commonwealth, when fonts from several adjoing parishes were also degraded. Fortunately for this parish the leading families always have taken great interests in the fabric of the church, for as the Lady Roos set up an altar in her day, the Kirchevalls who held the manor in succession since the Reformation *(sic)* – set up a new font in the church in commemoration of Restoration of Monarchy and Episcopacy.

This font is a very well-known and oft illustrated example. DR Cox says '*... the most striking Restoration font in England is the one in Orston Church, Notts., which is a fine piece of carving, partly after medieval model, but at the same time showing considerable originality'*.

In my opinion the design follows neither the mediaeval model, not the group of dated fonts with which it is sometimes classed, for it is clearly a Stuart copy of the Tudor font at Bottesford, one of the very few fonts set up during that decadent period.

That the Bottesford font was made by the craftsman of the Renaissance who was commissioned to set up a tomb to the 2nd Earl of Rutland (obit 1563) – is placed beyond doubt by comparisons between pedestals of font and tomb.

The font at Orston was originally placed against the craftsman of the Renaissance who was commissioned to set up a tomb to the 2nd Earl of Rutland (obit 1563) – is placed beyond doubt by a comparisons between pedestals of font and tomb.

The font at Orston was originally placed against the western pier of the south aisle, and that is the reason why one of the panels is blank. The carving on the font panel bears a unique arrangement of three tulips in a vase issuing from the centre of a Tudor rose – probably meant to be emblematical of the Trinity. Another panel contains an inscription and date:-

Given
By Mrs.
Constantia
Kercheval
Feb 7
1662.

The contrast between the virile gothic work of the pre-reformation periods, and the lifeless post reformation work is very noticeable in the tower, which, according to a date cut in the stonework was rebuilt in 1766. I can find no record of the earlier tower, but the inference is that its removal was due to the treacherous nature of the foundation, before referred to. The Churchwardens account book (1686-1789) contains item after item of expenditure on the steeple, the bells, the clock, and the porch.

An ominous entry occurs under date October 23rd 1722, '*...the Towns people of Orston are not satisfied without further advice to pay all the charges of the Steeple, without the Parish';* and again in 1749*, 'Paid when Mr Gamble viewed the steeple'.*

Above the internal doorway leading to the tower a painted frame of the Royal Arms (King George III) is fixed. Faint traces of the Creed, the Commandments, the Lord's Prayer and the Royal Arms are also discernible above the chancel arch. The belfry contains four bells dared respectively, 1599, 1621, 1622, 1730.

Externally the effect of the church is marred by the insignificant tower. The old walls of the nave and chancel were built in thin random courses of blue lias limestone quarried locally; the dressings in Lincolnshire drawn from a distance.

On the central pier of the south aisle is an old stone which contains a 'scratch dial' and a consecration cross. In the re-building this stone was re-set upside down.

The north aisle was underpinned and restored by the Society for Protection of Ancient Buildings in 1914, when much of the window tracery was renewed. The embattled parapet, being ruinous, was removed. A beautiful foliated cross at the NW angle, but the cross head was long since removed.

I can remember making a sketch of the village stocks (January 1874), which stood beside the churchyard gate on the south side but they have now gone almost out of memory; while all that remains of the village is a block of stone which now serves as a 'fender' by the roadside.

The font.

Medieval wall painting in St Mary's Church

CHAPTER 18
A SEVENTEENTH CENTURY ECCLESIASTICAL FINANCIAL SCANDAL

The expenses of maintaining and running the church with all its ancillary activities were financed by a tax levied by the churchwardens on the inhabitants of the parish.

Among the claims that came before the Archdeaconry Court at Nottingham was an action (it was called a libel) by Henry Hall, a churchwarden of Thoroton, against William Beane and Hugh Hickson, the churchwardens of Orston, for making a false levy for the repair of the Orston parish church which in 1661-62 was without many of the requisite ornaments, including a font, a prayer book and a surplice. The church fabric also required urgent repair. In the past the neighbouring parishes or chapelries of Thoroton, Scarrington, Staunton, Screveton and Car Colston had, on at least one occasion, come to the rescue of Orston and contributed readily and willingly to the repair of its church and to the purchase of ornaments which it had been unable to meet. There was some justification for this as Thoroton, Scarrington and Staunton were at that time classified as chapels of ease within the large parish of Orston.

Unfortunately, the Orston churchwardens had foolishly assumed that their neighbours would again render assistance, and so they attempted to establish a precedent for the levying of further assessments upon them, not only for repairs and purchase of ornaments but also for current expenses, such as dues payable at archdeaconal visitations, fees of apparitors (ecclesiastical court officials) and even for expenses incurred in collecting the assessments.

This was a most mischievous design because it involved the connivance of Rev Ezekiell Diglane, who was not only the vicar of Orston but also the curate of Thoroton and Scarrington and had written up the accounts.

Alert to the intolerable situation, Hall championed the cause of the five churches and accused the churchwardens with

> *'having plotted and framed the unlawful levies for none other end and purpose than in that the said inhabitants & parishioners of Orston aforesaid had first upon malicious device and practice amongst themselves & wherein & whereby endevouring to bring some evill & unjust & unlawfull custome to the charge of these parishes'.*

They had also, it was claimed, spent the proceeds upon *'many vain and idle expenses, regaling and delighting themselves in vain pleasures and journeyings'.* Unfortunately the outcome of the claim is unknown.

St Mary's Church circa 1905.

CHAPTER 19
ORSTON HALL

by Paul Barnes and Gill Smellie

Orston Hall is a rectory house originally owned by the Dean and Chapter of Lincoln who also owned the Church (even though it was not their diocese). Camden, 1637 (shown in Chapter 3) indicates a building on the site. The present building is mainly late 17th century. It was re-fronted in the mid-eighteenth century, part of which was altered in the mid-nineteenth century. The billiard room was built on in 1919. There are two interesting inscriptions. A rainwater head is inscribed 'G.G.1796' and a lead pump is inscribed 'F S A 1759'.

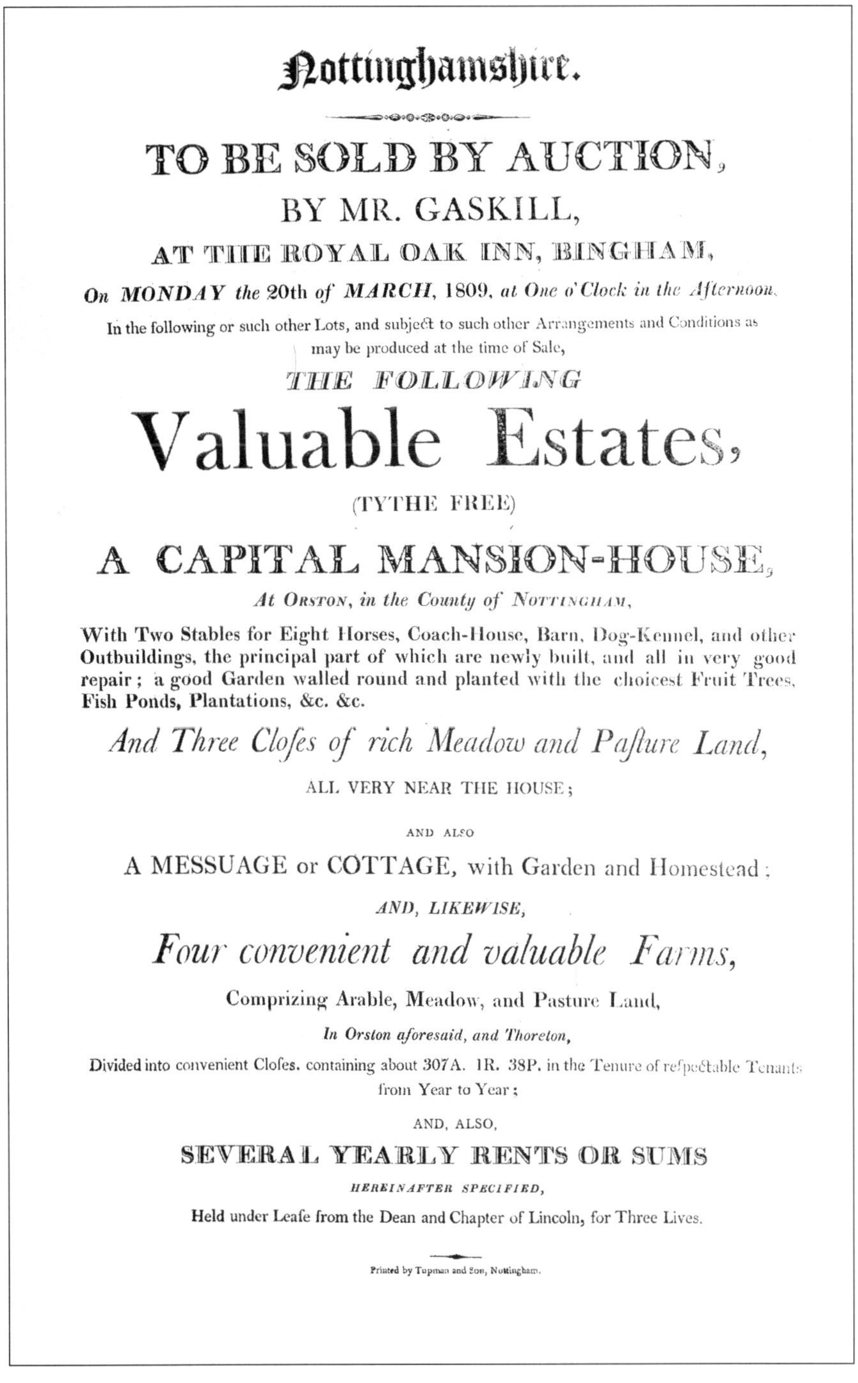

Nottinghamshire.

TO BE SOLD BY AUCTION,

BY MR. GASKILL,

AT THE ROYAL OAK INN, BINGHAM,

On MONDAY the 20th of MARCH, 1809, at One o'Clock in the Afternoon,

In the following or such other Lots, and subject to such other Arrangements and Conditions as may be produced at the time of Sale,

THE FOLLOWING

Valuable Estates,

(TYTHE FREE)

A CAPITAL MANSION-HOUSE,

At ORSTON, in the County of NOTTINGHAM,

With Two Stables for Eight Horses, Coach-House, Barn, Dog-Kennel, and other Outbuildings, the principal part of which are newly built, and all in very good repair; a good Garden walled round and planted with the choicest Fruit Trees, Fish Ponds, Plantations, &c. &c.

And Three Clofes of rich Meadow and Pafture Land,

ALL VERY NEAR THE HOUSE;

AND ALSO

A MESSUAGE or COTTAGE, with Garden and Homestead;

AND, LIKEWISE,

Four convenient and valuable Farms,

Comprizing Arable, Meadow, and Pasture Land,

In Orston aforesaid, and Thoroton,

Divided into convenient Clofes, containing about 307A. 1R. 38P. in the Tenure of refpectable Tenants from Year to Year;

AND, ALSO,

SEVERAL YEARLY RENTS OR SUMS

HEREINAFTER SPECIFIED,

Held under Leafe from the Dean and Chapter of Lincoln, for Three Lives.

Printed by Tupman and Son, Nottingham.

Sale notice, 1809.

The Kerchevals (see Chapter 23) probably lived in the Hall for the second half of the 17th century and most (if not all) of the 18th, sub-letting from the Chappell family, the lessee of the Dean and Chapter of Lincoln. In 1809 it was sold by the Dean and Chapter at auction (it was described as a capital mansion house) to Mr Middlemore, a Nottingham banker. After Mrs Susanna Middlemore died in 1849, Orston Hall was sold and William Marshall, a farmer from Kilvington who had already leased land on the estate since 1809, became the owner. William and his wife Mary lived at Hill House and also owned a property at Thoroton. The Marshalls had one daughter Catherine who was married in 1849 to John Fisher, and the 1851 Census for Orston shows that the Fishers were living in the Hall at that time.

When William Marshall died in 1872, Orston Hall was left to Catherine, and the Fishers continued living there and farming the estate until 1891 – 40 years at least! The Fishers had one daughter, Florence, who was married to Frederick Swire in 1889 in Orston Church. They lived at 'Manfield House' in Orston (previously 'Hill House, and subsequently renamed as 'The Gables'), until they moved to live at The Hall in 1901.

Ownership of the Hall passed down to Florence Swire after Catherine Fisher died in 1904. The Swires had two daughters, Marjorie and Kathleen, and the family lived at the Hall until 1912. At this time it was let, and an interesting Sale notice shows that most of the contents were sold at an Auction. The era .of the Marshalls` ownership was coming to an end, perhaps because both Frederick Swire and John Fisher died in 1913. Florence sold Manfield House and the Hill Farm land in 1917. Orston Hall and Estates were sold to Mr & Mrs Frank Burton in 1926. They lived at The Hall with their family until 1956, when it was bought by Mr C. B. Gibson who still occupies it.

It is interesting to note that the Dean and Chapter of Lincoln, who held the Leasehold Estate for 'three Lives' from 1856 until 1870, were ordered by the Ecclesiastical Commissioners through an Act of Parliament to sell the Leasehold estate back to Orston. This was done in William Marshall`s lifetime. The 'three Lives' referred to were- Thomas Bean the Younger, William Fillingham Parr and George Henry Gillott.

A deed of 1710 provides interesting details.

> *'A particular account of the Real Estate of Sale Mr John Kerchevall deced Devised by him to _ Athorpe Esq and John Town to be sold for payment of his debts as legacies as far as att psent thes^n^ - Althorpe & John Town can discover & sett for the Estate aforesaid .....*
>
> *In Orston in the County of Nottingham the parsonage house being a capital messuage consisting of Nineteen or Twenty Rooms & three very good cellars, having also out offices to bake. Brewheash Dress Meat & besides a large yard & stack yard with convenient Barnes Stables & other Outhouses And likewise adjoyning to the house an Orchard containing ab^t^ two acres of ground and Replenished with above Two hundred Thriving ffruit Trees of the best Sorts of Apples Pears Plombs Cherryes Quinces and Mulberry's beside wall ffruit and vines; and adorned with a pleasant Summer house and in part of the Avenues with Walnut Elm Ash and other Trees to which also belongs a Croft or Paddock of above an Acre of Ground and a Dovecoat well stored woth good pigeons*
>
> *In Mr Kerchevalls own hands A piece of Ground now used for a garden & nursery containing abt half an acre called the Vine Yard lying over against the said parsonage & wch are now standing abt seventy young Ash Elm & Cherry Trees Worth yearly 00.10.00. ...'*

Orston Hall maids, circa 1930.On the right is Lillian Aram who later became Mrs Spencer, for many years the owner of Orston's shop.

John Henry Fisher outside the Hall.

The present owner of Orston Hall, Mr Barry Gibson and his late wife, Mrs Fran Gibson, 1990.

Florence Swire, Catherine Fisher and unknown outside the Hall, 1901.

Florence Swire, daughter of Catherine Fisher, 1901.

Orston Hall, circa 1870.

Orston Hall, before the addition of the billiard room in 1919.

CHAPTER 20

CONDUCT AND MORALITY: THE ARCHDEACONRY COURT AND THE CRIMINAL COURTS

There is another aspect of the influence of religion at a local level which extends to personal beliefs, conduct and morality. Orston came within the Archdeaconry Court of Nottingham which regulated the spiritual and moral matters of its parishes. Their efficacy depended on the vigilance of the churchwardens who were entrusted with the task of reporting offenders. Punishments involved public apologies in church and the ultimate punishment was excommunication. Common offences regarding public morality were: fornication or suspected fornication, attempting chastity, adultery, incontinence, cohabitation, intruding amongst women, claiming to have had sex, living apart from wife, begetting a bastard, keeping company with women, drunkenness, scolding, blasphemy, sorcery, usury; regarding church services: not receiving communion, working on the Sabbath, football/alehouse in service time, not attending church, recusancy; regarding ecclesiastical jurisdiction: harbouring offenders (of the ecclesiastical courts), failure to present offenders; and (regarding church maintenance by the churchwardens) failure to maintain it, decay to the rectory and not repairing the churchyard boundaries.

In a rare statistical survey of the Nottingham Archdeaconry Court for the period 1606-1609, Orston appeared very near the top of those parishes with the largest number of cases. It was probably top for its size. The 'top ten' were:

Parish	*Cases*
Nottingham (all parishes)	127
Newark	95
Mansfield	83
Blyth	40
Warsop	37
Stanton	34
East Retford	27
Basford	23
Orston	21
Sutton-on-Trent	19

The Court could not work without the help of the churchwardens and clergy. The high ranking of a parish was not necessarily because of the low moral (especially sexual) standards there. Instead, it was more likely to be due to the vigour of its informants. The vicar at that time was Arthur Hargrave.

St Mary's Church with the stocks in the foreground at the end of the 19th century.

Of course, these were offences at the religious level. With the demise of the Court Leet (that part of the Manor Court to consider petty offences and civil affairs in the manor) from the 14th century onwards the secular aspect was increasingly considered by the local courts. The Orston and Thoroton Manor Court records show that while such offences were still considered here in the mid-17th century, by the start of the 18th century they were not.

Fines and offences in the 17th and 18th centuries according to the Nottinghamshire County records

Drunkenness

There were many indictments and presentments for the offence of drinking and drunkenness, the charge in several instances being brought against clergymen including Arthur Hargreave of Orston.

Illegal arrests

Persons were exempted from arrest while attending a church service. On 6 April 1635 Thomas Wiseman of Orston was presented for executing a warrant on Thomas Cariby '*in the parish church there'*.

Allegiance

In the County Records there are many instances of persons being '*committed to the Common Gaole until they shall take the Oaths of Allegiance and Supremacie'* and for 'refusing' and 'denying' to take such oath. Included is John Kirchwall, gent (1691).

Stocks

Imprisonment in the Stocks was a frequent form of punishment for petty larceny, idle and bad behaviour, vagrancy etc. The prison was a more expensive method. The term of imprisonment was usually for a few hours only but a long imprisonment was sometimes ordered. On 13 April 1607 John Peck of Orston was ordered to undergo imprisonment in the Stocks '*for the space of one day'*.

Commons and Fields.

There were many indictments or presentments, including Thomas Ludley of Orston on 3 October 1642 '*for chasing the sheep of William Marshall being on the Comon'*.

Lewdness

Keeping a bawdy house and open and scandalous lewdness were indictable by common law and many such cases also went before the Archdeacon's Court and dealt with by church law.

At Newark on 12 July 1775 it was recorded that '*Elizabeth the wife of John Wylie of Orston (was) brought into Court from the House of Correction at Southwell under a Committment of Mr Justice Carpenter charged with being a Person of Lewd Life and Conversation and a common Disturber of the peace and for refusing to find sureties for her Good Behaviour is recommitted to the aforesaid House of Correction untill the next Session or until she shall thence be discharged in due course of Law and pays her fees to the Court'*.

Watch and Ward

This very ancient liability was becoming a dead letter in the 18th century and there appear to have been only two cases of prosecution for failing to carry out its duties. Watch was by night and Ward by day. By the Statute of Winchester watching was only compulsory from Ascension Day to Michaelmas and the Watch was set by the Parish Constable. The Constable, however, could set a Watch at other times and the Justices also had power to order a Watch to be set and every able-bodied man was bound to take his turn properly weaponed or to find a substitute.

The first case was that of John Smith of Whatton in 1710. The second was at Newark on 12 July 1732 when Harvey Goostry and Robert Hoyes both of Orston were presented by the Constable for refusing to watch in the night time. They submitted and were fined 6d. each.

CHAPTER 21
LOCAL GOVERNANCE AND THE POOR LAW

This chapter uses documents relating to the Poor Law that have been handed down to Mr Edward Breedon.

The manor was the first unit of local administration. However, with its demise in the sixteenth century and onwards, the parish, as both an ecclesiastical and civil unit of governance gained in importance. The pivot of local government became the parish vestry. Its exact functions varied from place to place as parishes were more or less left to their own devices, subject only to the degree of supervision thought appropriate by the local Justices of the Peace (JPs).

The vestry selected its churchwardens, ex officio overseers of the poor, overseers of the highway and drew up shortlists from which the JPs selected constables. (The office of JP dates back much earlier- to 1341 when the Keepers of the Peace, agents of the king, became Justices with power to hear cases as well as to bring them. In the 14th century, there were four or five per county. As their duties and functions increased, for example, to preside over Quarter Sessions, so did their number and by 1565 there were thirty or forty per county).

The work of the churchwardens was not solely ecclesiastical. They had civil responsibilities, notably the application of the Poor Law, the destruction of troublesome animals and birds and the administration of local charities. The parish constable(s) was responsible for law and order, various administrative matters concerning the militia, the collection of national taxes, the relief of itinerant vagrants holding passes and the physical removal of others, the execution of J.P.'s warrants and many others.

The Poor Law

The most difficult and intractable problem facing all communities was the relief of poverty. During the 14th to 16th centuries the wool trade helped to provide Britain with wealth and large tracts of land were turned over to sheep farming. This led to an underclass of poor wandering the countryside seeking work, settlement and charity. An increased population and a series of famines led to an increase in poverty and the passing of a series of acts between 1563 and 1601 known as the poor law.

The 1563 Act categorized the poor for the first time into: those deserving social support (the elderly, the very young, the infirm, and families who occasionally found themselves in financial difficulties due to a change in circumstance) and the undeserving (those who had turned to crime to make a living, such as highway robbers and pickpockets, migrant workers who roamed the country looking for work, and individuals who begged for a living) who were to be treated harshly. The 1572 Act introduced the first compulsory local poor law tax and the 1597 Act created the post of Overseer of the Poor. The 1601 Act consolidated the earlier acts.

The effect of these acts was to introduce a system of poor relief. The Overseers of the Poor were required to levy a poor rate on the parish householders to provide support for the poor. For obvious reasons, vagrants were not welcome anywhere! See the photograph of the sign opposite. One way of providing for the poor was the provision of money, food and clothes to paupers whilst they lived in their own or a relative's home. This was known as 'outdoor relief'. In order to qualify for relief from the parish, an individual needed to be 'legally settled': born there of settled parents or having lived there for three years, although after 1662 an individual could be thrown out within 40 days. There were other ways to qualify: having served an apprenticeship to a legally settled man for seven years or being hired by a legally settled inhabitant for a full year. (As a result, most single labourers were hired from the end of Michaelmas week until the beginning of the following Michaelmas). Children of poor families, orphans and widows children were often apprenticed at the parish's expense to masters, either in the parish or elsewhere. If they served their full term of seven years then their legal settlement would be at the place of their master's settlement. Girls were usually apprenticed until they attained 21 or got married and boys until they were 24. Such an apprenticeship would be confirmed in a 'Parish Indenture', an important document sworn before the local JP by the Overseers of the Poor and the Churchwardens, placing on the master a legal obligation to feed, clothe and train the child in his trade for the duration of the contract. See the example below

> *This Indenture made the seventh day of March in the third year of the reign of our sovereign Lord George the Second..... that John Maltby, John Wiseman church wardens of the parish of Orston in the county of Nottingham and William Branston overseer of the poor of the said parish by and with the consent of His Majesties Justices of the Peace for the said county whose names are here unto subscribed have put and placed and by these presents do put and place William Older a poor child of the said parish, apprentice to Henry Davis of Orston husbandman with him to dwell and serve from the day of the date of these presents until the said apprentice shall accomplish his full age of twenty four years according to the statute in that case made and provided: during all which term, the said apprentice his said master faithfully shall serve in all lawful business according to his power, wit, and ability; and honestly, orderly, and obediently in all things demean and behave himself towards his said master and all his during the said term and the said Henry Davis for himself, his executers and administrators, doth covenant and grant to and with the said churchwardens and overseers, and every of them, there and every of their executers and administrators, and their and every of their successors for the time being by these presents, that the said William Older the said apprentice in some honest and lawfull calling he will instruct & teach to the best of his knowledge and shall and will during all the term aforesaid, find, provide and allow unto the said apprentice, meet, competent and sufficient meet, drink, and apparel, lodging, washing, and all other things necessary and fit for an apprentice. And also shall and will so provide for the said apprentice that he be not any way a charge to the said parish, or parishioners of the same; but of and from all charge shall and will save the said parish and parishioners harmless and indemnified during the said term. And at the end of the said term, shall and will make, provide, allow and deliver unto the said apprentice double apparel of all sorts, good and new, (that is to say) a good new suit for the holy-days, and another for the working-days. In witness wereof, the parties above said to these present indentures interchangeably have put their hands and seals the day and year above-written.*
>
> *Sealed and delivered in the presence of us Christopher Clarke Robert Brackson.*
>
> *We whose names are subscribed, justices of the peace of the county aforesaid do hereby consent to the putting forth of the above said William Older, apprentice, according to the intent and meaning of the indenture aforesaid, Jacob Charlton Langford Colin.*

Women changed their legal settlement on marriage, adopting their husband's legal place of settlement. If a girl married a certificate man in her own parish and he died, she would automatically be removed to his place of legal settlement along with their children. If someone could not satisfy these requirements, they could move into a new parish using a 'settlement certificate' but only if their home parish would be prepared to issue one. See the example below

> *To the Churchwardens and Overseers of the poor of the parish of Orson in the county of Nottingham and the churchwardens and overseers of the poor of any other parish whatsoever.*

We the churchwardens and overseers of the poor of the parish of Bourn in the division of Kesteven and county of Lincoln do hereby certifye you the churchwardens overseers of the poor and inhabitants of Orson aforesaid or any other place whatsoever that we do own and acknowledge Robert Hoyes and his wife to be inhabitants legally settled in our parish of Bourn. And we also promise for ourselves and successors to receive them and provide for them according to the statutes in that case made whensoever they shall become chargeable to your said town of Orson or any other parish or place whatsoever. Unless they shall in the meantime have gained a legall settlement with you or elsewhere. In witness whereof we the present churchwardens and overseers of the poor of Bourn aforesaid have hereunto respectively sett our hands and seals this fiveteenth of day of December in the fourth year of the reign of our sovereign Lord George the second of Great Britain King Defender of the Faith 1730.

John Lowe, William Mason – churchwardens

Witness our hands who were present at signing this certificate Richard Woulds, Robert Huffer.

This was effectively a form of indemnity issued by the home parish stating that the person and his family belonged to it and that it would be prepared to take them back at its expense if they became chargeable to the new parish. Because of the expense of removal, it was unlikely that a home parish would issue a certificate for a parish a large distance away. A settlement certificate was only valid if it bore the seals of the overseers of both parishes and that of the local JPs and was not transferable. If an individual or his family became reliant on parish relief and was unable to satisfy the requirements for legal settlement, he would be removed to the place of his last legal settlement. If no settlement certificate was in force then a 'removal order' would be applied for from the local JPs. This would usually involve an 'Examination as to Settlement' carried out before the JPs and the overseers of the poor to ascertain a person's last place of legal settlement. See the examples below

Whereas Martha Winfield having got into the Parish of Orston in the County of Nottingham and complaint being made to the Parish of Whatton her legal settlement being there that they shall remove her Except they have a certificate from that parish. Now we the Churchwarden and Overseer of the poor of the said parish of Whatton do own alone & Certify that the said Martha Winfield is our legal Poor and we do Certify that she nor her Child when born shall be any expense or any way Chargable or belong to the said parish of Orston.

Given under our hands this 19 day of march in the Year of Lord 1783
Thomas Gelstra churchwarden
Thomas cheetham Overseer of the Poor.

....

The examination of William Goodwin of Whatton in the County of Nottingham, Labourer taken upon oath before us the reverend Thomas Beaumont and the Revd John Storer clerks two his Majestys justices of the peace in and for the said county this 1st day of February 1821 .... being his last legal place of settlement.

This examination on his oath saith that he is of the age of twenty years or thereabouts that he was born as he has heard and believes in the parish of Whatton aforesaid of parents legally settle there. That after an hiring and service with Mr Wm Aruall of Sutton in the parish of Granby for a term short of a year he was hired by Mr William Green of Orston Field in the parish of Orston in the said county to serve him in the business of husbandry for one year which service he duly performed at Orston aforesaid – that he was then hired by Mr Thomas Maltby of Orston aforesaid to serve him in the business of husbandry for one year which service he duly performed there

– since which period he hath never been hired for a year or served a year in any other place or rented tenement of the value of ten pounds a year or upwards or served any parish office or done any other act deed matter or thing whereby to gain a settlement – that about nine weeks ago he was married to Mary his present wife and that they are now residing in the parish of Whatton aforesaid and are actually become chargeable thereto.

Taken before us and adjudged to Orston
Thos Beaumont
John Storer Junr.
The mark of Will Goodwin X

....

Received the 5th march 1788 of Wm Maltby – Overseer of the Parish of Orston – the sum of 5½ Guineas for the purpose of providing them with one substitute to serve in the Nottinghamshire Regt of militia; we also engage to Indemnify and free the said Parish from any after Ballott, occasioned by Deathe, Desertions, promotions, non Discharged for Misbahaviour etc; during the term of five years.
John Collinshaw
} Lients Notts Militia
John Smith

It was not until the nineteenth century that the parish government passed away. Under the Poor Law Amendment Act of 1834, the responsibility of the parish for the relief of poverty ceased and was replaced by poor-law unions and elected boards of guardians. Compulsory church rates were abolished in 1868, the office of parish constable disappeared in 1872. The remaining secular functions of the parish vestries were transferred to parish councils from 1894.

Sign outside Hill Farm (now The Gables), probably early nineteenth century. The reference to 'No vagrants' is due to the Poor Law in which the villagers supported their unemployed.

CHAPTER 22
EDUCATION

(The first two paragraphs have been updated by John Winfield).

Orston Primary School has about 100 pupils aged between four and eleven years old. It still occupies the site to which it moved in 1939. Since then much has changed: the school building has undergone two major extensions. It now has five classes, in addition to children attending 4+ compared with only two classes in the 1950s. It has all the conveniences of a modern school – outdoor play park, computers with internet connections and transportation to sports activities – all with the appropriate level of security needed nowadays.

Since World War II, its head teachers have been Miss Haslam followed by Mrs. Chambers, Eric Dix, Robert Lee and, since 2006, Sarah Moore all supported by many other individuals too numerous to mention by name - teachers, governors, cooks, caretakers, dinner ladies, secretaries, sports coaches, parent helpers etc.

The previous school, now known as the Old School, was located on Launder Street and is used as offices for Carlin Construction. The Old School dates back to 1848 when an earlier building on the same site used as a school was taken down. The origins of that earlier school are not known although it is known that a Thomas Lowe was schoolmaster in 1832 and there was an 'Orston Academy' in the 1840s. Above the porch roof of the Old School is an inscription *'W.E. Gray 1848'*. This coincides, but not perfectly, with the entry in White's Directory of Nottinghamshire that the schoolmaster was Edward E. Gray.

The Old School had about 50 children. They worked in three groups, except for religious education, physical training, singing and picture study when they worked as a whole. They left at 14 until 1936 when this was changed to the age of 11 to go to Bottesford Senior School. In 1951 Granby Primary School closed and its pupils were transferred to Orston. By 1954 the number on roll had risen to about 75. They were taught by two full-time teachers and one part-time. Substantial extensions to the original building were made starting in 1966 bringing about the school that we know today.

The school log book dates back to 1924 and provides fascinating insights both into the inter-war years and life in Orston during the last war. Here are some of the entries.

1924
24 October Room bitterly cold - allowed children to stamp, clap hands -marching etc to try to get warm. Room only 38 degrees at 10.30 a.m.

16 December A very dark, foggy day - unable to see books etc - singing - recitation, play taken instead of usual lessons in the afternoon.

1926
16 July The first three days of this week were extremely hot. Children nearly fainting for want of drink of water. No water on premises, borrowed a bucket & a cup. Nearest drinking water over a mile away. Mrs Walker who lives behind the school gave the children a drink of rain-water until other arrived.

1927
18 March Children taken to Sports Field for Games instead of having them in the road.

1928

27 March Received notice that all the Elton children must be excluded after the end of this week as the school is over-crowded. There are 66 children on Registers & only two teachers.

1929

11 January Dennis Cheetham left to attend Bottesford School. Woodwork etc is taught at Bottesford Sch & parents are anxious that their children should avail themselves of any craft that may be useful to them. (Wood & metal-work for boys & cookery etc for girls. This school offers none of the above).

11 June On the day of inspection the work of the school was seriously disturbed from 11 a.m. till noon by the ringing of the peal of six bells in the Church which is within a few yards of the school. It is earnestly hoped that the Managers will represent to the proper authority the inconsiderateness of holding bell ringing practices during school hours.

27 July One child buried this afternoon. She died last Friday evening. This is the second death from Scarlet Fever.

1932

10 July Leaflet on training of left handed children: these to be trained to use right hands except in very obstinate cases where ambidexterity should be the aim.

1933

22 March Repeated trouble occurs because the lady who lives over the way objects to the noise of the children playing in the street. The infants are now allowed to play on the vicarage lawn: the juniors and seniors at the west end of the street only.

1934

8 Jan Fifty seven children on the roll. Miss Kathleen Mabel Walker, aged 14, appointed as Rural Pupil Teacher.

1937

3 June The smells occasioned by the passing of the cows immediately in front of the school became so objectionable that the school doors had to be closed.

1938

28 Sept The School Nurse (Miss Preedy) excluded two infants, R. & D. Buckingham, for 3 days because of verminous heads.

1939

4 Sept This afternoon 12 Sheffield Evacuee children attended from 2-4 on the advice of Mr White for the purpose of acquainting them with the new conditions.

12/13/14/20 Sept Air Raid Drill

16 October Mrs Burton called to distribute new gas mask containers.

1940

4 June Head teacher visited the village hut where 48 senior boys and 4 teachers from Yarmouth are temporarily accommodated.

10 June Classes I & II of Orston School accommodated in Infant room. Evacuees have use of Junior room.

Senior section to use Staff Room for certain periods. Evacuees also have use of Old School and Village Playing Field. There are now 47 Yarmouth boys [1 junior, 1 infant, 45 seniors] and 4 masters.

7 Oct A long time was spent this morning in practising an indoor scheme of air raid drill, to be resorted to in case of a warning being given too late for children to "scatter" in safety. The signals are:-
1. Three loud clangs of school bell - "scatter".
2. (If planes can be heard) Three sharp blasts on whistle - "take your indoor places".

1941
6 Jan During the holidays the school field was ploughed ready for potatoes.

21 Oct A Naval Mine was dropped in the village at 10.05 p.m. last evening. A great deal of damage was done in the village and several people injured.

23 Oct 4 workmen arrived from Shire Hall to dig up the potatoes on the field. Evacuee boys helped to pick them up and place them in temporary "pies".

1943
1 March Mr Manser collected 3 cwts 6 stones cabbage from school field for delivery to East Leake Feeding Centre. The roots were left in the ground to "sprout" again.

1945
8 & 9 May The school was closed for two days on the occasion of the cessation of hostilities in Europe. To celebrate VE day the children attended voluntarily a short service of thanksgiving at school and afterwards paraded round the village singing and playing their percussion instruments and carrying flags and red white and blue flowers. A display of maypole and country-dancing on the green, which was watched by many of the villagers, concluded the proceedings. The flowers were laid on the grave of an airman of Orston.

25 Sept On arrival at school this morning we found that cattle had been on the garden, destroying almost all the green vegetables, and in the playground, during the weekend. The owner brought two prisoners of war to remove the droppings.

Orston School, 1897

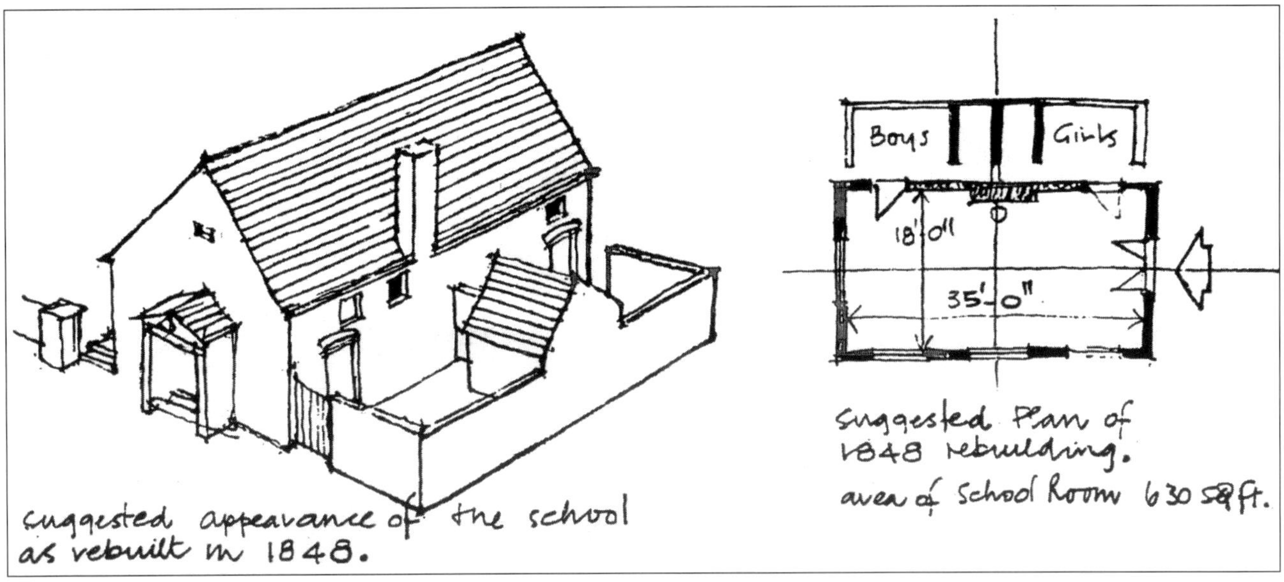

Orston Old School (John Severn)

The Old School building today – now the offices of Carlin Construction Ltd.

(below) Cover of an Orston Academy book

Orston School, 1912.

Orston School children with church bells, circa 1920.
See text at end

Orston School circa 1947. Back row: Ivan Spencer, Jean Walker, Marina Scotney, Bobby Baxter, Barbara Baker, Leslie Lovegrove, Edna Wakefield, Mrs Thornhill (infant teacher). 3rd row: Miss Haslam (head teacher) Frank Barks, David Baker, Brian Caunt, Bernard Wakefield, Margaret Buckingham, Wilf Patchett, Eric Wakefield. 2nd row: Raymond Foster, Herbert Wakefield, Barbara Mart, Cyril Patchett, Pat Baker, Colin Teasdale (evacuee), Betty Baker, unknown. Front row: Unknown, Terry Graveney, Rosemary Beevers, Michael Caunt, Phyllis Wakefield, Harry Wakefield, Lorna Barks.

Orston School children outside the Old Vicarage, circa 1913.

Orston School, 1925. L to R Back Row: Miss Fisher, George Cloxton, Alan Quartermaine, Arthur Baker, Roy Mills, Albert Baker, Lewis Moore,
Middle: Kathleen Breedon, Sheila Bates, Joan Scotney, Doreen Cheetham, Ethel Scotney.
Front: Daisy Wood

CHAPTER 23
FAMILY CONNECTIONS

Kercheval *by Rosemary Ruck*

The Orston family with the greatest claim to fame in the twentieth century must be the Kerchevals. (There have been various spellings of the name over the centuries). A famous son of this family, Ken Kercheval, better known to millions as Cliff Barnes of the celebrated TV series 'Dallas,' chose Orston church for the blessing of his marriage in 1986 and the christening of his grandchild in 2006.

Ken Kercheval's marriage blessing in St Mary's Church, 1986.

The Kerchevals were an important family in Orston, particularly in the 17th century. The earliest recorded members of the family were Walter Kerchevell, who was vicar from 1515 to 1524, Hughe and William mentioned in 1585 and 1597 in archdeaconry records and John Kercheval who died at Orston in 1595. A branch of the family were living in Hawksworth in the 17th century, but it seems that the Orston Kerchevals may have come originally from Balderton as the records of the court baron reveal that William Kercheval de Balderton, who died in 1606, held property and land in Orston. His heir Hugh Kerchever (or Kerchevall), who was aged 13 at the time his father died, sold ' a messuage, one close and four bovates of land' in Orston in 1613 and a close called 'Belhome' in 1627. Other deeds of 1613 record his sale of land in Mill field, Osier field, Coleman field and Beck field. The Manor Court records of 1641 refer to Hugh Kercheval of Balderton suggesting that he held land, but did not live, here.

The Kerchevalls are the only gentry in Orston to be entered in the Herald's Visitations of 1693. These enquiries recorded the pedigrees of families entitled to bear coats of arms. The family lived in the rectory and records of the hearth tax of 1664 and 1674 reveal that, having six hearths, the Kerchevalls possessed far and above the grandest house in Orston. Mrs Constantia Kerchevall, whose will was dated 1669, donated the splendid Restoration font in the church which is inscribed with the date 7 Feb 1662.

Most is known about her eldest son John Kerchevall, who Thoroton tells us 'held the tithe as his father and grandfather before him had done.' The Manor Court records of 1652 refer to John Kerchevall and imply that he was resident in Orston. His grandfather Hugh, by his will of 1639, left 10s to the church and 10s to the poor out of the tithe of corn and hay of the parsonage, as did his father in 1660. John Kerchevall was responsible for collecting the payments of monthly assessment to the parliamentary

KERCHEVALL OF ORSTON

No proofe of any Armes made

+ Arms: *Sable, three horses courant in pale argent*

+ Qu. for proofe of the Armes

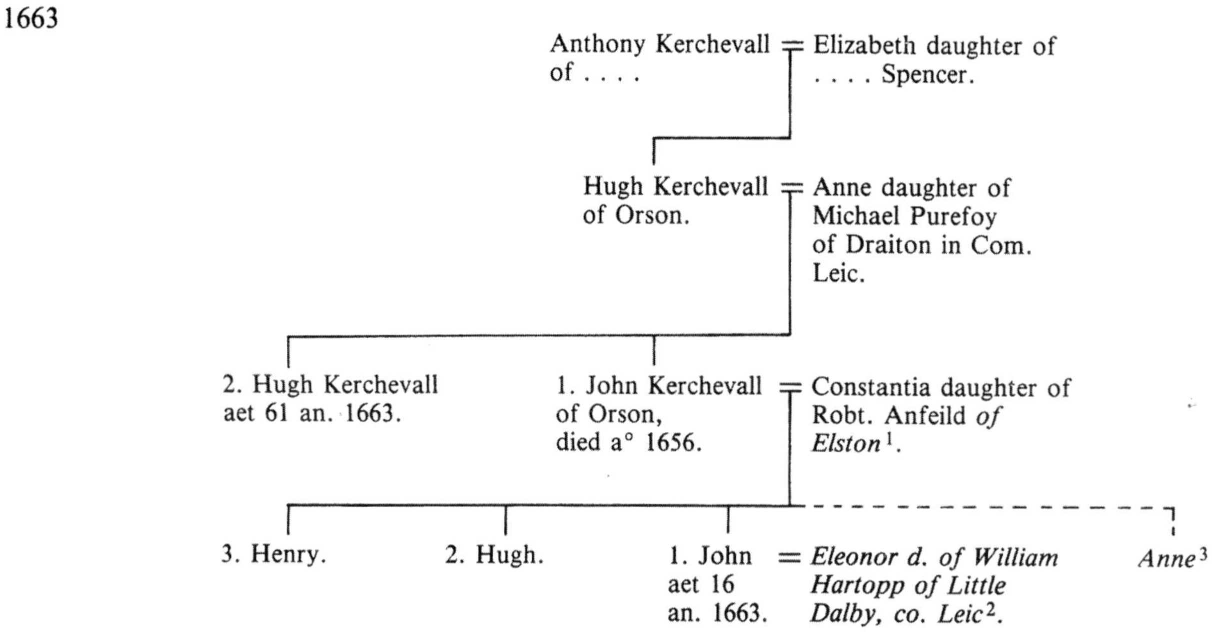

Certified by Hugh Kerchevall.

[1] Mar. lic. 21 May 1642 (N).
[2] d. 25 May 1695 (M.I. Orston).
[3] Licensed to marry John Challand of Orston, yeoman 17 Sep. 1664 (N).

Kerchival: visitation pedigree, 1693.

army during the civil war. His memorial in the church porch states that he died on 23rd September 1721, aged 75. Monumental inscriptions survive for Elinor his wife who died 25 May 1695 and for Constantia, one of their daughters, who died in 1681 and is buried in the church. Their other daughters were Elinor, born 1683, another Constantia, born 1684, whose son, John Charles is left land in his grandfather's will and Dorothy, born 1686. In deeds dated 1717 Henry is named as the eldest living son of John Kercheval, however, he must have died before his father, as it is William Kerchevall who succeeds as heir in 1721.

John Kerchevall's will reveals the extent of lands and property owned by the family in Orston, Flawborough and Thoroton, both freehold and on lease from the Dean and Chapter of Lincoln, and also property and land in Kirkby Underwood near Bourne, Lincolnshire. The leasehold estate alone had a total yearly worth of over £200. The will also suggests an educated man, as John bequeathed a writing desk and all the books in his study at Kirkby and in his study at Orston to his son Samuel Kerchevall.

The 'Particulars of real estate' devised by his executors, give details of the parsonage house (see Chapter 19), the windmill (see Chapter 25), Dovecote close with dovecote and barn, Holmes close, the Two close, meadow called the Penny and Farthing, Slades meadow, Thoroton close, the land of William Kerchevall called the Vineyard near the churchyard and the names of thirteen tenants of this estate.

The Kerchevals appear to have left the village by the late 17th century. A branch of the family remained in Balderton and at some point Kerchevals went off to America to found the family of which Ken Kercheval is a son. Tradition has it that originally two brothers went from England in the late 1600s, reaching Virginia around 1697; Diana Kercheval Bennett has recently published a book in the United States entitled 'The Kerchevals in America' about the establishment of that family in the new world.

Thomas Maultby's gravestone in St Mary's churchyard.

The family living in Orston for the longest time: the Maltbys, famous Quakers

This was undoubtedly the Ma(u)ltby family. Lasting over 450 years, the last Orston Maltby, Mr G.C., died at the Chestnuts in 1922. The first was William Maultby who moved to Orston from Millgate, Newark in around 1490.

The history of the family, a branch of which emigrated in 1698/99 to join a Quaker settlement in America is documented in a book '*Early Maultby with some Roades History and that of the Maulsby family in America, descendants of William and Mary Maultby, emigrants from Nottinghamshire, England to Pennsylvania'*, E. Barkland, Baltimore, 1909.

William and Mary Maultby were two of the early Quaker converts and during the years that followed the Conventicle Act 1864 suffered greatly. By this act all persons who met in greater numbers than five, for any religious worship other than the Common Prayer were punished by fine, imprisonment and transportation on a third offence. A return or escape from banishment was punished by death. In 'Besse's Sufferings of Friends' the following records occur

> *'May 28th 1676 William Maultby of Orston.- For a meeting held about the same Time at the house of Rowland Dabney, they took from Edward Richardson, of Kilverton, a Blacksmith, not only his Hay and Corn, but also his Bedding, his Children's apparel and even the working Tools and Utensils of his Trade, to the value of 16l'.*
>
> *'And from William Maultby, Robt. Bullivant and John Smith they took goods to the amount of 1l. 15s'.*

Two months earlier

> *'The 28th day of the 3d moneth, 1676. For being at a peacabl Meeting at Rowland Dabney's house William Maultby of Orston had 7 Strike of Barley taken from him worth about 17s. by Warrant from Robert Thoroton called Justice. Christopher Dent and robert Wycam Informers, taken by William Dawson, constable and Hugh Lamb, Officer'.*

And again in 1676

> *'Goods were taken from William Maulsby and two others valued at £1.15s'.*

And in 1694

> *'William Maultby of Estwood (Meeting) in the County of Nottingham had hay and a goose taken from him to the value of 5s. by Peter Lollywell priest of the Towne aforesaid'.*

This William was probably the son of the former who emigrated in 1698.

Not all Maltbys emigrated and the Orston connection continued. They appeared as either yeomen or farmers and held important positions in the village, e.g. churchwardens. But perhaps the family is nowadays most famous not for their Quakerism but for Thomas who died on 8 March 1881 aged 101 years and 101 days.

The 20th century: the Wakefield family

Probably the most interesting Orston family in the twentieth century is the Wakefield family. James and Elizabeth Wakefield originally came from Earlesfield in Grantham, although Elizabeth was raised in Flawborough. James was a steam-ploughman by trade. They had eighteen children, two of whom died in infancy. The family moved to Orston in 1930/31, taking up residence in New Row (where Chapel Garth now is). The family moved to the new council houses on Lombard Street when they were built. Three of the children, Herbert, Fred and Edna still live in the village, as do some of their children and grandchildren.

The Wakefield family. Fred and Jack are missing as they were in the army.

View of Hill Top before housing, James Wakefield with Herbert and Kate Wakefield in the foreground

CHAPTER 24
CHANGING OCCUPATIONS AND TRADES OVER THE LAST 150 YEARS

Using census data which are available for every ten years, it is possible to trace changes in occupations since 1841 when the first census was conducted.

1841
Most people worked on the land as agricultural labourers etc. Boys from the age of 15 tended to be sent to local farmers to work and girls at 15 to be female servants. Some jobs provided a local service, e.g. saddler, joiner, dressmaker, blacksmith, tailor, shoemaker, bricklayer, wheelwright and carpenter. Unusual occupations included cordwainer, chain woman, straw bonnet maker, framework knitter and lace runner. Most people were born in Orston.

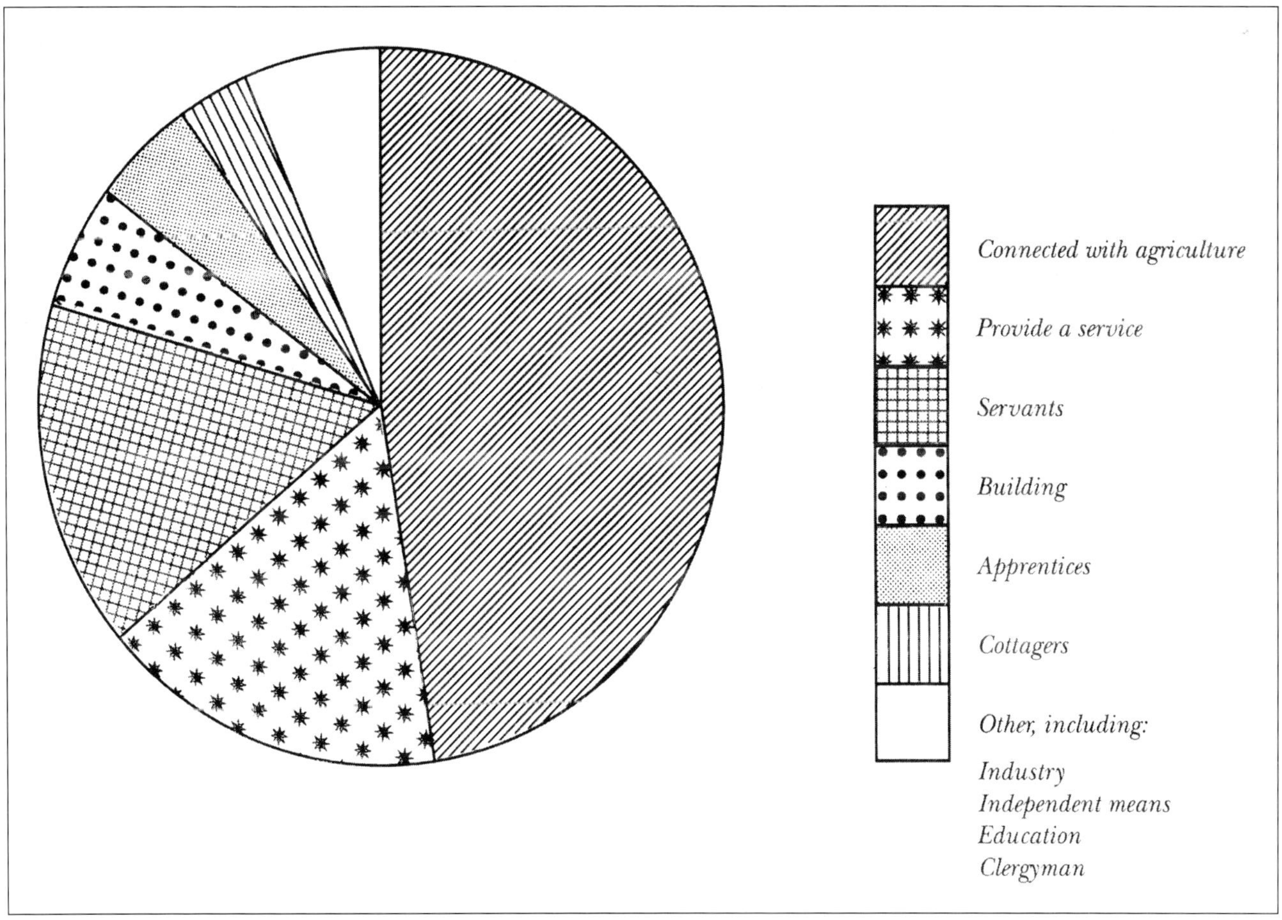

Pie chart showing occupations in Orston, 1841.

1891
Again, most people still worked locally on the farms or provided local services, e.g. saddler, tailor, bookmaker, wheelwright, farrier, coal dealer, miller, publican, dressmaker, shoemaker, baker and chair woman. Some people were employed on the railway and in the plaster works, both established since 1841.

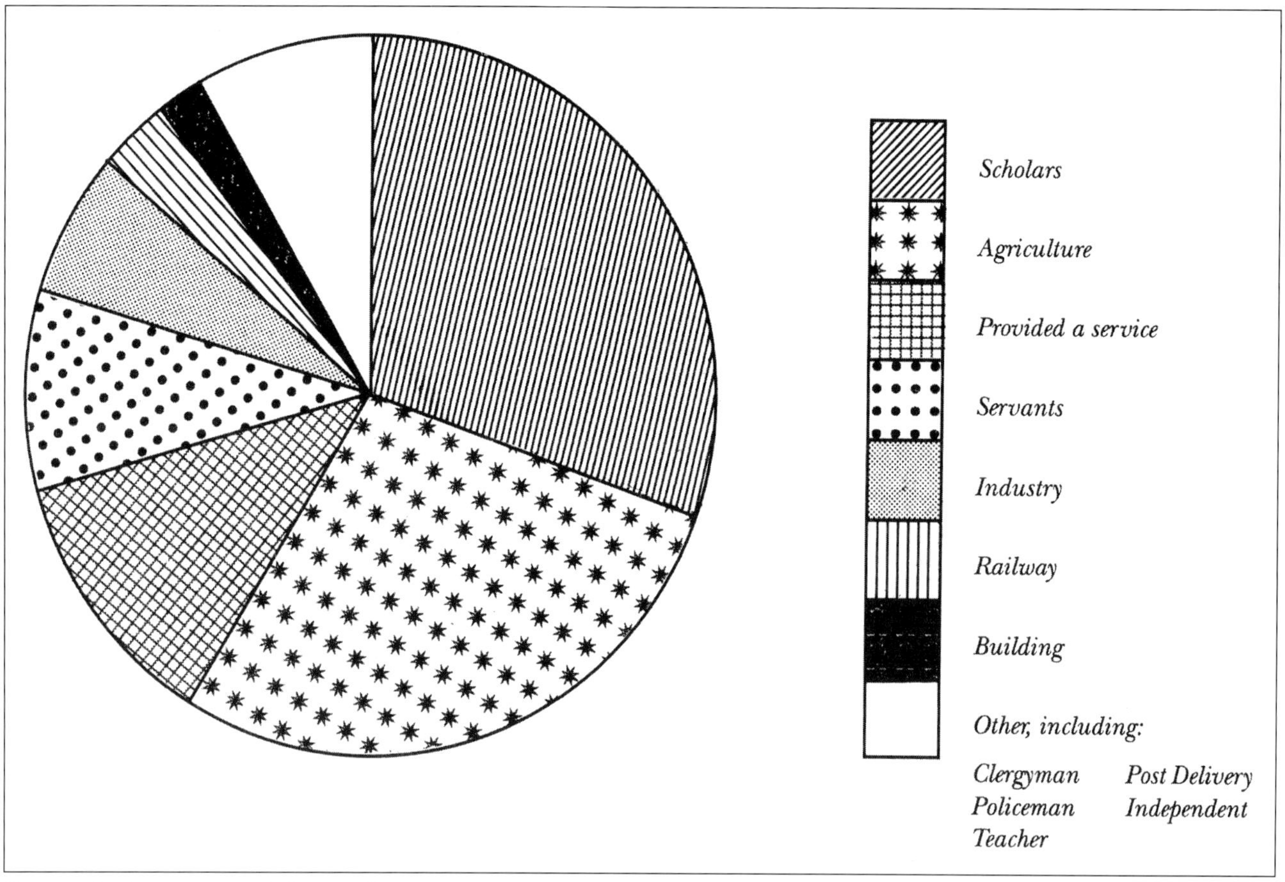

Pie chart showing occupations in Orston, 1891.

1946

Because the census is not publicly available until 100 years have elapsed, the electoral role was used with the help of Mr Bernard Johnson.

With the arrival of the railway more people worked out of the village, in Nottingham at Boots and the lace factories and as silk stocking workers. They were called the Bright Boot Gang by the local farm workers. Others cycled to nearby villages, e.g. Barnstone Cement Works, and nearby farms. More local businesses appeared, such as a barber's shop, a post office and a corner shop. There was also a builder, undertaker, teacher, road sweeper and scrap iron dealer. People also began to set up small holdings and poultry farms. Mr Lewis at Yew Tree Farm was the first farmer to put milk in bottles.

Unusual occupations included aircraft engineer, a chauffeur (to the Burtons at Orston Hall) and a cheese salesman. Probably the most unusual job was that of Alfred Telford who wrote obituaries. If the family cried when they read the poem he knew he had done a good job. The more they cried, the more he charged.

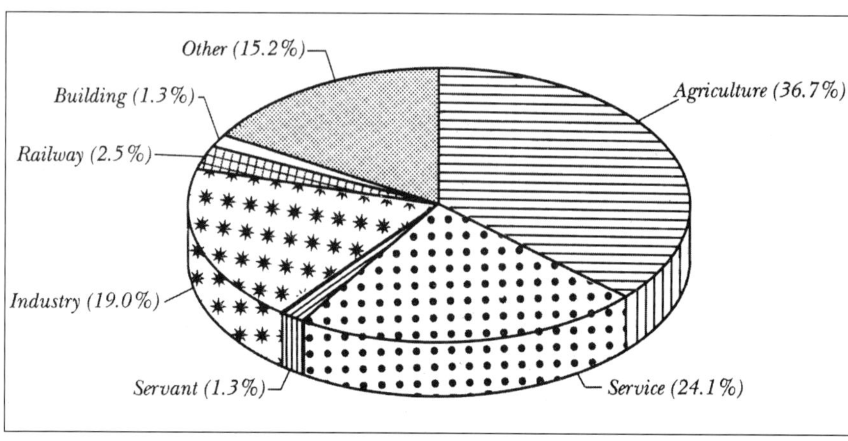

Pie chart showing occupations in Orston, 1946.

1995

Class 4, Orston Primary School conducted a questionnaire. They received replies from 23 households, about one sixth of the village. Ten of the 23 families (44%) arrived within the last ten years; of these, three people work in the village. Six families have lived here between 10 and 20 years (26%), three between

20 and 50 years (13%), and four for more than 50 years (17%, Maule, Johnson, Moore and Smeeton). Out of these, only three people still work in the village, two of whom work on farms.

2008

With the help of some villagers and the electoral roll, I surveyed the occupations and other demographics of current Orston residents. We were able to cover 95% of households in the parish. Here are the results.

We found that a significant proportion of the village is now retired. Although there are no statistics for 1995 to compare this with, I suspect that the proportion has increased, as it has nationally with the retirement of baby boomers. Regarding occupations, agriculture has yet to be replaced by a dominating single industry. The analysis shows Orstonians being employed in a wide variety of industries and sectors reflecting national employment tendencies. There are significant numbers in retailing, public administration, health and education. Despite the decline of these industries, there is a significant number of individuals working in manufacturing and agriculture in some way.

Analysis of the main occupations in Orston in 2008

	%
Agriculture	2.7
Education	7.2
Electricity, gas, water etc	0.7
Extra-territorial organisations, e.g. army	0.7
Financial services	2.4
Health & social work	6.1
Manufacturing	3.8
Property, construction etc	5.5
Private households, e.g. cleaning	2.0
Public administration	6.5
Retailing	8.9
Telecommunications, IT etc	1.0
Transport, storage, communications	1.7
Other industries/sectors	3.0
Student	6.5
Housewife (to an employed partner)	8.5
Retired	32.8
Total	100.0

Distances travelled to work by Orston residents in 2008

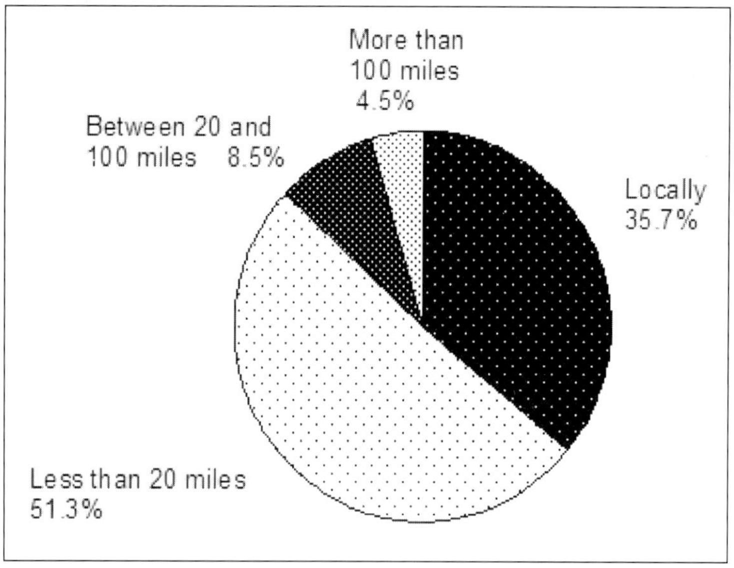

It is interesting to see the distances they travelled to work. A significant number actually worked locally. Probably, this has increased since 1995, as a result of a number of successful new businesses starting up in Orston. However, more than half work outside but within 20 miles. Most of these will be in, or around, Nottingham. Probably, the most interesting statistic is that 4.5% work more than 100 miles away. Whilst most of these will be in London, not all are and some travel considerably further. No doubt this is a developing trend, although the notion of the East Midlands as a commuter belt for London has been with us for some decades now and, to some, this statistic may be regarded as disappointing.

It is also interesting to see to what extent the village comprises families who have been here for more than one generation and the number of 'newcomers' and how this compares with 1995. Although the 1995 survey was much smaller, a comparison of the data suggests that there are significantly fewer new families (30% compared with 44% have arrived here within last ten years). Perhaps, this adds to the impression of an ageing population.

Length of time of families have been resident in Orston in 2008

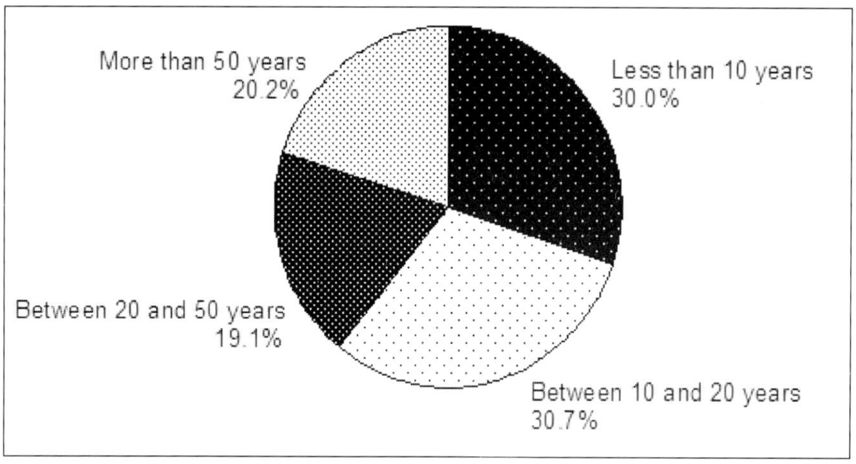

The trend over the last 150 years is clear. Only a relatively small number of people now work locally and very few on the land. Services which were provided at one time are no longer required (as people shop in the towns) and the businesses that do exist, do not necessarily employ local people any longer. Instead, people commute to work. As transport becomes easier, individuals are likely to commute even further to work. Some travel huge distances. On the other hand, as electronic communications get easier, less people need to travel at all to get to work.

CHAPTER 25
INDUSTRY AND BUSINESS IN THE 20TH CENTURY

It should not be thought that during the 20th century Orston was entirely dependent on agriculture for its employment and prosperity. Although gypsum mining had virtually finished by the start of the 20th century (see Chapter 15) milling was soon to flourish. This chapter describes the development of the corn milling business in Orston and mushroom farming here during the second half of the century.

Orston Windmill and Milling in the 20th century; William Maule and Sons. *Based on material written by Patricia French, John Wilkinson and Beryl Maule.*

> *'Th. Mason, tenant. One strong and well custom'd windmill in very good repair & wth 2 pair of mill stones & other proportionable geers worth yearly 08.00.00'.*
>
> - deed devising Mr John Kerchevall's real estate, about 1700.

Although the above is the first documentary evidence of a mill at Orston, there would have been a mill to grind grain for flour and foodstuff from medieval times. Probably the first mill was a water mill and later a wind mill. For obvious reasons, the windmill would be situated on the highest point in the parish. In the case of Orston, this is at the far end of Mill Lane. The first mill to be erected on the site was a wooden post-mill. It was owned by a Mr Leake, who combined the businesses of miller and baker. His trade was so good that the post-mill became inadequate for his needs, so he erected a much larger, tower mill.

Tom Maule bought the mill in 1868.He took in most of the of the local farmers' grain to grind it for both bread making flour and animal feed which was delivered to farms throughout the Vale by a horse and dray. William Maule joined his father in the business in the late 1880's. After Tom Maule died William decided that expansion was necessary. He left his house in Launder Street and built a new mill and house, The Limes, on what is now known as Hill Top. The old wind mill was left redundant.

Around 1909, a Mr. Partington from New Zealand, was on holiday in this country. He had heard about the Orston Mill and as he required many replacement parts for his own mill back home which was of a similar type, he decided to make contact with William Maule. After much discussion, Partington decided to buy all of the mill's mechanism, together with two sets of Granit Grinding wheels. Mr Maule transported all these pieces with his steam drive lorry and trailer to the railway station's goods yard, two miles away. It then went by steam ship to Auckland. Despite Mr Partington's fears that the Germans might sink the boat before it got to Auckland, all the pieces of the mill arrived safely and the Partington Mill started up again in 1916 producing flour for his biscuit factory until 1950.

Soon after William Maule had started up the new business he was joined by Mr. Harry Blackburn, from Easingwold, as a traveller for the firm. After a while, Harry left William and went into business on his own at the Old Maltings, Lombard Street. By this time, Horace Maule was working for his father. Eventually, Harry Blackburn bought the farm and house at the top of the hill (on the left) and went into farming. William Maule then bought the Old Maltings from Harry, but before this it was used during the first World War (1914 – 1918) as a Drill Hall and P. O.W. Camp.

At first, of course, the only transport was Horse and Dray. Two shaft horses drawing the load, but if it was a big load (3 to 4 tons) there would be a gear horse to lead. For smaller journeys there was a miller's cart with one horse. Delivery was a 20 mile radius, Old Dalby etc. All the feed, offal etc. would come from Hull to Elton Station and be collected by dray and put into stock ready for when the farmer required it. Life was very hard – no lifting gear in those days – everything had to be done by hand. The raw materials; maize, palm kernel cake, soya, sorgum (substitute for maize), cotton and linseed cake (this weighed 12 or 14 lbs per slab) and lots more, would come from different countries: Egypt, Africa, U.S.A. and Canada. Bill Baker, the drayman, used to have to get up at 5.00am to feed the horses and prepare them for the day's deliveries. This would take all day, leaving at 6.00am. The horses would have to be fed – probably at John Graves, Old Dalby, or Nether Broughton, before the trip back. William would regularly go to markets at Melton, Nottingham etc. to buy horses. Horace remembers going to Melton with his father to buy a horse and he had to walk home with it – 17 miles. This was not very easy, and quite often the horses took some handling. He also remembers having to get up very early to drive cattle to Nottingham or Grantham markets.

The Windmill, Mill Lane.

Partington's Mill, Auckland, NZ.

After a while, they bought their first lorry. Bill Baker, the drayman, wouldn't have anything to do with this, so Horace had to drive it. There were no tests in those days. The first lorry was steam – coal fed. It was quite difficult to drive. Ted Maule helped out as he understood more about steam. Ted on the driver's side, Horace steering it. It was very difficult to keep the steam up. Two had to turn the jet on to get plenty of steam especially when travelling up Stathern Hill, or else you wouldn't make it. Often they would have to camp out at night because of a break-down. They then bought an Austin Lorry - solid tyres. 'Pug-nosed'. Radiator in the cab, in front of you – very hot in the summer. These were apparently designed to go to Russia because of the cold weather there. Then they purchased a Ford six wheeler – with pneumatic tyres. They eventually worked four lorries and at busy times hired extra transport. Grinding, rolling and splitting was done every day and often at night too. At first an oil engine for grinding was fitted, but as business flourished, a big electric motor was purchased.

The grinding of barley, wheat etc (for animal feeds) was done on greystones – weighing about a ton each. These had to be replaced periodically as they wore away. These stones also had to be sharpened (called 'stone dressing'). This was an awful job and often the flint became embedded in the hands of the person doing the stone dressing.

The Limes, circa 1950, the residence of William and later, Donald Maule.

William Maule and Sons Ltd prospered and was the largest employer in the village, if not the area, at certain times. However, with the decline in agriculture during the 1970s, the firm began to contract. Grinding at the top mill ended and eventually became only a distributor of animal feed. It was wound up in March 1981. Top and Bottom Mill became warehouses for various businesses. In the 1990s Top Mill was finally converted into apartments. Bottom Mill is currently being demolished to make way for new houses.

'The Bottom Mill', 1968.

In 2001, John Wilkinson visited Auckland. He discovered that the mill had been razed to the ground. However, two sets of grinding stones had been saved and were in the Ministry of Transport and Technology Museum.

On the site of the mill, there was a Sheraton hotel but in the lobby John found a brass plate referring to the mill. The lounge was now called the Mill Room and the restaurant called Partingtons. However, when he returned in 2005, the hotel had changed hands and was part of the Langham group. It had undergone yet another refurbishment and the brass plate was missing. Instead, was a glass case containing the National Heritage book of New Zealand windmills which lay open at the page relating to the Orston Mill.

The Limes and 'Top Mill', circa 1968 with Hill Farm in the background.

Kavell's Mushroom Farm

Roland Shepperson, who worked at the Kavell's for much of his life, in conversation with Brian Harrison.

What was the Mushroom Farm is located a few hundred yards from the start of Bottesford Lane on the left hand side towards Bottesford. Nowadays, it is a collection of warehouses used by a variety of businesses. Although it is mainly on one side of the road, in recent years it spilled over to the other side. It was built on the original site of the RAF camp.

Leo Kavell fled his native Poland to join the RAF as a pilot in the Polish Squadron. He made many flights over Orston and, after the war ended in 1945, he bought the camp and set up the mushroom farm. He began in a small way using the existing buildings. Profits were ploughed back into the business in the form of new sheds and brick buildings, most of which we see today. Local people were recruited to pick the mushrooms and build the sheds. Also, as production increased, mechanization began to take over - fork lift trucks, tractor and lifting devices to empty the boxes, anything to make work easier.

Roland joined the staff in 1962. There were ten women pickers including Phyllis Wakefield, destined to become Mrs Shepperson. The ten men on the staff mixed the growing compound by hand. This was a mixture of sugar beet pulp, gypsum granules, fertilizer, and horse manure which was packed in boxes to be sterilized with steam. After cooling, the mushroom spawn was added. Two weeks after germination, peat was added to the top of each box. After ten days, harvesting started and continued for six weeks. The spent compost was then sold as a soil improver to gardeners, nurseries and golf clubs.

Neville Foster, a few years younger than Roland and also from Orston, worked there after leaving school. After two months watering compost, they asked him to go on the mixing gang. He asked for more money, was refused, so parted company.

One of the many jobs Roland did was to weigh the mushrooms into 31bs boxes. These would be taken to wholesale markets in Nottingham, Mansfield and Sheffield. They were also sold to callers. Later, in the 1990's, they were packed in punnets for the supermarkets.

Christmas time was always special at the Mushroom Farm. Mr Kavell gave a party for his workers. All the food and drink was on the house. Everybody left with a hamper containing festive goodies and most years Roland found a bottle of Scotch secreted in his hamper. During the 37 years Roland worked for Kavells, he always found it to be a happy work place and he made many friends as well as finding a wife.

Leo Kavell took two Polish ladies as wives and produced two children. He made many trips back to his homeland. He retired to Edwalton and died at the ripe old age of 92 years. David and Sarah Mehigan took over at the farm and in 1999 stopped growing mushrooms, turning the buildings into industrial units.

Mr Rowland Shepperson weighing mushrooms.

CHAPTER 26
LEISURE

The 19th century and earlier

Before the 19th century, leisure activities were largely based on the seasonal cycle of the farming community and the religious festivals such as Christmas, Easter and harvest providing opportunities for merriment. This changed in the 19th century, at least in the cities and towns. There, factory owners saw holidays as a waste of valuable production time, and therefore lost profits, and the bibulous festivities associated with these as undesirable for their workforce and their need for reliable and sober employees. As a consequence, hitherto blood-thirsty, brutal and rowdy leisure activities were replaced by polite, inhibited, orderly and more tender-minded pursuits. These were often 'improving recreations' centring on education and the development of such things as subscription libraries, Mechanics' Institutes and philosophical societies.

The drum from the Battle of Waterloo which was played in village processions

Villages such as Orston were unable to share in these advances and, probably, leisure activities did not change so radically. Unfortunately, not much in terms of documents exists for earlier centuries and it is only possible to speculate from the glimpses that we have of that period.

Feasts

The Odd Fellows Club feast was always held on the first Friday in June. The Parish Feast was on the first Sunday after September 19th. It flourished in Victorian times but later declined and was superseded by an August flower show which, with its accompanying dancing and sports, drew large crowds from neighbouring villages.

Music

In addition to the musical element at organised feasts, singing was taken so seriously and organised to such an extent that documents survive from as early as 1782 when a 'society of singers' at the parish church was formed. In 1790, the 'society of psalm singers' documented its constitution as follows:

> *The Society of Psalm-singers at Orston have agreed to observe the following:*
> *Articles and Rules in 1790: vis, 1 That all the members shall meet together at each Wednesday in the evening at 7 o clock from April 5th to November 1st and at 6 o clock all the rest of the year; and every member absent shall forfeit 1 penny.*
>
> *2. That William Willson shall ring or cause a bell to be rung during 5 minutes before the time of meeting and every member who does not attend before 2 stanzas of any psalm be sung shall be deemed absent and forfeit accordingly.*
>
> *3. That during 6 weeks in harvest no member shall be obliged to observe the first and second article nor pay any forfeit for being absent.*

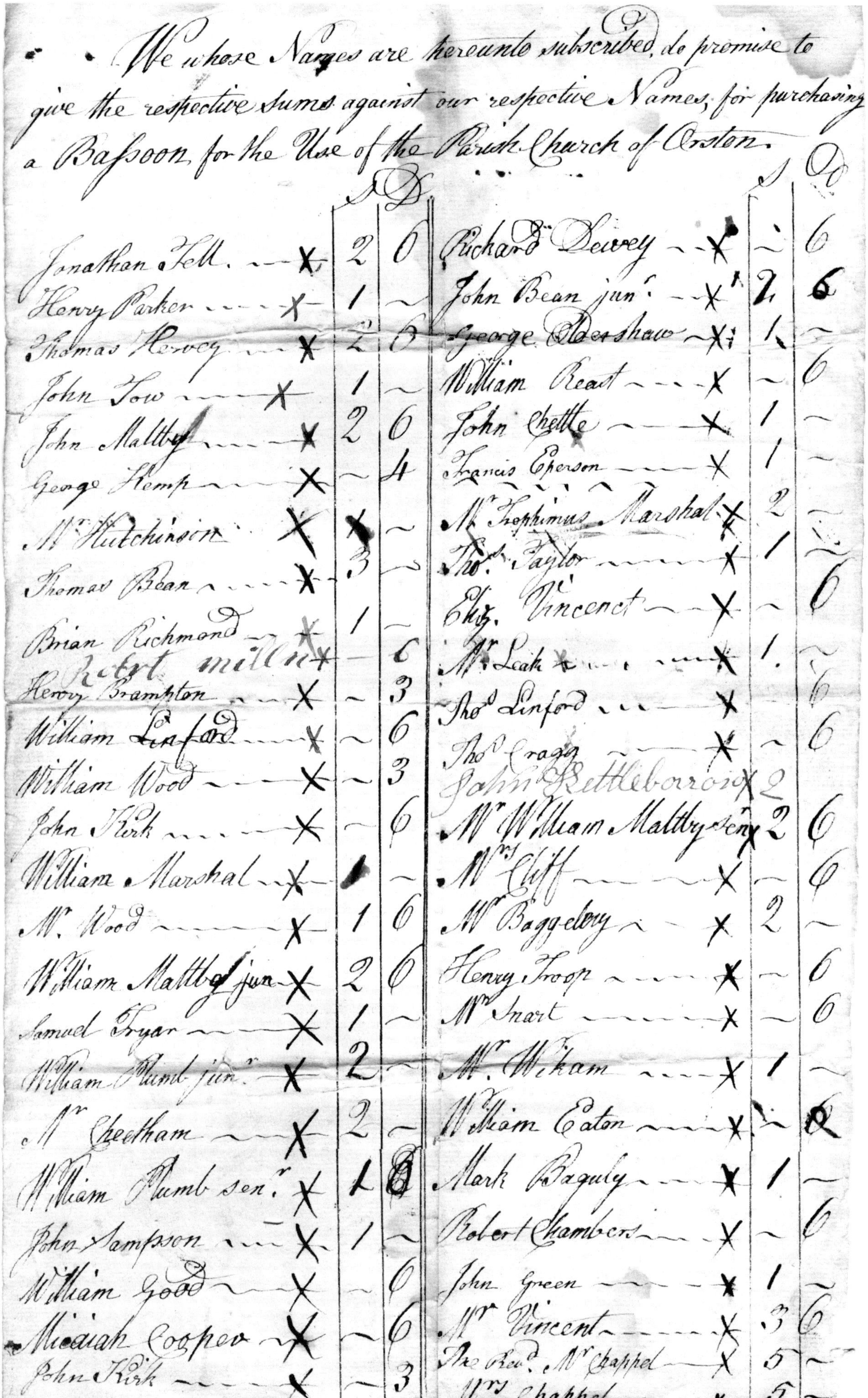

We whose Names are hereunto subscribed, do promise to give the respective sums against our respective Names, for purchasing a Bassoon for the Use of the Parish Church of Orston.

		S	D
Jonathan Fell	X	2	6
Henry Parker	X	1	–
Thomas Hervey	X	2	6
John Tow	X	1	–
John Maltby	X	2	6
George Kemp	X	–	4
Mr Hutchinson	X	[illegible]	–
Thomas Bean	X	3	–
Brian Richmond	X	1	–
Robert Miller	X	–	6
Henry Brampton	X	–	3
William Linford	X	–	6
William Wood	X	–	3
John Kirk	X	–	6
William Marshal	X	[illegible]	–
Mr Wood	X	1	6
William Maltby jun	X	2	6
Samuel Pryar	X	1	–
William Plumb junr	X	2	–
Mr Cheetham	X	2	–
William Plumb senr	X	1	6
John Sampson	X	1	–
William Good	X	–	6
Micaiah Cooper	X	–	6
John Kirk	X	–	3

		S	D
Richard Dewey	X	–	6
John Bean junr	X	2	6
George Aldershaw	X	1	–
William Reast	X	–	6
John Chettle	X	1	–
Francis Eperson	X	1	–
Mr Theophinus Marshal	X	2	
Thos Taylor	X	1	
Chas Vincent	X		6
Mr Leak	X	1	–
Thos Linford	X	–	6
Thos Cragg	X	–	6
John Kettleborrow	X	2	
Mr William Maltby sen	X	2	6
Mrs Cliff	X	–	6
Mr Baggeley	X	2	–
Henry Troop	X	–	6
Mr Smart	X	–	6
Mr Wickam	X	1	–
William Eaton	X	–	6
Mark Baguly	X	1	–
Robert Chambers	X	–	6
John Green	X	1	–
Mr Vincent	X	3	6
The Revd Mr Chappel	X	5	–
Mrs Chappel	X	5	–

List of subscribers for the purchase of a bassoon for use in the Parish Church, costing £3.13.6, 1773.

4. That every member shall at all times attend the meetings on Sundays so far as he can make it convenient but whoever is absent in time of divine service shall forfeit 1 penny.

5. That no person being absent on account of sickness shall be liable to the above forfeits.

6. That any member cursing or swearing shall forfeit 1 penny.

7. That William Willson shall be secretary and John Green treasury.

8. That every member shall signify his consent to these articles by subscribing his name to this paper which contains a memorandum of unanimous agreement to observe these rules.

William Willson
John Green
Richard Heart
George Harve
John Low
John Osow
John Willson
William Willson
Thos Trimbery
Thos Leak
Wm Fell
Thos Marshall
Francis Cox his mark
Thos Fell
John Mills
John Shell

Friendly societies *by Julie O'Neill*
Friendly societies evolved in the eighteenth century as self-help organisations through which working people could provide for their own needs in times of hardship. Members made regular, usually monthly, contributions in return for weekly pay when illness prevented them from working. Funeral benefits were also paid when the member, or his wife or children died.

Records show that there were ten members of friendly societies living in Orston in 1813-15. It is not known to which society they belonged but it is likely to have been one in another village, possibly Whatton where a society had existed since 1807. Orston does not seem to have had its own society until a Fraternal Society was established at the house of Thomas Baguley at The Royal Oak (nowadays the Durham Ox) on 24 September 1836. The club still existed in the mid-1860s but its absence in other records suggest that the society had probably closed by 1875.

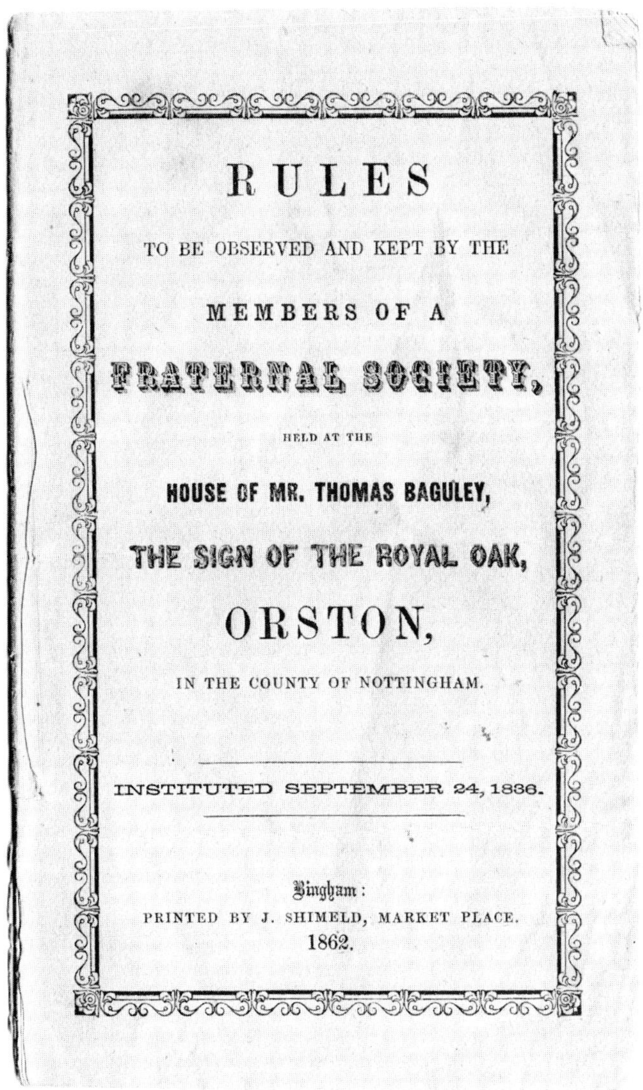
RULES
TO BE OBSERVED AND KEPT BY THE
MEMBERS OF A
FRATERNAL SOCIETY,
HELD AT THE
HOUSE OF MR. THOMAS BAGULEY,
THE SIGN OF THE ROYAL OAK,
ORSTON,
IN THE COUNTY OF NOTTINGHAM.

INSTITUTED SEPTEMBER 24, 1836.

Bingham:
PRINTED BY J. SHIMELD, MARKET PLACE.
1862.

Cover page of the Orston Fraternal Society's rule book, 1836.

A printed set of rules to be observed by members exists which reveal that the club met monthly. Members were admitted between the ages of 18 and 35, provided they were in good health and did not belong to another benefit society. Newcomers were elected by the existing members.

Each year the society appointed a Father, two Stewards, four Assistant Stewards, a Clerk and a Committee of nine members. Each member had to take a turn at being a Steward or else face a fine. Only the Clerk received payment for his work – one sovereign a year for keeping and regulating the books.

Funds and records were kept in a locked box which required three keys to open it. One each was kept by the Father and the two Stewards and the box was only to be opened in the presence of at least four members.

Members were entitled to benefits after one year of membership. In 1862, sick entitlements were generally ten shillings a week for 12 weeks, six shillings a week for 12 further weeks, and four shillings a week thereafter. The rules allowed for reducing these amounts in times when the Society's funds were low. If funds reached as little as £30 sick payments could be suspended, but funeral payments would continue to be made.

A sum of £3 was provided for the funeral of a member and £2 for his widow, or a friend who arranged the funeral if there was no widow. No payment was made for the funeral of a member who died by his own hand, but the payment to the widow or friend could still be paid. Members were expected to attend the funerals of other members carrying black staffs, but this was not required in the event of suicide. Funeral payments were also made for the deaths of the wife and legitimate children of members - £3 for a wife, £1 for a child aged between one and fourteen years old.

On reporting illness, the Stewards would visit the sick members at home. The club retained a doctor to attend to the sick for which he was paid 2/6 per member yearly.

Fines were imposed for a variety of acts or omissions. The landlord where the club met had to ensure that a fire was kept in the club-room during the winter months or be fined (1/-), members could be fined for refusing to take up office as Steward (1/-), for being a key holder to the Box but not turning up on Club night (2/6), losing a key (6d), interrupting other members while speaking (6d), abusing or taunting other members for being in receipt of funds from the box (2/6), coming to the meeting or to funerals 'disguised in liquor', quarrelling or laying wagers with other members (6d), failing to attend the annual feast day parade or funeral of a brother member (6d)

Members could also be excluded or heavily fined for activities undertaken while in receipt of box-funds - drinking in a public house more than 6d worth of drink, undertaking paid work or being more than half a mile from home without permission. Members would be expelled if they voluntarily joined the army or navy but not if they had to serve because of being pressed into service or drawn by ballot to serve.

In about 1843 another friendly society was established in the village with its base at the Durham Ox, which is nowadays Churchside Farm, on Launder Street. (This apparent confusion between the two public houses is understood when it is recognised that when the Durham Ox closed down around 1920, the Royal Oak took its name. This was the Launders Lodge, no. 156 of the Nottingham Ancient Imperial United Order of Oddfellows. The Nottingham Oddfellows was one of the Orders that developed in the nineteenth century creating networks of lodges that were affiliated members of an Order, but independent within it.

The Launders Lodge was established in Orston at a time when the Nottingham Order was expanding rapidly. It was one of twenty established in 1843. The Launders Lodge had 68 members in 1870, 65 in 1894, 58 in 1905, 76 in 1910 and 57 in 1912. The Lodge met monthly on every fourth Monday between

7pm and 9pm at the Durham Ox where members came to pay their subscriptions, discuss lodge business and enjoy a social evening. Officers of the lodge consisted of a Grand Imperial, Vice Grand Imperial, Warden, Tyler, three trustees, a treasurer, a Secretary, two stewards and a committee of management.

The rules of the lodge were similar to those of the existing Fraternal Society. Fines were imposed for breaking lodge rules, such as being late for meetings (3d to 6d), refusing to serve as an officer of the lodge, failing to attend the lodge meeting, entering the lodge room 'disguised in liquor', or casting reflections on the birth, trade calling or circumstances of a brother member (all liable to a fine of 1/-), upbraiding another brother, visiting a public house while in receipt of sick visits, re-commencing work after sick leave without giving written notice (all liable to a fine of 5/-). Members found guilty of serious offences, such as defrauding the lodge or working while in receipt of sick benefit were liable to fines of up to 21/- or expulsion from the society. Despite so many potential offences, only one fine was noted in the account book (in 1893, J.Richards 2/6).

Membership of the lodge was restricted to men aged between 16 and 40 who were in good health. New members had to be proposed by an existing member. An entrance fee, which varied from 2/6 to 10/- according to age, was paid and thereafter a monthly contribution of between 1/4 and 1/9, according to age, was paid. In return, a member would receive 10/- per week for twelve weeks when illness prevented him from working; the weekly allowance was then reduced to 7/- for 12 weeks and to 4/- for the subsequent 12 weeks. After that time the Management Committee would review the case. Payment was not made for any illness or injury thought to be the result of improvident actions. Rule 36 excluded illness arising from venereal disease or from injuries sustained in running, jumping, fighting or wrestling for gain or by being the aggressor in any affray or quarrel. Funeral benefits, to which the members were entitled after belonging to the lodge for one year, were £6 for the member and £3 for his wife. In addition to these benefits, the lodge paid a 2/- pension to elderly members.

'The anniversary', more often known as 'Club Feast Day', was the most important part of any friendly society's year and was often the most important social event in the village calendar.

The Fraternal Society's anniversary was celebrated on the second Friday in June. Members would meet at the club-house with staffs in hand to walk to church for a service before returning to the club-house for the feast itself.

Similarly the Launders Lodge rule book for 1895 specifies the first Friday after 14 May for its anniversary, although in earlier years, the feast was held in June. On Feast Day the annual meeting of the lodge would be held, the accounts presented and a dinner provided for the members. It is not known whether the Launders Lodge had special regalia for its feast day, but they did buy a flag in 1871 and a band was hired for the feast day procession each year from 1870 to 1887 at a cost of around £2.10.0. on each occasion. The lodge also paid for the ale and other expenses of the feast until 1883 when the regulations prohibited such expenditure.

On 16th June 1865, the *Nottingham Review* carried a report of anniversary celebrations in Orston. The Oddfellows held their feast at the Durham Ox on 2nd June. The weather on this occasion was unfavourable as heavy rain had fallen the previous night and continued during the day, which put a dampener on proceedings. The Old Sick Club held their feast at Baguleys on 7th June but this year the procession to church was not so large as usual, several members being absent from sickness and other causes. The Calverton Brass Band attended on both occasions and delighted the company with their music, executed in their usual style.

The 20th century

During the 20th century much of the organised leisure activities centred on the village hall. Some, of course, were organised around the church and chapel. There was also a men's reading room in the grounds of the hall on High Street. But, of course, in the 20th century leisure activities were no longer all in the village. With the motor car and improved public transport, villagers could pursue their leisure activities elsewhere.

The Red Triangle Club, later Orston Village Hall.

The original village hall came from Kegworth in 1918. It had previously been a YMCA hut. It was placed on the site of what we now know as the village hall and was to be called the Red Triangle Club.

In 1941 a bomb landed on the field behind the Red Triangle, exploded and totally flattened it. All that remained were the iron stove and a few beer bottles hiding beneath it. (Drinking alcohol in the club was not allowed).

Soon after the war, a new brick building was erected, financed by compensation from the War Office and loans from William Maule and Frank Burton. The building continues today, although rearranged. The billiard table has long gone and, recently a small extension has been added and the ground extended. In addition to the many private functions, such as wedding receptions, it is used for badminton (various clubs use it), Brownie Club meetings and, of course, a variety of social events organized by the Village Hall Committee

William Maule and an unknown lady opening a gymkhana in the Park field (opposite the Hall) circa 1950. Mrs Burton of Hill Hall is seated.

The opening of the Village Hall. L to R: Mr Sutton, the srchitect, the Duchess of Portland, Maurice Thornhill and Harry Mart..

Kath Walker with sister Jean outside what is now called Orchard Cottage with the old wooden village hall in the background, 1936.

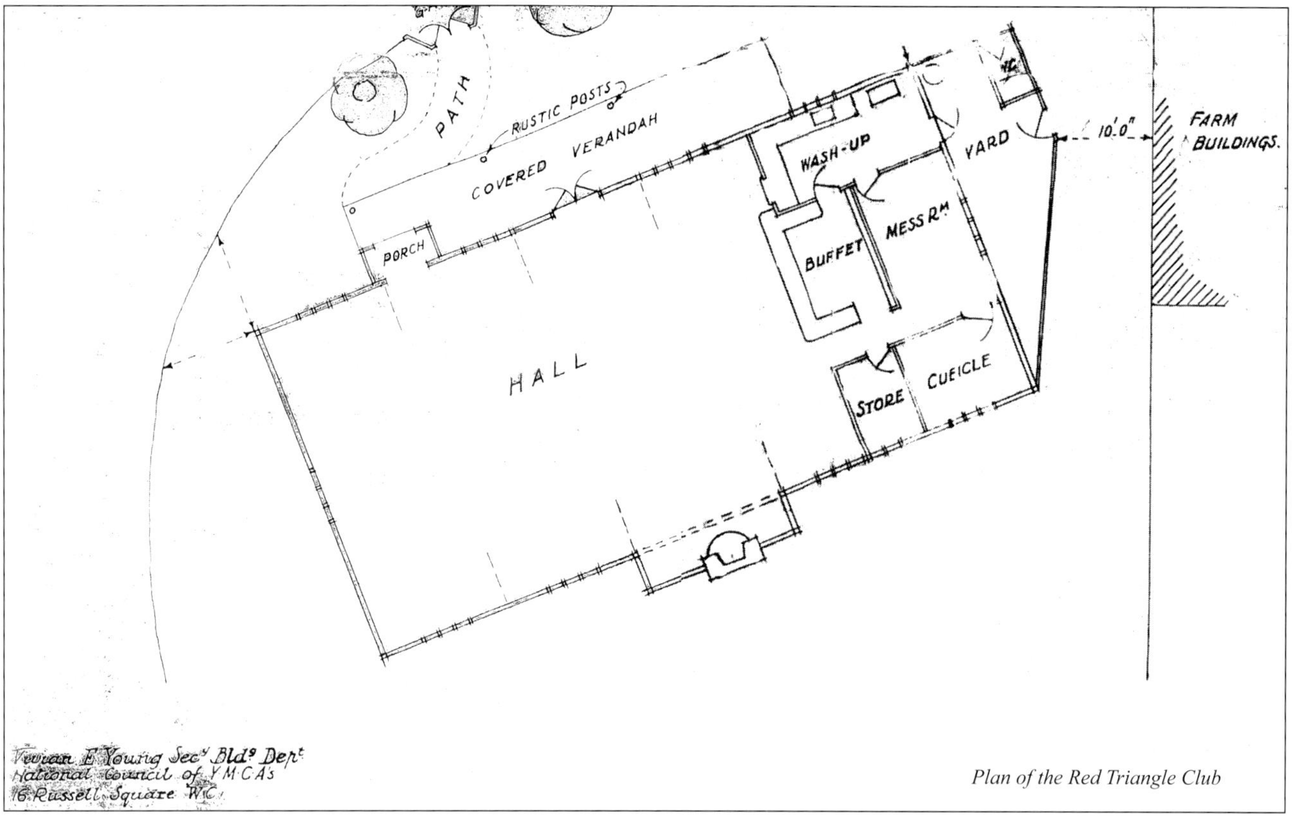

Plan of the Red Triangle Club

ORSTON.

RED TRIANGLE CLUB.—The members held a convivial social on Tuesday, and there was again a very large attendance. A most enjoyable evening was spent. The proceedings opened with a few dances, and Miss Nix, of Hawksworth, was at the piano. Mr. Bernard Maule, who has been of great assistance to the Club at these socials during the season sang four songs, including a duet with Miss Woolley (who was making her first appearance as a vocalist), in his usual pleasing style. Mr. Bentick, another new friend in the village, also sang, and left a good impression. Miss Moor, who is well known in the surrounding villages, sang two songs very effectively. Mr. Wilson played three violin solos, and was accompanied on the piano by Miss Higginbotham. Mr. Horace Sharp, of Aslockton, sang several songs in his characteristic manner, and there was no mistaking the fact of the popularity in which he is held at Orston. The secretary of the Club, Mr. Telford, did all he could to uphold the reputation of the "Red Triangle" members by his vocal powers, and received due recognition. Miss Higginbotham, the mainstay of the musical life in the village, accompanied all the songs, with the exception of Mr. Maule's, who was very ably provided for by his sister, Miss Doris Maule. A musical travelling parcel, which caused much merriment, was secured by Mrs. Vince. The singing of "God Save the King" brought to a close one of the most pleasant and successful evenings held in the Club.

Red Triangle Club - press report, circa 1937

Orston and Thoroton Women's Institute *by Jean Purdy, its president*

Our WI was formed in 1928, originally as Thoroton WI. Twenty two ladies paid a subscription of two shillings (10p) on the 5th December of that year. Of the twenty two members, seventeen lived in Thoroton, three in Orston and one each from Hawksworth and Staunton.

Numbers fluctuated over the years, but there were always several members from Orston, leading to the change of name, in the early 1940's to Thoroton and Orston WI. At the annual general meeting in 1947, it was decided to change the name of the institute to Orston and Thoroton and to hold the meeting in Orston, from where the majority of members came.

Over the years, meetings have been held in various venues – the village hall, the school, the chapel schoolroom, and now, the chapel; and at different times on various days of the week. We meet currently at 7.30 pm on the second Monday in the month.

A huge variety of speakers have educated, informed and entertained members over the years. Competitions and roll calls were

WI outing, 1949-50.

a common feature of earlier programmes. The roll call was when every member was expected to stand up and speak on the chosen topic. For example, in 1933 this was 'what our men folk think of the WI. Changing times and attitudes brought an end to the roll call in the 1950's.

WI's are always known for excellence in cooking – as true today as in WW2, when Thoroton and Orston WI served as a preserving centre. Fruit was brought to the centre for 'co-operative preservation'. A wide variety of jams and jellies were made and in October 1941 218 lbs were produced!

For several years Orston and Thoroton WI invited pupils from an inner city school in Nottingham for a day in the country – seeing the animals, going for a walk, and being served a wonderful tea.

More recently, members became involved with the making of story sacks to enrich children's enjoyment of books, and tactile books for partially sighted and blind children. Of course, over the years members have enjoyed a huge number of visits locally, regionally and nationally. Some members have even visited our twinned WI in Carterton, New Zealand, with whom we have corresponded for over twenty years.

Membership of Orston and Thoroton WI is still strong, and, as well as upholding the original objectives of the WI – to educate, entertain and inform - we are proud of our role as representatives of women across a broad spectrum of British life and culture. The WI has become proactive in making our voices heard on fundamental issues that lie at the core of our society.

Other forms of entertainment

Of course, a description of the activities of formally constituted organisations is only part of the picture. In addition to visiting performers at the village hall, from time to time the village itself has put on entertainment. Probably the most notable is in the early 1950s when a group of villagers, the most prominent being George 'Jeff' Jeffcott, Thomas 'Robbie' Robson, George Abrams and Marina Scotney presented a number of reviews and comedy shows. They were also responsible for the Orston Song, the subject of the next chapter.

The Durham Ox skittle team with Miss Leicester on Robbie's knee, 1969.

CHAPTER 27
THE ORSTON SONG – 1950S

At the end of the last chapter, it was mentioned that during the 1950s a group of villagers put on reviews and comedy shows. They were also responsible for 'At Old Orston in the Vale' which was sung to the tune 'Much Binding in the Marsh'. It was probably written mainly by 'Jeff' Jeffcott with 'Robbie' Robson, George Abrams and Marina Scotney lending a hand. Here it is, followed by some explanation.

1. At old Orston in the Vale,
Built upon a river called the Smite,
At old Orston in the Vale,
It really is a dreary place at night,
The fact we have no street lights in our streets is very sad,
Although the courting couples here all seem very glad,
But when you put your foot in something soft it makes you mad,
At old Orston in the Vale.

2. At old Orston in the Vale,
At courting now you see we're really classy,
At old Orston in the Vale,
We try to make a friend of every lassie,
There is a sweet young lady here, she's known to all of us,
She travels to her school each day, not by train but bus,
Her name is little Jeannie and on John she's got a crush,
At old Orston in the Vale,

3. At old Orston in the Vale,
In a field near here was found some hidden treasure,
At old Orston in the Vale,
Our digging now will give a greater pleasure,
The history books all tell us that King James was short of dough
And some poor chap to fight for King and country had to go,
He hid his money in the ground and then came back no more,
At old Orston in the Vale.

4. At old Orston in the Vale,
At football we're the best in all the nation,
At old Orston in the Vale,
Our supporters often cause a big sensation,
They stand there weekly by the lane and boy, they've got some pluck,
A player slips and tumbles down his face stuck in the muck,
If one of theirs it serves him right, if ours it's "oh bad luck"
At old Orston in the Vale.

5. At old Orston in the Vale,
Another game that we play here is tennis,
At old Orston in the Vale,

So come on Jill and Jack and James and Dennis,
Our courts and our pavilion win many a jealous glance,
And who knows you may be the next for a Beat and Ralph romance,
At old Orston in the Vale.

6. At old Orston in the Vale,
At cricket too we are a great attraction,
At old Orston in the Vale,
They flock to see us when we are in action,
Our wicket-keeping opening bat's the best round here by far
And Mr. William Maule the Miller is his loving pa,
And who sits watching by the gate but Skipper in his car,
At old Orston in the Vale.

7. At old Orston in the Vale,
The wealthy folk now all have television,
At old Orston in the Vale,
The ones without all view it with derision,
The television owners all stay at home each night,
The others mournfully proclaim it's sure to spoil your sight,
But they'll come knocking at the door to view the next big fight,
At old Orston in the Vale.

8. At old Orston in the Vale,
We have the Sunday papers that we like,
At old Orston in the Vale,
Delivered by our Mary on her bike
Whenever she is leaving one she pays a chatty call,
For hours our papers with her bike are propped against a wall,
But grumble when she's late, and you don't get one at all,
At old Orston in the Vale.

9. At old Orston in the Vale,
There is a lad who sleeps above the shop,
At old Orston in the Vale,
When school is done his courting has to stop,
Although he looks so very shy, he's quite a lively youth,
This tale he really can't deny because it is the truth,
At school each day he puts his arms around a girl called Ruth
At old Orston in the Vale,

10. At old Orston in the Vale,
Our village transport is getting up to date,
At old Orston in the Vale,
There is no reason to arrive there late,
Kids going to their school each day for education's sake,
Or Simon off to Elton with a mighty thirst to slake,
Don't ever think of walking, they use Alec's shooting brake,
At old Orston in the Vale.

11. At old Orston in the Vale,
Whenever there's to be a local wedding,

At old Orston in the Vale,
Housewives forget their pots and pans and bedding,
From all their nooks and crannies the curious cronies creep,
Behind the blinds in Chapel Street there's many a cautious peep,
Poor husbands have to hear it all before they go to sleep,
At old Orston in the Vale.

12. At old Orston in the Vale,
Mrs. Pearson is our Club caretaker,
At old Orston in the Vale,
She also is a real good coffee maker,
She rushes round with ash-trays at all the local do's,
And shouts to table tennis players 'What about your shoes',
And pity poor old Cyril when he tries to have a snooze,
At old Orston in the Vale.

13. At old Orston in the Vale,
At darts & doms we're getting quite proficient
At old Orston in the Vale,
If Dick wants double top that's quite sufficient,
But one night we must admit we had an awful scare,
Tom wanted double one, then threw two darts anywhere,
His third dart was a beauty & Dick shouted 'Gad',
At old Orston in the Vale.

Verse

1. In the early 50's there was an issue about whether the village should get street lighting.
2. The 'sweet young lady' is Jean Walker, later, of course, to marry John Smeeton.
3. This is a reference to the treasure trove found in Ransome's field in 1952 at the end of High Street, on the left hand side of the footpath to Thoroton.
4.
5. Jill, Jack, James and Dennis are not names of members of the tennis Club but names that fit the rhyme. Beat and Ralph Hawkins were Orstonians, the latter very much still alive in Chapel Street.
6. The wicket keeper is Donald Maule, William Maule's son. Skipper is Egbert Shepherd, Mary Breedon's father.
7. At the time, television was just coming into our homes so there was considerable status with owning one.
8. 'Our Mary' is Mary Cloxton. See Herbert Wakefield's section of Chapter 29.
9. The 'lad who sleeps above the shop' is Ivan Spencer. Ruth is Ruth Wilkinson from Sutton.
10. This is Simon Stewart who lived in New Row, off Chapel Street (now demolished and replaced by Chapel Garth). Alec was Alec Gilbert who lived in Flawborough and the owner of two shooting brakes he obtained from the army for the purpose. He ran a regular service taking drinkers from the Durham Ox to the Manor Arms at Elton.
11. Nothing changes!
12. The caretaker was Mrs Pearson, the mother-in-law of Mrs Pearson who lives at The Willows, opposite the Village Hall.
13. This is Dick Dry the star of the Durham Ox darts team, and Tommy Scotney, his wife's uncle.

L to R: ...Tommy Scotney, 'Robbie' Robson, George Abrams,, Marina Scotney, not known, Jeff Jeffcott

Marina Scotney and George Abrams

CHAPTER 28
SPORT

In the same way that the Victorian factory owners attempted to 'tame' traditional leisure activities in the interests of progress (and profit), they also attempted to tame sport, especially to outlaw some of the more blood thirsty traditional country activities such as badger baiting, cockfighting and dog fighting. On the other hand, hunting which was pursued by the upper classes, was acceptable. In the Middle Ages, the nobility hunted deer. Until 1795 deer still roamed free in Belvoir. Originally, the fox was considered as vermin and only gradually became the chief object of the chase. As early as 1539 foxes were being hunted in east Leicestershire but it was not a sport with any formal rules.

Today's popular sports, such as cricket, football, golf, and tennis, have similar origins in pre-Victorian times. However, this book is devoted to the history of Orston, and their origins are not discussed here. Below are brief histories of the main sports in Orston.

Foxhunting *by Barry Gibson*
Situated on the northern edge of the celebrated foxhunting Shires, it is not surprising that Orston over the years has become well acquainted with foxhunting and its followers. Territorially, the village is part of the Belvoir Hunt with the river Smite forming a boundary with that of the South Notts. Usually, the Belvoir would meet in the surrounding area every other Saturday and, prior to the war, it was very agreeable hunting country. However, two war time airfields constructed at Normanton and Bottesford had a somewhat detrimental effect on hunting but, being adaptable, the enthusiasts made the most of what was remaining.

In 1956 when Barry Gibson, a hunting enthusiast himself, bought Orston Hall, he instigated an annual Lawn Meet in the field opposite the house. This proved extremely popular, not only with the mounted followers but also with the local inhabitants who were only too happy to partake of the traditional stirrup cup provided by the host. Some very enjoyable runs often followed the meet, and hounds usually found a fox lurking in the old plaster pits which then ran over the A52 into the Granby and Redmile areas.

Recent legislation outlawing foxhunting has not had the effect its promoters wished. Quite the contrary, hunters have shown a remarkable increase in numbers, even though, to conform with the law, hounds have to follow an artificial 'man laid' scent. Even the most confirmed 'anti-hunters' agree that the legislation was drafted in an ill-conceived manner making it difficult to interpret accurately, but making it quite easy for an enjoyable form of hunting to continue yet still remaining within the law.

Although the Belvoir Hunt does not visit Orston quite so frequently nowadays, The Beagles with their enthusiastic foot followers still meet regularly in the village and with the same constraints as Foxhunting have some enjoyable sport. How long this will continue is anybody's guess. Hopefully, one day we will see the legislation more sensibly amended or better still repealed. In the meantime, in the words of RS Surtees' hero Mr John Jorrocks, 'Tell me a man's a foxhunter and I loves him at once'.

The Hunt with the Hall in the background.

Cricket *by Peter Henson (Who wishes to thank John Cope for details of the first reported cricket match.)*
The earliest recorded game of cricket by Orston took place in August 1820 against Whatton. Orston won 'contrary to expectations'. It was a two innings match and probably took place on the Well Field. It is likely that cricket was played in the village well before then. Orston was a large village and would have been able to support a team.

Until 1926, cricket was played on the Well Field. This was to the north of Smite Lane between the two bridges. The sports field was then moved to Spa Lane by arrangement with Mr Frank Burton the owner of Orston Hall. Apparently Mr Burton did not like the sound of sport so close to his house. The pictures show Mr Burton at the gate of the new ground and players preparing to play their first game at Spa Lane.

The pavilion that had been used at the Well Field was mounted on old iron reaper wheels and towed to the new ground by two horses provided by Mr Walker (the gentleman in the photograph wearing a cap with a cricket bat at his feet) and placed against the hedge at the east side of the ground.

All the games at this time were played during weekday evenings or on Saturday afternoons and never on a Sunday. This was reserved for chapel or church.

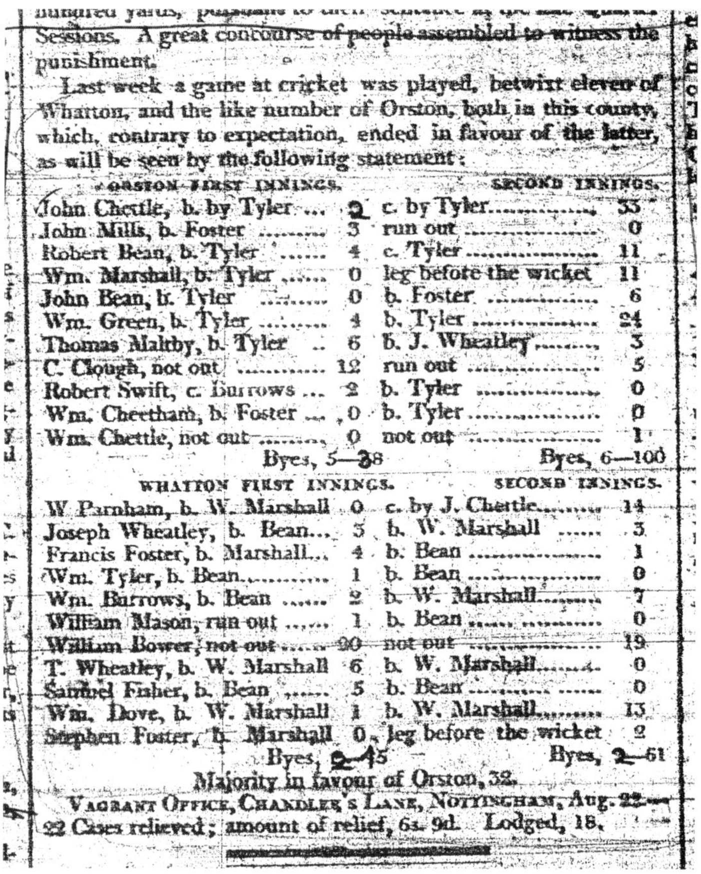

Sessions. A great concourse of people assembled to witness the punishment.

Last week a game at cricket was played, betwixt eleven of Whatton, and the like number of Orston, both in this county, which, contrary to expectation, ended in favour of the latter, as will be seen by the following statement:

ORSTON FIRST INNINGS.		SECOND INNINGS.	
John Chettle, b. by Tyler ...	2	c. by Tyler..............	35
John Mills, b. Foster	3	run out	0
Robert Bean, b. Tyler	4	c. Tyler	11
Wm. Marshall, b. Tyler	0	leg before the wicket	11
John Bean, b. Tyler	0	b. Foster	6
Wm. Green, b. Tyler	4	b. Tyler	24
Thomas Maltby, b. Tyler ..	6	b. J. Wheatley.........	3
C. Clough, not out	12	run out	5
Robert Swift, c. Burrows ...	2	b. Tyler	0
Wm. Cheetham, b. Foster ...	0	b. Tyler	0
Wm. Chettle, not out	0	not out	1
Byes, 5—38		Byes, 6—100	

WHATTON FIRST INNINGS.		SECOND INNINGS.	
W. Parnham, b. W. Marshall	0	c. by J. Chettle.........	14
Joseph Wheatley, b. Bean...	5	b. W. Marshall	3
Francis Foster, b. Marshall...	4	b. Bean	1
Wm. Tyler, b. Bean............	1	b. Bean	0
Wm. Burrows, b. Bean	2	b. W. Marshall.........	7
William Mason, run out	1	b. Bean	0
William Bower, not out	20	not out	19
T. Wheatley, b. W. Marshall	6	b. W. Marshall.........	0
Samuel Fisher, b. Bean	5	b. Bean	0
Wm. Dove, b. W. Marshall	1	b. W. Marshall.........	13
Stephen Foster, b. Marshall	0	leg before the wicket	2
Byes, 2—45		Byes, 2—61	

Majority in favour of Orston, 32.

VAGRANT OFFICE, CHANDLER'S LANE, NOTTINGHAM, Aug. 22.—22 Cases relieved; amount of relief, 6s. 9d. Lodged, 18.

Newspaper report of the first reported cricket match at Orston, 1820.

During WW2 a 'blister' hangar was erected on the cricket ground where the present club house stands. This was used as a dispersal hangar for the small emergency airbase on Bottesford Lane. Altogether there were six or seven blister hangars in the area. When cricket club members were putting in some new land drains in 1981 there was a loud rattling and grinding from the digger and up came two huge concrete blocks. It was discovered that these were the bases of the post supports for the landing lights of the aerodrome.

Frank Burton, May 1926, opening the gate to the new sports field on Spa Lane

Group at the opening of the new new sports field on Spa Lane, 1926.

Cricket was played on the ground during the war, mostly by military personnel who were based in the area. One of the 'local rules' was that if the ball went into the blister hangar it was a four but if it hit the fence or the outside of the hangar it only scored two. This rule was needed as the hangar went well into the field of play and the boundary was very short on that side.

In 1959 the wicket square was doubled in size. However, the best wickets were on the old part of the playing surface. A new and bigger pavilion was built in the early 1960's. It was extended in 1970 to incorporate a larger seated tea room, a kitchen and larger changing rooms. When the ladies of the club served sit down teas instead of the normal plated tea at cricket matches it was the talk and envy of visiting teams.

At about this time Orston could, if needed, field a team made up entirely of left handed batsmen.

Orston was one of the founder members of the Newark Cricket Club Alliance League in the 1980's. Although it had always been able to field a strong side, by village standards, it was during this period that the team was perhaps at its strongest. It won the Newark league several times and the Cope Cup four years back to back. It also won the highly prestigious Ransome Trophy, beating Collingham in the final. At that time, Collingham had no less than four Nottinghamshire players in their side.

Orston had the privilege of providing four players, including the captain, for the Newark League team when they played against the Australian Club touring team. Much to the surprise of the Australians who had beaten most English league teams, they came unstuck against the Newark League who beat them easily. The Aussies admitted they had underestimated the Newark side but said it would not happen in the future. However, when they next toured four years later and Orston again provided four players, the Newark team was again the victor.

The club suffered a major blow when the club house, the new score box and many items of equipment were burnt down due to arson. Nothing survived other than a chair and a photograph. For nearly two seasons the club had to use a Portacabin. With the help of Gunn & Moore, the club was able to obtain a new pavilion from ATV, the television company which had just finished filming the series 'Outside edge', a comedy about cricket.

As with many clubs, it became harder to get local players. The existing players grew old together and retired. People moved away to work and with the lack of cricket played in schools, younger members were scarce. Because of lack of members, Orston CC was wound up in 1998.

Orston CC, 1907.

Presentation of the Ransome and Marles cup to (left) Peter Henson, Orston CC captain, 1985.

(above) Cricket team, circa 1946 Back row (L to R) Ted Caunt, Norman Scotney, Wilf Baker, Horace Walker, George Cloxton,,not known, Front row (L to R) Horace Maule, Ben Wilds, Maurice Thornhill, Jim Carlisle, Harold Walker, (on ground) Norman Parish.

Orston CC, circa 1955 L to R. back row: Peter Simester, Les Wakefield, John Smeeton, Mike Pragnell, Terry Graveney, Ken Maule, Middle row: Bill Baker, Robbie Robson, Donald Maule, Eric Walker. Front row: Charlie Pearson (umpire), Jean Walker (scorer), Harry Wakefield.

Tennis *by Peter Henson*
Orston Tennis Club was founded in the early 1930's by some keen locals. Two grass courts were prepared in the north east corner of the sports ground on Spa Lane.

A small wooden shed was used as a pavilion. Tennis was never played on Sunday, as it was the custom that this day was set aside for Church or Chapel. Members travelled by bicycle from as far away as Hose bringing with them plates of food to be shared with a cup of tea, boiled on the Primus stove. If you arrived early, the chances were that you could be called upon to push the grass mower or asked to wheel the white line machine to get the courts ready for play.

A new larger pavilion was built in 1953 with gents' and ladies' Elsan toilets. Membership in the 1950's climbed to over thirty including a number of junior players. Many of the members obtained their kit or rackets from jumble sales held in the area. Sports clothing was not easy to come by because of rationing. Games were played against East Bridgford, Bingham, Bottesford and Radcliffe on Trent.

Jean Smeeton outside the Tennis Club pavilion, circa 1950.

It was the custom in the first week of July to play a Club Championship. The ladies of the club provided strawberry and cream teas for everybody. One of the village highlights in the early 50's was the Tennis Club's New Years Eve Supper in the Village Hall. All the village was welcome. Food was provided by the ladies of the club followed by games and dancing.

Owing to the number of members and only having two courts a third court was laid down in 1960 at a cost of £300. This court was never played on. Between 1960 and 1964 the membership fell to such a level that the club was no longer viable. It could not afford the new wire netting. The club was wound up in 1964.

An attempt was made to re-start the club in the 1980's but, because of the distance of the sports field from the village, there was insufficient interest and insurance was too expensive.

Golf *by Tony Benton*
The Golf Society was formed in April 1999 when it was agreed to hold a knock out competition for people living in the village. The first year it was won by Frank Pavett with Kathy Rusby the runner up. The following year it was expanded with The Durham Ox donating the main knockout trophy. A plate knock-out competition was also held and a golf day. All current and past members and any one who had a business in the village and regular patrons of the Durham Ox, were invited. This has continued to this day. The past winners of the Durham Ox

Presentation of the Durham Ox Golf Trophy to Patrick Newton by Tony Benton, 2003.

Trophy are: 2000 - Lance Ward, 2001 - Tony Benton, 2002 - Tony Benton, 2003 - Patrick Newton, 2004 - Nigel Rusby, 2005 - Nigel Rusby, 2006 - Andy Tongue, 2007- Andy Tongue.

Badminton: Nigel Rusty and Andy Holmes

Badminton *by Peter Henson and Tony Benton*
When the billiard table was removed from the Village hall in 1954, it opened up the space to allow Badminton to be played. It was not until about 1963 that a club was formed when Terry Graveney rounded up a group of village teenagers and taught them to play. This they did once a week until about 1967 when the club joined the Newark and District Badminton League. The club continued to grow, fielding both a ladies and a gents team and two mixed teams.

The Village Hall used to have eight pendant lights suspended from the ceiling. These were useful guides for home players to judge their whereabouts on the court while still following the flight of the shuttle. This 'home advantage' was lost when the hall was refurbished and the lights removed.

In 2002, the Newark League introduced a ruling that players could not play for two teams unless they played in an adjacent league. This had the effect of preventing the ladies from playing in the two mixed teams causing some of the men to move to new clubs and reducing the number of teams from four to one.

The club still plays on a Monday night during the winter with League matches on Wednesdays. Orston also has another Badminton club that was formed in 1983 to play friendly games between its members on Tuesdays.

An Orston football team outside the Durham Ox, circa 1950.

Orston Football Club, 1952
L to R. back row: Arthur Glenn, David Otter, George Tindale, John Marsden, Johnny Clarke, Eric Walker, George Abrams, Geoff Flack. Front row: Bob Patchett, Alec Dowse, Phil Price, Robbie Robson, John Smeeton.

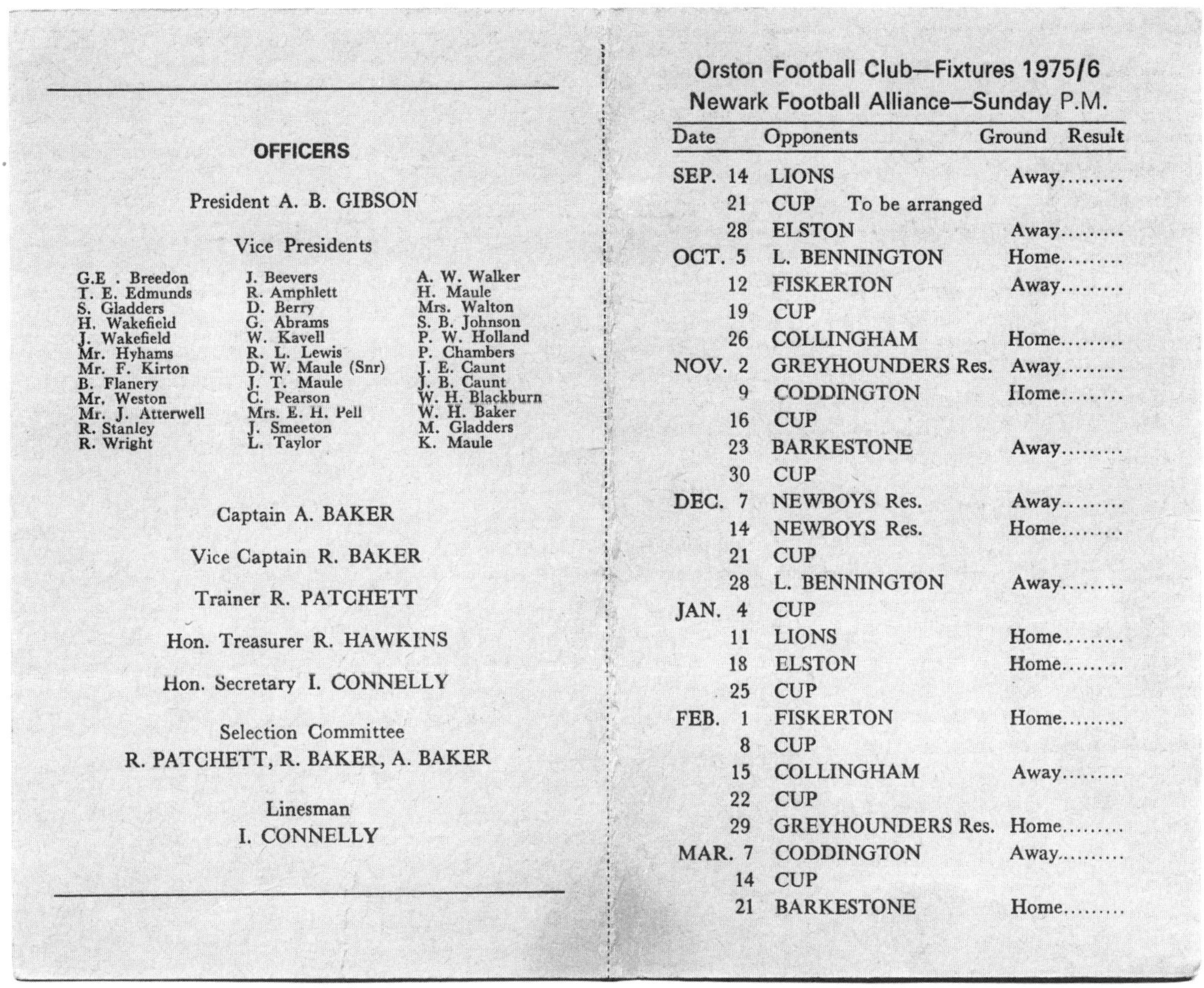

OFFICERS

President A. B. GIBSON

Vice Presidents

G.E . Breedon	J. Beevers	A. W. Walker
T. E. Edmunds	R. Amphlett	H. Maule
S. Gladders	D. Berry	Mrs. Walton
H. Wakefield	G. Abrams	S. B. Johnson
J. Wakefield	W. Kavell	P. W. Holland
Mr. Hyhams	R. L. Lewis	P. Chambers
Mr. F. Kirton	D. W. Maule (Snr)	J. E. Caunt
B. Flanery	J. T. Maule	J. B. Caunt
Mr. Weston	C. Pearson	W. H. Blackburn
Mr. J. Atterwell	Mrs. E. H. Pell	W. H. Baker
R. Stanley	J. Smeeton	M. Gladders
R. Wright	L. Taylor	K. Maule

Captain A. BAKER

Vice Captain R. BAKER

Trainer R. PATCHETT

Hon. Treasurer R. HAWKINS

Hon. Secretary I. CONNELLY

Selection Committee
R. PATCHETT, R. BAKER, A. BAKER

Linesman
I. CONNELLY

Orston Football Club—Fixtures 1975/6
Newark Football Alliance—Sunday P.M.

Date		Opponents	Ground	Result
SEP.	14	LIONS	Away	....
	21	CUP To be arranged		
	28	ELSTON	Away	....
OCT.	5	L. BENNINGTON	Home	....
	12	FISKERTON	Away	....
	19	CUP		
	26	COLLINGHAM	Home	....
NOV.	2	GREYHOUNDERS Res.	Away	....
	9	CODDINGTON	Home	....
	16	CUP		
	23	BARKESTONE	Away	....
	30	CUP		
DEC.	7	NEWBOYS Res.	Away	....
	14	NEWBOYS Res.	Home	....
	21	CUP		
	28	L. BENNINGTON	Away	....
JAN.	4	CUP		
	11	LIONS	Home	....
	18	ELSTON	Home	....
	25	CUP		
FEB.	1	FISKERTON	Home	....
	8	CUP		
	15	COLLINGHAM	Away	....
	22	CUP		
	29	GREYHOUNDERS Res.	Home	....
MAR.	7	CODDINGTON	Away	....
	14	CUP		
	21	BARKESTONE	Home	....

Orston F.C. fixtures and officers, 1975/6

CHAPTER 29

SOCIAL SATIRE, 1880 - 'GRAND EXHIBITION OF BURDS AND HANIMALS AT HORSTON'

GRAND EXHIBITION OF BURDS AND HANIMALS AT HORSTON.

July 1880

BURDS.

SPEACH BY THE KING-FISHER.—Be it enakted that all the feasts mun be in one wick, as I axed all tother birds and they want it. I shall [illegible] allow [illegible] [illegible] shuting gallaries, or any thing of that sort to s[illegible]n in street, as I mun have room to fly round every morning. I shall not allow anyone to [illegible]ve land beside me, as I ave orthority over all other birds, and if you obey my orders you sha[illegible] have plenty of malt for paying for, and I'll sell you bear cheaper than the publicans, (here here) and I'll have John Mayfeld for my edge cutter agen, and I'll not be father in lor to clu[illegible] as I have been, but I'll be as good as a mother and pay my subkription as usual, and not dror[illegible]t out as i sed, (here, here) and when my yung bird is fliged you shall have bear 20 yeers of ag[illegible], (loud aplorse), the horses shall eat grass in front of church, and I'll allow all of you to tak[illegible] in logers. I'll allow Bro. Cocks and sister Mat hen to sell stockins and lace but do nowt before church time on sunday mornings, and I'll allow club fokes to go into my butiful grounds as my ornt used to let 'em do, but if you offend me I'll send you all to Bingam as I did Bro. Dickards, but I'm sorry to say I had to pay, (pretty mess), and I'll put manure agen my pomp so that none of you can fetch any worter, and wen I lok it up you munner pick i[illegible] as you did aforetime, (no, no,) and I'll pay wages when you gets your leg broke and hed a[illegible] the subscripsions with a pound, as I gen note when keeper's child wor fetched home, and [illegible]woodna lend a cart to fetch her from station. (here, here).

HANIMALS.

THE GREAT FISH.—[illegible] been [illegible] here and [illegible] allowed any other fish to get fat, I've swollerd everything I could get old of. I've just got a coyfish to get a good bite for me agen big stone, and totner fish was as quite as a Lamb while I got it. I hed a swim to Bingam tother day, and new publican got in water and I bit him, and it cost ten bob to get out, and I batted my fins, and waged my tail as a dog does when its a bone. But best of it was a Sturgon fish came up Smite, and a smorley fish, a worley fish, a stuat fish, a hand fish, and some other small fry got it and brought it to me, and I kollerd it and tode em to put it in brewhouse, snd I loked it up and they wanted it back, they thort I was fool big enuff to be katched with a hook like that, but I sed, no, its mine, or else I'll send you all to Bingam for trespas, and I kut it up and sent bits to all big fokes, but they wor none for baker, nor for keeper's child, nor for any poor fokes, and not a smell for them fools as katched it, they didna no as I could bite like that, but they know now.

THE CHANGING SEEN.

Jackson will be Station mester insted of Johnson. Post orfice will be fixed at 4 lane ends as there's a good traid got now. Willows will be put on side of Smite. Mayfeld will be turned to June. Uncle will be clean washed and shaved and have on a new white shirt [illegible] occasion. The windmill will be stopped as the miller loves the grove best. Deafy will [illegible] [illegible]tal. Durham Ox turned to Durham Hefer. Royal Oak to Elm tree. High street put on bottom. Church put agen Ranters' Chapel. The vermin killer will turn keeper. The villa[illegible]e tailor will make a new seccond-hand suit of clothes. Cheatem will cheat em no more. Parafin will be 10d. a galon. Dolly Verdon will have six new dresses on. Grume will carry a bag of beans without lettin it fall on master's leg. The edge will be finished in Smite lane. Fieman will get £40 and a new leg. The buth for club will be put in a field agen some closits. The grocer will put on his blacksmith's apron again. Bingam Band will play and not break down: tune "See the konkering hero comes."

The hole to konclude with a grate bunfire, wh[illegible]e the great fish will be roasted and the king-fisher plucked and fried. In case of ackident [illegible]e runaway shopkeeper has kindly konsented to preside.

GOD SAVE THE KUEEN.

The satirical pamphlet was common in the eighteenth and nineteenth century. Famous authors include Jonathon Swift and Daniel Defoe. Although public issues were often the subject, many others were local and anonymous. This one is typical and is, presumably anonymous.

Even though many of the references are lost in time, the thrust of the pamphlet is obvious: it is attacking the pomposity and arrogance of the 'well to do'. Nevertheless, with the help of the 1881 census, trade directories of the time, it possible to unravel just a few.

The 'kingfisher' was John Fisher, the owner and occupier of, what we now know as 'The Hall'. The 1871 census describes him as a farmer of 900 acres (1 square mile is equal to 640 acres. Altogether there are 1,800 acres in Orston). He was by far the largest landowner living in the village at the time and, given the position of the Lord of the Manor who not only did not live here but owned considerably less, John Fisher was undoubtedly the 'village squire'. Here, he is asserting himself as the top bird ('king') and what he will and will not allow and what he will and will not do.

John Mayfield was a humble agricultural labourer who lived at No 1 Chapel Street. Presumably at some time Mr Mayfield worked for John Fisher and was sacked. Hedge cutting in those days was done manually by means of a hedge knife and regarded as a skilled task.

Presumably, as the squire, John Fisher could exercise his rights to prevent grazing of horses on the green outside the church. He must have acted to prevent one/some of his tenants taking in lodgers. He must have owned many terraced houses in the village which were used by his servants and farm workers. The reference to Bingham is probably to the workhouse. It is likely that Mr Fisher would have had the power to send someone there.

'I'll put manure agen my pomp' refers to having placed manure next to the pump in the Holme field near the Hall that villagers used to get drinking water. Presumably, the last few sentences refer to various mean acts he is considered to have done.

The first line of the 'HANIMALS' section reads 'For a long time I've been swimming here and not allowed any other fish to get fat ……'.

In 'THE CHANGING SEEN' (scene) section, 'Cheatem will cheat em no more' probably refers to Mr John Cheatham, the grocer although Joseph Cheetham was the sub-postmaster (in addition to being the parish clerk and school master). There were three or four 'grooms' in the village, men employed by the gentry and the largest farmers to take care of their horses or a stable. Presumably, the reference here is to the groom at the Hall. The tailor is probably William Magson, great grandfather of our own Eileen Harrison! Unfortunately, I have not been able to discover who Dolly Verdon was.

The final paragraph suggests that there will be a large bonfire at which the kingfisher will be killed and eaten over which the runaway shopkeeper would appear to be keen to preside.

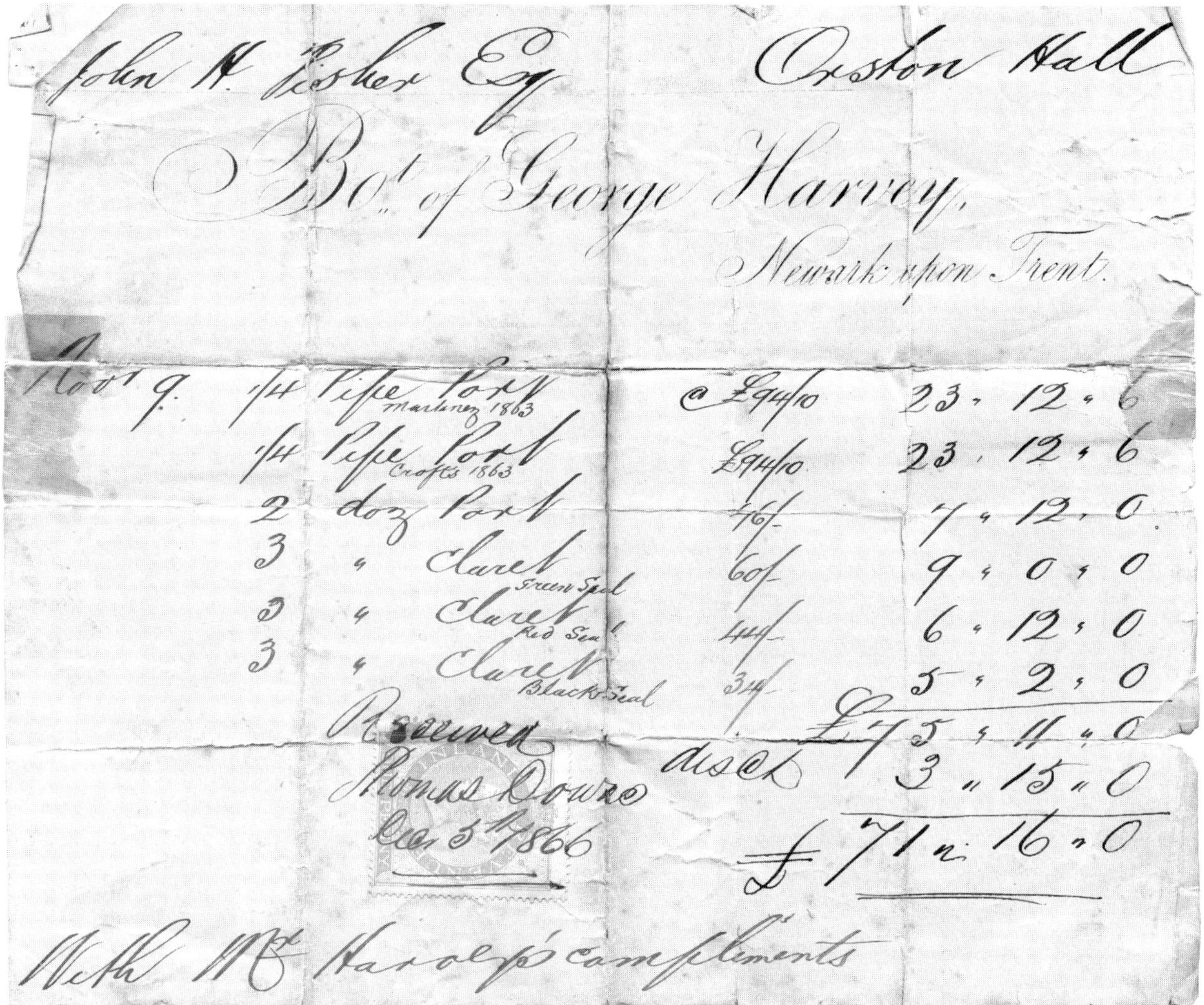

John H. Fisher Esq Orston Hall

Bot. of George Harvey,

Newark upon Trent.

Novr 9.	1/4	Pipe Port Martinez 1863	@ £94/10	23 . 12 . 6
	1/4	Pipe Port Crofts 1863	£94/10	23 . 12 . 6
	2	doz Port	76/-	7 . 12 . 0
	3	" Claret Green Seal	60/-	9 . 0 . 0
	3	" Claret Red Seal	44/-	6 . 12 . 0
	3	" Claret Black Seal	34/-	5 . 2 . 0
				£75 . 11 . 0
			disct	3 . 15 . 0
				£71 . 16 . 0

Received
Thomas Dowse
Dec 5th 1866

With Mr Harold's compliments

It appears that John Fisher was a formidable drinker of port and claret. £71-16-0 in 1866 is equivalent to £4,862 in today's prices, although we do not know how often he placed an order with George Harvey. A 'pipe' of port was 105 gallons (115 gallons if it was from abroad). Both Croft's and Martinez port (10 years old) can be bought today - at £32 and £9.35 a bottle, respectively.

William and Rebecca Magson, circa 1925.

CHAPTER 30
LIFE IN ORSTON IN 1900

Notes from an interview by Elizabeth Smeeton of her grandmother, Edith Walker in 1978 when she was 87 years old.

Shops

There was a general stores and post office, a draper's shop and boot repair shop, a saddler's and boot shop and a sweet and tobacco shop. A notice was displayed in one shop which said *'Please do not ask for credit as a refusal might give offence'.* There was an annual sale of china, crockery etc held on village green.

Other food and services

Milk was delivered to houses straight from farms. Churns were carried in hand cart, later by pony cart. Butchers brought meat from Aslockton and Bottesford in horse-drawn carts. There was a bakery in the village. Bread could be collected or delivered. The postman walked to the surrounding villages to collect and deliver mail. Paraffin and candles were sold at the local shop. Trucks brought coal by rail to Elton and Orston station. It was then delivered by horse-drawn carts to houses. It was later sold from coal merchant's yard in village. There were two Pubs in village: The Durham Ox and The Royal Oak.

Livestock

Most households kept a few hens and some fattened a pig for household use - bacon and hams were salted for use later. Pork pies were hand raised, brawn made, haslet, and pigs fries – liver, kidney, chopped meat covered with a skirt (rather like netting). Home-rendered lard made from pig's fat was used for pastry-making and frying. Many of the products were shared with relatives, friends and neighbours.

Pets

My grandma can only remember having a guinea pig.

Water

Drinking water was fetched by bucket and yokes from the village pump on the outskirts of the village and on Bottesford Lane from, what was called, Promised Land. Domestic water was collected in butts or tubs and during shortage bought for ½d. a bucket from houses where there was a well or cistern. Water from the Spa in Spa Lane was used for medicinal purposes.

Medical service

The doctor lived in Bottesford. He came to Orston by bicycle, later by motor bike and much later by car. Most people walked to his surgery 2½ miles away in Bottesford.

Church life

The local school was a C of E school. The vicar was a regular visitor. There were two teachers. Children attended Church three times each Sunday. One party 'A treat' once a year. The village reading room was used by the men folk for cards, whist drives and billiards. This was organised by the Vicar. There was no work on Sunday. All clothes and boots and shoes had to be cleaned by Saturday evening ready for church on Sunday.

Children's Games

They played whip and top. Hoops were made by the local wheelwright. Children also played shuttlecock and battledore [the term to describe, what we refer to today as 'Badminton', a 'battledore' was the racket], marbles, hop-scotch and skipping.

Transport

There was a carrier's cart once a week to Nottingham and Newark and a pony and trap to market on market day. The first motor car in the village was owned by the Squire from the Hall.

Farming

Horses were used for ploughing and cultivators which were used after harvest to prepare land for sowing. The threshing machine was local. Men walked to neighbouring villages with threshing machine for 2s. 9d. a day. There was a mill for grinding corn on Mill Hill. It was eventually sold and shipped to New Zealand. There was a pinfold where stray animals were put.

Other work

Lacework for women was fetched from Nottingham by train in a three wheeled trolley. Some worked at the Plaster pits. The buzzer sounded at 1.00 pm each day.

ORSTON is a township, village and parish, bounded on the west by the river Smite and on the east by Leicestershire, 1 mile north from Elton and Orston station on the Nottingham and Grantham line of the Great Northern railway, 5 miles east-north-east from Bingham, 9 south from Newark and 115 from London, in the Newark division of the county, Bingham wapentake, petty sessional division, county court district and union, rural deanery of Bingham, archdeaconry of Nottingham and diocese of Southwell. The church of St. Mary is a building of stone with freestone facings, in the Norman and Perpendicular styles, consisting of chancel, clerestoried nave of three bays, aisles, south porch and a low tower of Norman date at the west end containing clock and 4 bells, dated respectively 1599, 1621, 1622 & 1730: there is a piscina and a mural monument to the family of Kercheval (1695); in 1889-90, the south aisle and porch were entirely rebuilt and other restorations made, at a cost of £940: there are 344 sittings. The register of Orston dates from the year 1589 for all entries, and that of Thoroton from 1583. The living is a vicarage, with the chapelry of Thoroton annexed, joint net yearly value £277, including 95½ acres of glebe, in the gift of the Dean and Chapter of Lincoln, and held since 1873 by the Rev. Thomas William Swann M.A. of Caius College, Cambridge Here are small Wesleyan and Primitive Methodist chapels. The Ladies' dole of £1 14s. 6d. is distributed yearly. Gypsum stone abounds here, and there are manufactories of plaster of paris. A short distance from the village is a spa or mineral spring, said to be highly beneficial in scorbutic complaints. Earl Manvers, who is lord of the manor, and Mrs. John Henry Fisher are the chief landowners. The soil is strong clay; subsoil, clay. The chief crops are wheat, beans, barley and peas. The area is 1,955 acres; rateable value, £4,678; the population in 1891 was 408.

Parish Clerk, Joseph Cheetham

Post Office.—Joseph Cheetham, sub-postmaster. Letters arrive from Nottingham at 7 a.m. & 4.15 p.m.; dispatched at 5.50 p.m.; sunday, arrive 8.20 a.m. (callers only); dispatched, 3.45 p.m. Postal orders are issued here, but not paid. The nearest money order office is at Aslockton & telegraph office at Bottesford, 3 miles distant

National School (mixed), erected in 1848, for 78 children; average attendance, 40; Miss Clara Mary Goss, mistress

Carrier.—William Shipsides, to Nottingham, sat.; & Newark, wed

PRIVATE RESIDENTS.

Fisher John Henry, The Hall
Maltby Chas. Wm. Chestnut house
Price John A. The Villa
Swann Rev. Thos. Wm. M.A. (vicar)
Swire Frederic, Manfield house

COMMERCIAL.

Baker Arthur, wheelwright
Belvoir & Newark Plaster Company; works, Orston sidings, G.N. Rly
Breedon George, farmer
Cheetham Annie Elizabeth (Miss), shopkeeper
Cheetham John Edwin, farmer
Cheetham Joseph, farmer & clerk to the parish council, Post office
Cheetham William, blacksmith
Clayworth Thomas, farmer, Manor fm
Colston Mary (Mrs.), dress maker
de Wilton-Holmes Capt. Samuel C. Royal Oak P.H
Ellis Alfred, saddler & harness maker
Fryer Frank, cowkeeper
Hickman William, cowkeeper
Houseley Frederick, farmer
Lane John, shoe maker
Lovegrove Thomas, baker
Magson Thomas, tailor & draper
Maltby Thos. Ludlow, farmer&maltstr
Maule & Morley, machine proprietors & millers
Oliphant William, cowkeeper
Parnham John, shopkeeper
Shipsides William, carrier
Smith John William, coal merchant & grocer
Swanwick John, cowkeeper
Taylor Adeliza(Mrs.),Durham Ox P.H
Tyman Betsy (Mrs.), shopkeeper
Walker & Sons, coal merchants
Walker Frederick, carpenter
Wilson William, butcher
Worley John, cowkeeper
Worley Mary Ann (Mrs.), grcr.&bakr

Kelly's directory, 1900

Frank Walker and horse and cart on Loughbon, circa 1925.

Loughbon, with shop on the right, 1910.

Staythorpe House, 1909.

Staythorpe House, C..Eades, 1906

Maypole dancing on the Green, V-E Day, 1945

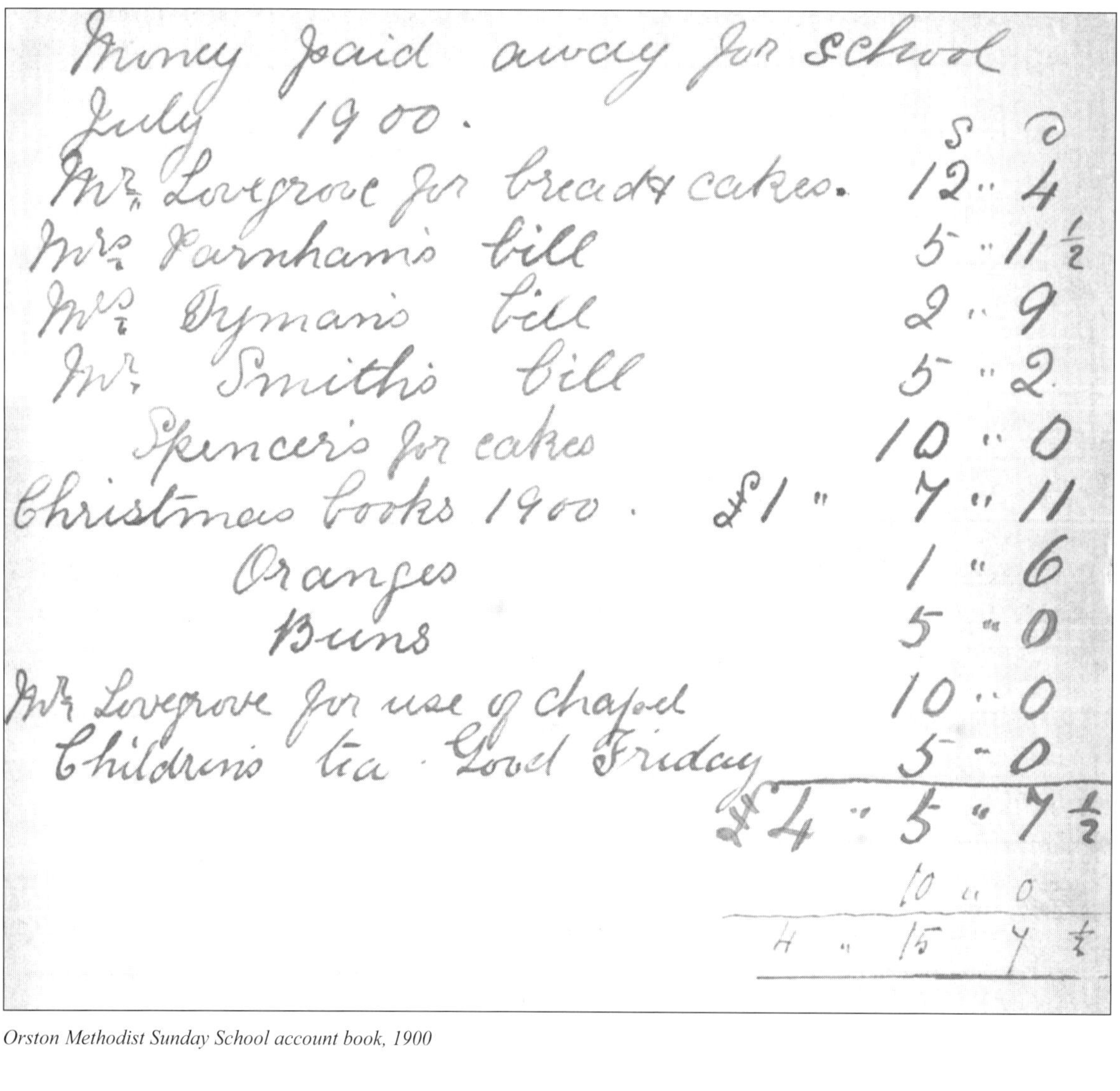

Money paid away for school
July 1900.

		s	d
Mr Lovegrove for bread & cakes.		12	4
Mrs Parnham's bill		5	11½
Mrs Dyman's bill		2	9
Mr Smith's bill		5	2
Spencer's for cakes		10	0
Christmas books 1900.	£1	7	11
Oranges		1	6
Buns		5	0
Mr Lovegrove for use of chapel		10	0
Children's tea Good Friday		5	0
	£4	5	7½
		10	0
	4	15	7½

Orston Methodist Sunday School account book, 1900

Cottages on The Green

Coal delivery, 1910, Albert Walker and Billy Baker (who worked at the old windmill).

CHAPTER 31
ORSTON BETWEEN THE WARS

This chapter comprises reminiscences by three Orston residents and an article in the *Nottinghamshire Countryside* about the village in 1937.

***Mrs Peggy Southwood** who lived in one of the cottages on Mill Lane from notes taken by Jean Smeeton.*

Utilities and amenities
In the coal shed we had a water butt. Out of this had to come washday water and water for washing hair (it had to be soft!). There were no taps: we had to lift water out in buckets. Water was heated in the copper. We had to fetch sticks out of hedges to light it. Washday was always on a Monday. We had bubble and squeak and rice pudding cooked in the side oven. Also irons were put in front of the fire to heat up. We simply relied on the weather to dry clothes; they would be strung across the kitchen overnight to dry.

We had a little kelly lamp to take to bed. The toilet was outside: we had to take a lantern up the garden. The produce show was the highlight of the year. I fetched milk from Staythorpe House Farm (Wilmot Walker) for other people. I took Colonel May's at night (he lived at the cottage near the railway station). I might get a slice of cake if I was lucky. Granny Walker (Eliza) weighed coal out in sacks. She was a very kind woman.

Guards used to see Mrs Sarah Lace Smith (who lived on the Row off Lombard Street where the author lives today) off the train at Orston with a big wicker trolley of lace for women to draw for extra money. She also took scissors to be sharpened somewhere in Hockley, Nottingham.

Mrs 'Lace Smith' who collected lace remnants from Nottingham for 'tatting' jobs for ladies in Orston.

School

I went to the old school on Launder Street. The teachers were Mrs Stokes and Miss Johnson. Rev Sturton, the vicar, came for prayers. The lads were little devils at the back!

Inkwells were in desks - someone was ink monitor. Woe betide you if you got ink on your white pinafores with frills on the sleeves. Uniform was green when older with an orange badge and trim. Boys and girls kept their hats in a box - there were plenty of nits about. The nit nurse came and then visited mothers.

At playtime we played in Launder Street - there were no cars then. We got shooed off people's fronts. There was no teacher on duty. We went home for dinner, except those who walked from Elton who brought their own. I left at 14 to work.

Summer holidays

We went to Burtons' Plantation (the wood at the south end of High Street) to frighten peacocks. We played Fox and Hounds in the woods. The boys went to the Reading Room when they got older. (The Reading Room was in the upper floor of the tithe barn in the grounds of Orston Hall almost opposite Launder Street. Access was up some outside steps on High Street). There was a Sunday School outing one day a year to Skegness. The sea was up as far as the black tower.

Mr Telford who lived in The Cottage on Lombard Street was not popular. He was ran-tan-tanned (residents gathering outside the house banging pans etc.) out of the village. He eventually left and built the house now called Telford on Station Road.

ORSTON is a township, village and parish, bounded on the west by the river Smite and on the east by Leicestershire, 1 mile north from Elton station on the Nottingham and Grantham line of the Great Northern section of the London and North Eastern railway, 5 miles east-north-east from Bingham, 9 south from Newark and 115 from London, in the Newark division of the county, Bingham wapentake, petty sessional division and union, Nottingham county court district, Bingham rural deanery, Nottingham archdeaconry and Southwell diocese. The church of St. Mary is a building of stone with freestone facings, in the Norman and Perpendicular styles, consisting of chancel, clerestoried nave of three bays, aisles, south porch and a low tower of Norman date at the west end containing clock and 4 bells, dated respectively 1599, 1621, 1622 and 1730: the number of bells has now been increased to 6 and all have been rehung at a cost of £388 by public subscription: there is a piscina and a mural monument to the family of Kerchevall (1695); in 1889-90 the south aisle and porch were entirely rebuilt and other restorations made, at a cost of £940: in 1914 the north aisle and nave were restored: there are 344 sittings. The register of Orston dates from the year 1589 for all entries, and that of Thoroton from 1583. The living is a vicarage, with the chapelry of Thoroton annexed, joint net yearly value £300, and residence, in the gift of the Dean and Chapter of Lincoln, and held since 1911 by the Rev. Charles James Sturton B.A. of Oxford University. There is a small Wesleyan chapel. The Ladies' dole of £1 14s. 6d. is distributed yearly. A short distance from the village is a spa or mineral spring, said to be highly beneficial in scorbutic complaints. Earl Manvers V.D., D.L., J.P. is lord of the manor. The land is held chiefly by small freeholders. The soil is a strong clay; subsoil, clay. The chief crops are wheat, beans, barley and peas. The area is 1,955 acres; rateable value, £4,786; population of the civil parish in 1921 was 327 and of the ecclesiastical in 1911, 461.

Parish Clerk, Albert Walker.

Post Office.—Miss Annie Elizabeth Cheetham, sub-postmistress. Letters through Nottingham. Whatton is the nearest money order & telegraph office

Public Elementary School (mixed), erected in 1848, for 61 children; Mrs. A. Stokes, mistress

Elton & Orston Station (Great Northern section of the London & North Eastern railway), Arthur Gilbert, station master. At this station is a telegraph office, with delivery on station premises, open on week days only

PRIVATE RESIDENTS.

Burton Frank Ernest J.P. The Hall. T N Bottesford 6
Maltby Mrs. Chestnut house
Maule William, The Limes
Price John A. The Villa
Sturton Rev. Charles James B.A. (vicar), Vicarage
Tate George Joseph, The Gables. T N Bottesford 12

COMMERCIAL.

Marked thus ° farm 150 acres or over.

Baker S. E. (Mrs.), wheelwright
Breedon George, farmer
°Brown Horace, farmer, Manor farm
Cheetham Annie Elizabeth (Miss), shopkeeper, Post office
Fryer Frank, cowkeeper
Hallam Frederic, agricultural implement repairer & blacksmith
°Higginbotham Wm. Henry, farmer
Lovegrove Reynolds, farmer
Martin Francis John H., M.R.C.S., L.R.C.P., D.P.H. surgeon (attends tuesday, thursday & saturday)
Maule & Morley, threshing machine proprietors
MAULE W. & SON, MILLERS & CORN & CAKE MERCHANTS. T N Bottesford 5
°Mellor William Edwin, farmer, Highfield farm
Morley John Hy. threshing machine proprietor, see Maule & Morley
Orston Red Triangle Club (Thomas Wilson, sec)
Savage Percy, farmer
Scotney D. P. & Sons, builders
Sharp W. T. & Sons, farmers
°Stokes George Bowne, farmer
Taylor William, Durham Ox P.H
Topham Morris, shopkeeper
°Walker Frederick & Sons, farmers
Walker J. & Sons, saddlers & harness makers
Wilkinson William, baker
Wilson Samuel & Thomas, farmers
Young Men's Christian Association (T. Wilson, sec)

Kelly's directory, 1925

Miss Kath Walker *(see Chapter22) who lived at, what is now Whitegates in Chapel Street.*

Utilities

There were wells in most gardens. Terraced houses had access to a shared well. This water was used for most household purposes. Some houses owned a soft water well (rain water). I remember this kind of water from The Willows, Lombard Street, where Mrs Pearson now lives, for a half penny a bucket. It was either pumped up or a bucket on a rope was used. Drinking water was fetched from the Holme Well (in the field between the Hall and the Smite next to the road). The pump had a fence round it to keep the beast away.

Prior to mains drainage we used an earth closet, a pit which was emptied periodically by us onto the garden. Later a closet pan was used which was still emptied by the household onto the garden. Later still, it was collected by the night soil lorry".

Lighting in homes was by paraffin lamp, either standing on a table or hanging from a hook on the ceiling. Paraffin could be bought from the corner shop (Loughbon and Chapel Street) or travelling van (Mr Baines from Bingham) who supplied most hardware equipment and came weekly. Candles were also used from room to room. The farm stables and cowsheds were lit by a storm lantern which was carried around. The lamp used in the church still hangs in the main aisle.

Cooking in homes was done using a side oven and boiler in the black leaded grate. Flour was fetched from Top Mill (on Station Road). My family kept a pig for home consumption. Pork pies were taken to the bakers (on the site of the shop at Beauvale Cottage) to be baked.

Societies

There were Mothers' Union meetings. My mother was a member. They were held at the Hall (Mrs Burton's) or at the homes of enrolling members - Yew Tree Farm (the first Mrs Lewis), the Woodlands (Mrs Sam Johnson). Later, they were held at the Old School, Launder Street.

Recreation

There were cricket, football and tennis clubs. They all used the ground on Spa Lane and were well patronised by locals.

The allotments were on Spa lane between the Sports Field and the Spa. There were other allotments opposite Windy Ridge on Station Road. Most households were self-supporting in vegetables and fruit. The produce show was held each year in the Village Hall. There was a Children's Section which specialised in a collection of wild flowers. This always made a wonderful display - from jam jars to bucketsful!

Leisure and Entertainment

The tennis courts were in the far corner of the sports field. The club was self-supporting with crockery etc. Matches with other clubs and tournaments were held. It was all very enjoyable. There was a library and reading room in the village up the steps to the top of the tithe barn in the Hall grounds on High Street. (The upstairs of the building opposite, on the corner of Launder Street and High Street, was used prior to the 1930's).

Work

My father, Frank, worked with my grandfather, Frederick, the churchwarden, who lived at Staythorpe House. The front part of the house was used to sell cycles and spare parts (puncture outfits etc). They also sold fruit, apples plums, damsons etc according to the season. Coal, in hundredweights or half-hundredweights as required, was sold from the yard. Truck loads of coal from the Nottinghamshire collieries were shunted into the sidings at Elton and Orston station and put in wagons from there and sold to houses.

The chapel between Staythorpe House and the Blacksmith's shop was used for general repairs and picture framing. The chapel had a balcony, reached by a ladder. It later became a garage.

In 1939 my uncle, Wilmot Walker, bought Staythorpe House Farm, which is now Mulhouse on Loughbon. He kept three horses. These were taken daily to a field near the end of Smite lane. Cows were also kept at the farm. Milk was sold from the kitchen each day in pint and half pint measures. Surplus milk was fed to calves or sent to the Co-op dairy in Nottingham.

Village Characters

A man was 'ran-tan-tanned' having been cruel to his wife. They lived at, what is now, the Old Cottage on The Green.

An old lady, who always wore black, wandered about. Nowadays she would have been cared for by the state. Miss Aspinall, who lived in a cottage near where the telephone kiosk stands, used to shout and scare us children.

Frederick Hallam, blacksmith, High Street, circa 1930.

The Church

The choir consisted of men, women and boys. The organist was Mr Billy Coulston who was blind. Later it was Miss Kate Bonser, Rev. Sturton's sister-in-law who cycled from Hawksworth for morning and evening services and choir practice. Anthems were sung at Easter, Harvest and on special occasions.

At a funeral the passing bell was rung to indicate death. The bell rang again to denote the age of the person as the mourners left the churchyard. The gravedigger was Mr Albert Walker helped by Mr Frank Walker.

Floral arrangements in the Church windows on special occasions were by individuals as is still the custom. At the Sunday School Chapel Anniversary, music was supplied by members from Bingham - violin, cello and organ. A rising platform was erected on the right of the main door to seat children - the younger ones on the lower levels, so as to be seen by the congregation. There were recitations, solos choir items etc.

The Old School

Children started at five; the leaving age was 14. In the mid-1930s children started leaving at eleven to go to Bottesford. There was no drinking water. This was supplied by Mrs Albert Walker from the cottage next door. Wet clothes were draped around the tortoise stove to dry before walking home. Mrs Stokes, who came by train from Radcliffe on Trent, was the head teacher, Miss Fisher the infants' teacher. She lodged with Mrs Albert Walker.

Country and maypole dancing regularly took place on the Vicarage lawn and in the Hall grounds.

The Hall

Staff lived in. During one period the cook, parlour maid and housemaid were all Bottesford girls. Later another resident couple were Cyril and May Fathers. Cyril was the handyman and butler, and May was the housekeeper.

Local Farmers

Church Farm on Launder Street - Lovegroves kept cows.
What is now Syringa Cottage on Chapel Street - Wilsons who made a living with a few cows.
Dovecote Farm - Higginbothams had cows and sold milk.
Staythorpe House Farm - Walkers also sold milk .
Manor Farm – Wagstaffs.
Hill Farm – Savages.

Shopping

The village had a number of shops. The corner shop and post office (Loughbon and Chapel Street) was run by Miss Cheetham assisted by Mrs Elsie Walker who was postmistress. The postmen were Billy Cheetham and Albert Walker. There was a small wooden shop in the entrance to the farmyard at, what is now, The Woodlands on Church Street. Mrs Sam Johnson sold mainly sweets. Fruit, vegetables and meat were for sale from Mr and Mrs Talbot at what is now the Old Cottage on the Green.

There was, of course, Walker's at Staythorpe house, a cycle shop and vegetables and fruit in season. Fish and chips were cooked and sold from a corrugated hut which stood near the entrance to the field at the edge of the village on the corner of Mill lane and Flawborough Road.

Earlier, there was a tailor's shop at what is now called Magson's cottage on Loughbon, named after the proprietors of the shop. (Mr Bampton from Thoroton remembers walking over the fields to fetch scraps of material to make pegged rugs). The bakers were Wilkinsons. The bakehouse was at, what is now Beauvale cottage on Loughbon. I remember them baking our pies after pig killing time. There was an annual sale of crockery etc on the Green. The blacksmith's shop was on Loughbon which has now been turned into a house. It was worked by the Hallam and Hardwick families. A wheelwright, joiner and undertaking business was situated at the junction of Loughbon and Mill Lane by the Baker family. There was a saddler's shop in the building adjoining what is now called Mulhouse on Loughbon. It was later used by a plumber from Bingham.

The Scotney family undertook building repairs. Tom, who lived at what is now the Old Cottage on the Green and Dan who lived in the cotttage next to the Durham Ox. They had separate businesses. Travellers [*at that time, sales representatives who took orders for deliveries were known as travellers*] also visited the village. A Co-op man from Bingham came for orders. Later in the week these were delivered. Burtons Grocers of Smithy Row, Nottingham, came in the same way. Potters Stores at Aslockton also fetched orders and delivered the same day. Doncasters from the Market square, Bingham sold drapery and household linen. Miss Taylor brought samples and came for orders. Goods were delivered later. Butchers from other villages included Mr Baxter from Aslockton, Mr Bugg (later Goodson) and Mr Miller (later George), both from Bottesford, and a Co-op van from the butchery department.

....

Bernard Johnson in the *Orston Newsletter*, Spring 2008.

I came to Orston from Thoroton Manor Farm in 1927, aged three. I recall all our furniture being loaded onto horse drawn wagons to be moved to our new home – Woodlands Farm, now the home of the Fords on the corner of Church Street and Loughbon. My father had lost a leg in the First World War but this did not deter him from all the usual farming duties, aided by crutches. Mother ran a village shop. By profession she was a dress-maker and milliner. She used to fetch the cows from down Smite Lane for my father to milk. I delivered the milk round the village before I went to school. I filled up jam jars or milk jugs left on the kitchen tables of the houses down Chapel Street, doffing my hat to the labourers' wives who lived there. We were more polite then!

Orston was very different - no piped water or sanitation or electric light. I remember Mr Burton, who lived at the Hall, coming round to ask my father to sign a petition against bringing electricity to the village claiming that the village would look like a 'blasted bird cage with all the wire around it'. Father gave him short shrift, pointing out that the village was kept awake at night by the sound of Mr Burton's private electricity generator.

The school was on Launder Street. Up the three steps the two nooks on each side provided room for 2 or three children – boys one side, girls the other. There was one big school room, divided in the middle by a blackboard. The older children were on one side of this divide, the younger on the other. Miss Raithby was a strict disciplinarian, keen on using the cane. I was used to being well-behaved. My father used to say 'A dog or a child that don't do as they're told needs squaring up'. I went to church three times a day on Sunday. I seemed always to be changing in and out of my Sunday best.

Ferreting was a great pastime. We used to send the ferrets down the rabbit holes so that the rabbits could either be shot by the older lads or trapped in purse nets. I can remember once, when we tired of ferreting, we played cricket on what is now the A52, using an oil drum as the wicket. On hearing a car coming, we could usually get one more bowl in before clearing the pitch. How times change!

My first job was farm labouring at 11/6p (58p) a week. I started work at six and finished at five. The great challenge was to work out when it was time to come home for lunch as we didn't have watches. The trains were a good time measure. I also recall being most impressed by a friend who improvised a sun dial with sticks and straw.

I started coming in contact with a wider world when I took a job building runways for the many airfields that sprang up in the area following the outbreak of war. My childhood world of Orston would never be the same again.

Nottinghamshire Countryside – October, 1937

ORSTON – Twenty five years ago George Bourne wrote a depressing description of English village life, under the heading "Change in the Village." It is a sordid picture of change – for the worse; it is the story of the decay of English farming, of the dreary monotony of village life, of the stagnation of the English countryside. Here is an antidote – not an isolated example, but one typical of much that is happening in Nottinghamshire to-day. It is a picture of Orston in 1937 – a picture produced by the combined efforts of members of the Orston Adult Education Class.

There is nothing at all unusual about Orston or its people. It is a typical Vale of Belvoir village, with its main street, cross road, Hall, Church, rather antiquated school, cottages and small farms. A casual visitor would pay little attention to it'; and, in fact, there is nothing of a sensational character happening in it today; but there is an almost invisible upheaval going on in its social life. And that is what makes it a typical village.

Not so long ago, it was a village of 334 people, all working in farming and kindred trades. To-day it is outwardly the same; it is a farming village, with allied occupations still in evidence; there is a mill, a blacksmith, a wheelwright and joiner and a saddler – quite a representative collection for these mechanised times. But in two respects there is a marked difference from the earlier days. One is in the number of people who go out of the village to other kinds of work – both in the district and in Nottingham. The other is in the disappearance of Orston's self-sufficiency of only thirty odd years ago. Practically every week, from Newark, Grantham, Nottingham, a horde of tradespeople descend on the village. The co-op van comes every day; Burton's call once a week; four butchers, four bakers and six greengrocers (who literally follow one another round the village) bring metaphorical coals to Newcastle; two hardware vans pay regular visits; varying tastes are catered for by the quaintly named cake-men, by the fish and chips van, the ice-cream cart, a wireless service, a chemist, a rag and bone and scrap iron merchant; and thirsts are quenched by a mineral water delivery and by the Home Brewery.

This is the mundane side of Orston's life. For Orston's leisure there is a varied assortment of activities. On the cultural side there is the regular series of weekly meetings of the Adult Education group, with its twenty members; there is the recently formed and initially successful Drama Society, which, in spite of some difficulty in persuading the men-folk to come out of their shells, boasts twenty one members, regular weekly rehearsals, and two performances of One-Actors in Orston and a neighbouring village. And there is the County Library branch with its fiction in the year.

Then, if you simply like being with people, quite informally, you will find all you want in that rather unexpected institution – the Y.M.C.A. hut, a post war growth, and a kind of village hall, club and institute rolled into one. It has sixty members of whom about half are ladies; it has open nights for table tennis, billiards and cards; there is a library for the use of its members, and a stage on which the Drama Society performs, and a succession of whist drives and dances. And if you happen to be a woman, with an occasional taste for the company of members of your sex alone, you have the choice (or combination) of the W.I., a flourishing and popular organisation, linked up with two other villages, the Mothers' Union and the Women's Conservative Association. As far as one can discover, these three organisations between them seem to have the support of a considerable majority of the adult female population of the village. Of course, they vary greatly in character – from the regular, open, semi-educational meeting of the W.I. to the irregular gatherings and trips arranged by the Women's Conservative Association.

Formal sport has its outlet in cricket, a traditional and popular sport in Orston, which does not seem to be losing any of its lustre – and on the three grass tennis courts; more generally there are the indoor games provided at the Y.M.C.A., and the darts, dominoes and really old skittle alley at the Durham Ox. Football does not seem to be in favour – except from the angle of the estimable Mr Littlewood. And, rather curiously, the children of the village seem to be about as badly off as they can be for recreational facilities. There is no children's field, no playground (the street is used for games and school drill) and practically no organisation is catering for the social side of the youth of school age – outside the Sunday Schools. The Feast is virtually extinct. But the red letter day in Orston is the horticultural Society's exhibition at the end of August, with its vegetable and flower show, sports and dancing. It is an unqualified success and draws crowds from neighbouring villages.

Mrs Higginbotham outside her cottage on the New Row, off Chapel Street, 1926. These have since been demolished and replaced by Chapel Garth.

And, when all the attractions of the village fall, there are ways of escape; bus facilities are poor, being confined to two days only, though there is the main road service between Nottingham and Grantham a mile and a half away. There are trains to both towns; and seventeen cars and six motorbikes in the village, and bicycles that probably number not less than 200. These suggest that movement out of the village is by no means rare. Well, that's Orston. Just an ordinary village – but changing...

Chapel Street, circa 1930.

Laburnum Cottage, 1925, Doris Caunt and John Maule

Feeding geese, circa 1920s

Cottages at the corner of Launder Street and Church Street, circa 1920.

Chapel Street, circa 1925.

Carlin House, High Street, 1927

Loughbon, circa, from Staythorpe house with Mill Lane in distance.

CHAPTER 32
Orston During The Last World War

by Brian Gunn

I came to Orston in 1940, two weeks before Dunkirk, aged nine. These are my personal memories, clearly not the whole story but very vivid.

The conflict affected Orston greatly, as everywhere else The call-up took away most young men and some young women. They went to every continent, mercifully all returned alive though some were hurt. Many came into the parish, from far and away. This movement of population disturbed the expected life pattern and family relationships of many.

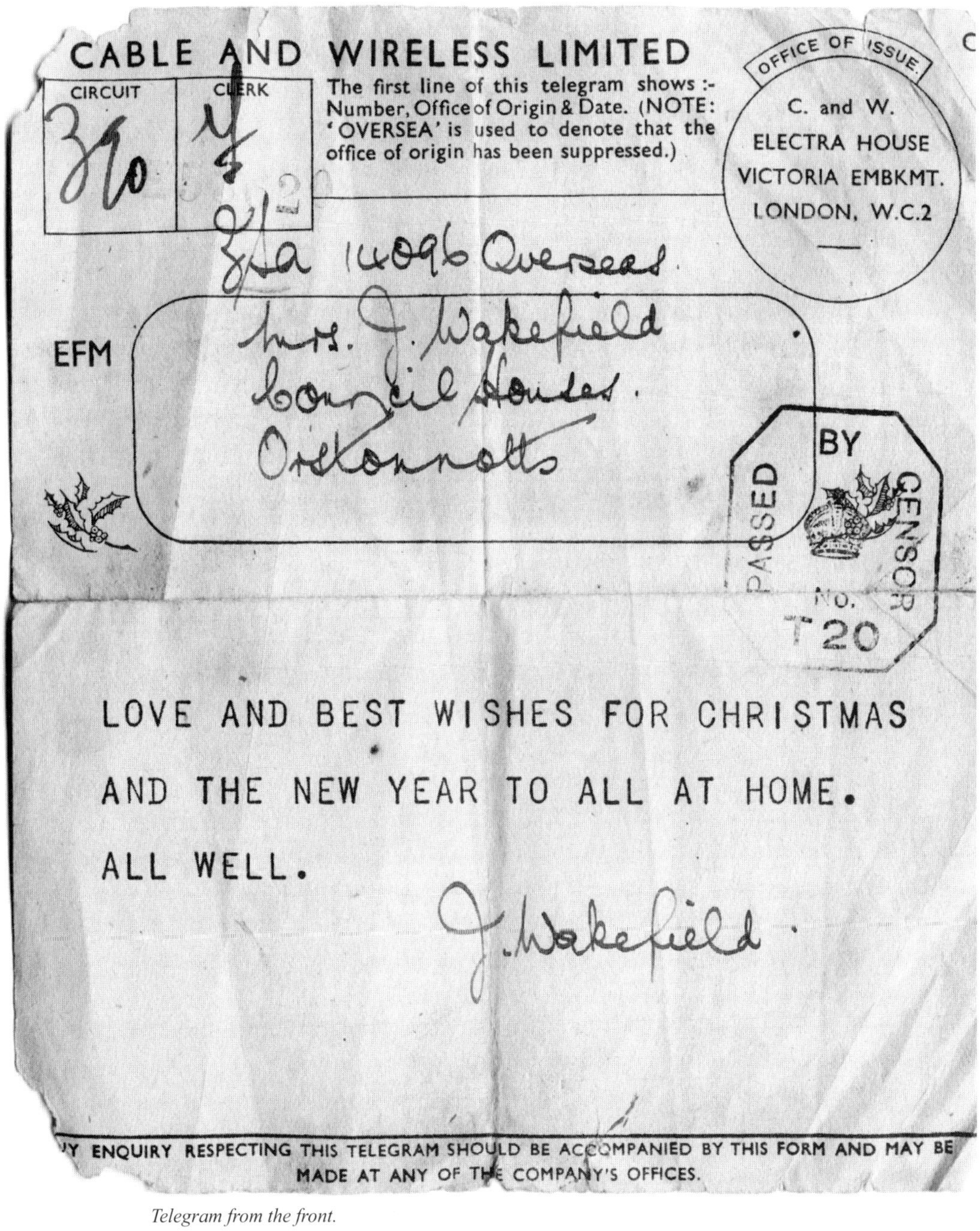
CABLE AND WIRELESS LIMITED

CIRCUIT: 380
CLERK: 4

The first line of this telegram shows :- Number, Office of Origin & Date. (NOTE: 'OVERSEA' is used to denote that the office of origin has been suppressed.)

OFFICE OF ISSUE
C. and W.
ELECTRA HOUSE
VICTORIA EMBKMT.
LONDON, W.C.2

GA 14096 Overseas.

EFM

Mrs. J. Wakefield
Council Houses.
Orston Notts

PASSED BY CENSOR No. T20

LOVE AND BEST WISHES FOR CHRISTMAS AND THE NEW YEAR TO ALL AT HOME. ALL WELL.

J. Wakefield.

…Y ENQUIRY RESPECTING THIS TELEGRAM SHOULD BE ACCOMPANIED BY THIS FORM AND MAY BE MADE AT ANY OF THE COMPANY'S OFFICES.

Telegram from the front.

Farming

In 1939 Orston was an all-grass parish, surviving the depression on the milk cow and keeping down cost. All were forced, some unwillingly, into mixed farming, growing a variety of crops with varying degrees of success. The organiser of this change was the War Agricultural Committee, made up of prominent farmers with a paid staff. This was usually known as the 'War AG' or 'Little Hitlers'. The committee directed cropping, maintained a pool of machinery, much of it imported and often hitherto unknown and provided extra workers for busy times. The changes initiated then have continued until the present day. The milk cow, once the great saviour, is now extinct in Orston.

Keep the Home Fire Burning

Food scarcity forced a 'Back to the Land' movement. Women and children scoured fields and hedgerows for anything edible or preservable. Fruit crops were carefully picked. Extra sugar was available for those willing to preserve and store. Vegetable gardening was a worthy occupation as was rabbiting. All who could kept poultry or rabbits. The cornfields were 'gleaned' after harvest by hand pickers collecting spilled grain. Many kept a pig under rigorous supervision from the Food Office. Monday was pig killing day during the cold months and the village rang with the victim's screams. The offal and meat that could not be salted was shared with other pig keepers or city relatives.

The School

The present building came into service at the outbreak of war. Four teachers looked after two classrooms. Two disappeared quickly, then the local children were concentrated into one room to make space for the evacuees. Staff was further reduced to the Head, Miss Berry, later Mrs Chambers. After a while a retired teacher Mrs Thornhill, returned to work to help. There was much prejudice against this at the time.

The Vaccies

I missed the first wave in September 1939. These soon returned home but a second wave came after systematic bombing of English cities began. We had boys aged eleven to fourteen from a tough district in Great Yarmouth. They were from a very different society to Orston, reared in conflict with the Police and they fought back resolutely. They had their own male teacher who sought to control them with a rod of bamboo. Their presence and stories were a culture shock and often a sore trial to the Orston people. There were some whole family evacuations too, when family groups left the city to spend the war in the country.

The Landgirls

These were young women often of urban upbringing, organised to help with the extra farm work. Sometimes they lived in a farm, more often they were based in hostels, available for emergency or gang work. Our nearest hostel was at Hawksworth. Sometimes their friendship with a local boy led to marriage and a permanent home in the country.

The Prisoners

Prisoners of War made a great contribution to the farm labour force. Like the landgirls they either lived on-farm or slept in-camp. During hostilities in Europe they were Italian, after VE they were German. Orston people treated them kindly and they responded to that, glad to be finished with the lunacies of war. The Germans were the most liked, being prodigious workers, good churchgoers and bringing a variety of very useful skills to the village. Close and lasting friendships grew between locals and prisoners, both platonic and amorous.

Dad's Army

Orston's Home Guard was led by Major Birch and Sergeant Thornhill. Outdoor drilling was done in the school yard, indoors they met in the loft in the Hall outbuildings. At first the men had arm bands and broomsticks, in time they acquired uniforms, gas masks and rifles. They were mainly older men and farm workers. However they would have fared as a fighting force, they saw their duty clearly and they did it.

The Camps

The first camp was on Station Road where the Drainage Board Depot now is. This was a Royal Artillery searchlight station with three powerful lamps and listening devices. There were two brick pillboxes nearby on the ridge. Later came the Royal Air Force camp on Bottesford Lane where the mushroom farm now is.

From the autumn of 1943 until June 1944 an American battery camped under canvas on land between Mill Lane and spa Lane. They had six 90mm Anti Aircraft/Field guns, mighty weapons indeed, which they never fired in Orston. They said the noise would be unbearable. They also had a self-contained mobile radar outfit. As their previous camp had been in Death Valley, California, the men found the Orston winter weather bitterly cold.

Outside the parish, beyond the railway on Bottesford Lane was a fuel depot spreading either side of the road. Millions of cans of petrol, grease and other oil products were stacked there. The depot had its own light railway system. Strictly speaking, local people needed a pass to get through to Bottesford but this was not usually insisted on, except during the occasional purge.

The Airfield

During the simmer of 1940 about 300 acres of land between Spa Lane, Bottesford and the Winterbeck were requisitioned as an Emergency Landing Field. Hedges were cleared, the ditches filled in and great quantities of stone were stockpiled to fill crates in a few weeks. The Air Force then held back for the rest of that summer until the crops had been cleared. Later on the camp was built and a fuel tank and pump installed. Six blister hangars were built; the four along Bottesford Lane with concrete floors which still exist. The two others never had a hard floor. No aircraft ever used these hangars, Barbed wire and trenches were set up in strategic places.

The field was used early on and later on for 'circuits and bumps', take off and landing training by a variety of aircraft, the most memorable being the very noisy Harvard type. In the middle period it was used for parachute training. Usually this was the dropping of supply baskets and cylinders filled with stone and gravel. Thc supply parachutes were gorgeously coloured to indicate their load. Those that fell off target were a great prize for home dressmakers, hungry for something pretty. Some fell right in the village, one, brilliantly coloured, gift wrapping the old pinfold on chapel Street. Sometimes parachutes failed to open, plummeting to the ground. Steel cylinders burst like bombs while the baskets buried themselves in the ground intact.

The real spectaculars were the mass jumps of men, the sky filled with the khaki canopies and the men floating down in great drifts, swearing loudly and shouting horribly.

For months the hard floored hangars were filled with factory-fresh Chevrolet lorries awaiting use in Europe.

Aircraft

Every type of allied war plane was to be seem over Orston. Keen young eyes could even pick out the first experimental jet planes high in the sky. Most numerous were the four engined British bombers based all round here, the twin-engined Dakota transports and the training planes using our own airfield. Most admired were the Spitfires and most beautiful the British Mosquitos and the American Mustangs.

The British heavy bombers test flew in the afternoon then loaded and took off from about 5.30, formed up and set off for the night's target. A shrewd guess could be made as to their destination by their direction. A big effort on a summer evening was an awesome sight, hosts of aircraft visible at one time, spread from horizon to horizon and the hundreds of engines roaring in unison drowning everything. We cheered them on, heedless of the misery and destruction they would wreak. They returned in the small hours, sweeping low and shedding quantities of anti-radar foil as flaps were adjusted for landing.

From somewhere to the north, American Flying Fortresses operated, setting off in a tight group of 36. Usually there would not be 36 returning. Stragglers would follow back, often showing visible damage. I remember one in particular so badly damaged one could not believe it could still fly, so much sheeting shot off that it was a skeleton of a plane.

There was much glider practice prior to D-Day. They did not as a rule land near here but one day a tow rope parted over the village, and the American Hadrian glider landed near Smite Bridge. I recall the lovely carpenter's shop smell of the interior and the pilot enthusiastically helping a landgirl with her hedge cutting.

One bad crash occurred in the parish, a fully laden Lancaster, just taken off from Bottesford came down near the Plaster Pits with stupendous explosion, instantly killing the entire crew.

Under Fire

Air raids gave a fine sight which most people turned out to enjoy. The probing searchlights, the lazily climbing flak, the vapour trails criss-crossing the moon, the flash of bomb bursts and the glow of Nottingham ablaze made a never-to-be-forgotten spectacle.

The bombs dropped on Orston were jettisoned as German aircraft were intercepted. One stick landed on the skerry between Bottesford Lane and the railway making a tremendous noise. Another stick fell into the soft clay near Robert's Pond and did not explode. No doubt they lie there to this day. In October 1941 a single large bomb fell between Hill Road and Lombard Street after machine gun fire was heard. It went deep before exploding, making an enormous crater. Most buildings in Orston were damaged, mostly roof tiles jumping off their laths, broken glass and collapsed ceilings. Severe damage was suffered by Hill Farm and Yew Tree Farm. Readers can see the repairs to the farm building to this day and the lopped-off tree opposite Yew Tree Farm. The village Hall, a wooden structure, collapsed completely. Again the village was spared loss of life, although some people were heavily bandaged.

Mock Battles

Two of these were memorable. The village was 'attacked' by a unit of the regular army and stoutly defended by the Home Guard. The battle culminated in a charge by the attackers across the churchyard towards the Durham Ox. The defenders knelt waiting under the churchyard wall opposite the pub door. They held their fire until the attackers leapt onto their gun muzzles. What a slaughter there would have been if anyone had had live ammunition.

Anther morning Spa Lane was packed at daybreak with hundreds of American airborne troops who had made a night drop and gathered at Orston to eat their wonderful field packs. I recall one bemoaning that he had landed in a 'creek'. 'I am all right but I have lost my shooter' he complained. Could that have been the submachine gun and ammunition found in the Devon at Shelton some years ago?

The Bells

Church bells were silenced after the fall of France, to be used only as a warning of invasion. This was relaxed for a celebration ring after victory at El Alamein. After that there was a steady succession of triumphs and finally total victory for which to ring out joyously.

Peace Returns

After the end of hostilities village life began to return to normal though much of the pre-war way had gone for ever. The last of the evacuees had left. The young veterans returned from all over the world and the troops packed up and left their camps and stations all round. As RAF Bottesford Lane fell empty, squatters moved into the huts.

About a dozen families came, some of whom still have a presence in the village.

The War Ag called in steam ploughing machinery, tore up the whole of the airfield and set it with wheat. The next summer the greatest expanse of cereal we have ever seen flourished. How was this to be harvested? When it was ripe 6 strange red machines arrived and fiercly attacked the crop. What a crowd of farming folk gathered to see the amazing sight. How the Little Hitlers strutted and preened How the old men shook their heads and said this would never be any good. A new age had arrived.

Cars laid up for the duration were coaxed back to unreliable life. The cattle and the hangar were removed from the Sports Field and the Tennis Club was painfully restarted. Kenneth Bampton had his new foot fitted and started to walk on it. Plans were made for a fine new village hall. Orston was turning its back on the dark days and preparing for the strange new era of peace.

L to R: Myra Leese, Bill Gayle (sitting front), Mrs Gale, Bob Kirton, Eve Kirton, Nellie Wakefield, Alice Kirton.

Ken Maule, Tom Wardle, Bill Wakefield, Elsie Glenn, Arthur Glenn.

Second World War Orston School children, evacuees on the back row.

CHAPTER 33
POST-WAR ORSTON

This chapter consists of a short newspaper article and reminiscences by three Orston residents.

> *The first impression one receives upon entering the village is that it is a bustling, energetic place, as villages go. Often there are one or two coal lorries near the post office, and one of them is usually backing into somewhere. Incidentally, if you should happen to call at the post office, be sure to wipe your shoes before entering.*
>
> *Aimless geese wander across the road near the telephone kiosk, the Durham Ox invites the thirsty traveller beyond the tall trees and so we approach the Hall. This is one of the oldest residences in the village, dignified in approach and bearing with very attractive gardens and tennis courts, surrounded by smooth green lawns and footpaths. I always look forward every year to seeing the little haystack appear in a corner of the meadow, as I do to enjoying the lovely display of flowerbeds, rose gardens and rockeries.*
>
> - Vale Traveller, Guardian 29/11/1949.

Barry Gibson

July the 6th 1956 was a milestone in my life when after an auction sale in Nottingham I found myself, a first time buyer in todays language, the owner of Orston Hall. There is a well known saying that any newcomer to a country village is not accepted by the locals for some twenty five years or more and although this may have been true in the village where I lived beforehand it was certainly not so in the case of Orston.

I was thirty years old at the time, about to get married and had recently left the army to manage my family business in Nottingham. In those days commuting sixteen miles to one's place of work was considered the extreme range, so there were only a handful of commuters like myself in the village, the rest of the population relying on agriculture and small local trades for their livelihood.

Public transport was very limited, the railway station being a mile away and buses only ran a limited service to local towns. This served to make the village a self contained community with its own thriving primary school, two shops and of course the traditional British pub. Other social activities centred around the village hall, parish church and the Methodist chapel.

Although things have changed over the years with more and more commuters coming and going, Orston has remained very much a self-contained community especially compared to neighbouring villages where most of the residents work in the local town or cities. After nine oclock in the morning until seven in the evening, their village is virtually deserted except for the old and the very young. The friendly atmosphere of the Orston community impressed me from the very start. I soon realized that some six families who had lived and inter-married in Orston for generations counted for a large proportion of the population and one quickly learned not to make derogatory remarks about one person to another as they were almost bound to be related.

It was not long before my wife and I found ourselves quite naturally involved in local activities. After a year or two I was asked to become a member of the school managers as they were then known, which I found fascinating and rewarding. At our first meeting, I discovered that the Head teacher and the

Chairman of the managers were not on speaking terms and therefore neither would attend a meeting if the other was present which necessitated quite a bit of diplomatic activity before each meeting. Nevertheless, the school was extremely well run and a happy one and comparatively free from the bureaucratic paper work and red tape which besets the governors today. However after thirty three years as a manager/governor and sometimes chairman, I reluctantly decided to resign to make way for younger people with more modern ideas to take my place.

At about that time I was also asked to become treasurer and church warden of the parish church. It had been united with Thoroton church for some hundreds of years, sharing a vicar who lived at Orston. The Church of England had found it difficult to find and pay suitable incumbents and I had not been a church warden long before I realized that some form of grouping was necessary such as was taking place in other parts of the country. Consequently, with the help of one of my co-wardens in Thoroton, we approached the Bishop of Southwell and were instrumental in grouping our two parishes with four other local ones to form the Cranmer Group. The principle was it was better to have a sixth share in a good and active vicar than a half share in a dud.

All in all this has been most successful and although we have seen congregations decline over the years, we have kept the church active and even non-churchgoers cannot fail to be impressed by the lovely medieval church of St. Marys situated as it is in the centre of the village.

Looking back over the years I consider myself extremely lucky to have been able to settle and bring my family up in Orston. To me the village has the same unique charm that it had when I first arrived nearly fifty years ago – long may it continue.

Herbert Wakefield *talking to Paul Barnes.*
There was one main shop, Spencers, on Shop Corner, (the junction of Chapel Street and Loughbon, now one of the White houses). Mr Chambers at Loughbon Villa (now called Beauvale Cottage) sold some things. The Post Office was at Staythorpe House, Walkers, which was also a coal and haulage business.

There were two mobile shops once a week: W. & H. Potters from Aslockton and the Netherfield Co-op. They sold everything. Hardstaff and Brown of Bingham (recently taken over by J. Sainsbury) delivered. Mr Hardstaff came round in his car taking orders for the delivery later in the week. Tommy Simpson, the baker from Bottesford came on Mondays, Wednesdays and Fridays. The Co-op took over from him. There were a number of butchers coming once a week: Bert Baxter from Aslockton, on horse and a high mounted trap, him on top, the meat underneath; Harry Bugg, later Goodsons from Bottesford, Johnny George, also from Bottesford, Paylings from Aslockton, Pride of Whatton and Pickfords from East Bridgford. There were also fishmen: Jack Wright from Bingham, later of course, our own Matty Gladders. There was no milk delivery, of course. Those who didn't work on farms and get free milk, collected it from Wilmot Walker's farm, behind what is known today as Mulhouse (see Chapter 13).

There were other visiting tradesmen: Mr Baines, paraffin and hardware, from Bingham and a haberdasher from Aslockton – the tallyman: we paid 1d. a week into the club. The chimney sweep, Bob Marshall, came in a pony and trap from East Bridgford. You could hear him in Orston coming over Speller Hill singing "Now the day is over". He used to whip kids' legs – in play, of course. He used to tie his horse up outside Mrs Cloxtons at Manor Farm Cottage. We kids got our own back. We tied the horse up to another gate!

There were many barbers: John Maule, who lived at what is now called The Final Furlong, Ken Bampton who lived on Launder Street, at what is now part of the other White House. A fish and chip van came round: Carol Bros from Hickling. I remember my dad sending my brother Harry to Bob Kirton with 6d. for a haircut. He came home with only one side of his head cut. My dad saw Bob the next day and told him off for only cutting one side. Bob replied that Harry asked for 3d. worth so as to buy himself some chips!

For a time, there was a chip shop run by Parnhams, in the village: in a "leanto" next to the black shed that housed Edward Breedon's farm implements on the site of, what is now, Ridgeway on Mill Lane. A cinema van came round in the summer months. We used to sit on the Green eating chips and watching films!

There was a joiner, wheelwright and undertaker: Harry Baker at The Woodyard (now called Loughbon) and a blacksmith, Arthur Hardwick, at what is now The Old Blacksmiths. They worked in conjunction with one another a lot, making and repairing wheels. I remember Harry Baker sending me to Mr Hardwick's for a long weight. I stood there waiting for about half an hour. Eventually, Mr Hardwick said, 'You can go back now. You've had a long wait!'

We had two newspaper sellers: Mary Cloxton who delivered the Sunday newspapers herself (she also lived in part of, what is now, the White House on Launder Street) and Philip Chambers and later John Maule. They employed delivery boys.

It is claimed that Mary Cloxton was the first to bring the information technology to Orston - from Grantham in fact, where she brought biros. On her rounds, she demonstrated how they worked and how they would make her indelible pencil obsolete as she did not have to lick them.

There were many other self-employed people providing services: Arthur Baker was the painter and decorator, Walkers delivered coal, which came to Orston railway sidings from Colwick. Maules, the millers, provided those who kept pigs and hens with animal foodstuff.

The new Village Hall to replace that blown up in the war was opened in 1951. It was largely funded by loans from the Burtons and the Maules. Because Maules were Methodists, no alcohol could be consumed on the premises in those days. The billiard table, located at the village end of the hall, was very popular. Dances were held on Saturday nights, whist drives were common activities during the week. The hall was also used, as it is today, for all sorts of activities such as concerts, plays, wedding receptions and village festivities. Nevertheless, it had to compete with the Durham Ox which at the time had a ballroom upstairs, a comfortable place for meetings. The Old School (see Chapter 22) was also used for smaller village functions.

Both the upper and lower mills were popular playing areas for kids, especially hide and seek. Popular games were, whip and top, marbles, hopscotch, snobs, go-cart making and scrumping. Some of us would go swimming in the plaster pits. The first pit on the left had a partitioned area specially for the purpose. Fishing in the river Smite was popular both for locals and visitors.

On bonfire night there was a large fire. Orston competed with Bottesford for whose fire lasted longer.

The village had a football team. We used to ride on Walker's lorry to support the team at away games at places such as Newark and Southwell. Seats from the Primitive Methodist chapel which was part of Walkers were put in the back of the lorry for us to sit on to watch the game. Tommy Scotney took cricketers to away matches in his cart.

There was a phone box on the Green. If we wanted to use it, we would have to go to the Post Office and ask Horace Walker to switch it on. Street lighting was introduced in the late 1950s. (See Chapter 27).

At the Methodist Sunday School Anniversary (see Chapter 16) we would travel round the village singing on Walkers lorry accompanied by a harmonium. Books were handed out each year to scholars for attendance.

The school was much smaller in those days. There were just two classes, about seventy or eighty children.

The teachers were Mrs Chambers (Miss Haslam deputised when she was pregnant) and Mrs Thornhill. We had the school dentist who came in a van and, of course, a 'nit nurse'. The dinner lady was Lilian Hardwick, Mrs Thornhill's sister. They lived together at, what is now Orchard House on High Street .

Every year there was a garden fete at the Hall. Burtons own brass band would play. The Burtons at the Hall owned Burtons foodstore in the Council House in the centre of Nottingham. The Coronation celebration decorations in the arcade were dismantled and displayed in and around the Village Hall. At Christmas, the Burtons gave hampers to most households and coins to the children. The Hall employed three gardeners, a chauffeur and three service people

Nevertheless, many worked in Nottingham. The platform was full for the 8.00 train to Nottingham. (Except in the winter when it was cold, when the commuters would huddle round the station master's fire). There was a train service (steam of, course) in those days not only to Nottingham and Grantham but also to Newark and Melton Mowbray, changing at Bottesford. There was a bus service to Newark and Nottingham run by Gash's of Newark and Lincolnshire Roadcar. On a Wednesday both companies' buses arrived in Orston at the same time and ran side by side to Newark. There were two buses a day, both ways, on Saturdays and one on a Sunday. Lincolnshire Roadcar first ran the school bus service. It was then run by Alec Gilbert in his two shooting brakes. (See the Orston Song).

After the war, the "army camp" on Bottesford Lane was commissioned by Bingham RDC for temporary accommodation. It was known as "Chinatown". It mainly comprised asbestos or wooden huts. Matty Gladders (later to become the fishmonger and to live at Mattys on Launder Street) was one of the few who lived in a brick building for the guard. I remember we boys used to go up to Chinatown in the evening. We watched Matty as he went out to get coal to light his fire. We would then put a dustbin lid on the chimney!

In the mid-50s, Chinatown was cleared. The asbestos huts went to Edward Breedon on High Street for hen huts. Leo Kavell bought the land and set up the Mushroom farm. (See Chapter 23).

A few houses had televisions. Spencers, the shop keepers, were probably the first. My mother went across the road to Gents in Moor Lane Farm to watch the Coronation in 1953.

There was huge transition to farming mechanisation in the 1950s. During the early part most farmers had horses: Blackburns (Manor farm), Baguleys (Hill Farm), Wilmot Walker and Ted Caunt at the top of High street certainly did. Threshing was a major occasion. The threshing machine would travel between farms and villages towed by an Oliver 90 or Field Marshall tractor from Burtons at Alverton worked by Horace Underwood and Jack Lambert. Threshing ended in 1960 when combine harvesters took over.

Barbara McCoy (nee Dry)

I came to Orston as a small child with my parents in 1949 to live with my grandparents. Tudor Cottage, Chapel Street, where Grandma and Grandad Scotney lived, was idyllic with ivy growing all over its mud walls. The front door opened more or less into the kitchen and just in front of the door was a dresser. Beneath the window was a large beautifully polished drop leaf table. At this, Grandma sat either knitting, sewing or watching the villager go about their business. Either side of the black lead fire-grate stood two easy chairs and a foot stool. There was a clock and a few ornaments displayed on the mantelpiece. At the left and corner of it, bits of paper were neatly filed. (Invitations and such like I think). Attached to one of the beams spanning the kitchen and scullery door hung Grandads gun which, like the table, always looked shiny and clean. The overall impression was of cleanliness and a homely atmosphere. It was a traditionally furnished, dark Victorian house and smelled wonderfully of coffee and lavender polish. (Grandma always had a pot of coffee bubbling on the range). Most of the cooking and baking was done in this room, though I do recall some kind of cooker in the scullery where the food was generally prepared. The scullery ran along the back of the house and was approached through the kitchen or the parlour. It housed lots of cooking pots, shiny pans and jam kettles. There was a white stone sink and sort of wire framed cupboard. Under one of the two staircases, the scullery maid slept, according to Grandma, (although I never saw her). My sisters would play hide and seek in this secret bedroom.

The parlour was my favourite room. This was full of lovely china. The walls were papered, it smelled of lavender polish and it housed the piano. When my sister Mell was only three or four, both she and I wanted to play the piano – Mell won. She had an alarming charm which always got me into trouble. Anyhow, she sat on a chair with her legs tucked underneath her and I stood by her side. As she pushed hard onto the keys, the chair toppled backwards, trapping her (left) leg beneath her. There was a loud crack and an ear piercing shriek emanated from her tiny body. Mum and Grandma raced in from the scullery as I vehemently pleaded my innocence, even though I had not been accused of anything. Mells leg was in plaster for quite some time. I still feel some sort of responsibility although I do not know why. Outside there was a large washroom with a wood-burning, brick-built copper, which was always brought to life on Mondays –Wash Day. Grandad had a huge fenced area for his hens, (which smelled appallingly) just beyond the washroom at the back of the house.

One memorable occasion was the Coronation in 1953. Orston was bedecked in red white and blue bunting which was strung across the road on telegraph poles and electric cables. To celebrate the event, a fantastic sports day was arranged (by whom I do not know). My handsome and very fit father beat the younger Ivan Spencer, who was expected to win, in one particularly exciting race. I can still imagine the feeling of one-upmanship and elation as Dad accepted his prize.

Sundays were wonderful in the early days. My mum would dress my sisters and me in frocks she had made and in the afternoon the whole family would go for walks. These were usually alongside Smite Lane but occasionally down the pits. On rare occasions, when it was especially hot, we would join other families engaged in the same activity – a picnic. We children all got together to paddle in the cool clean water of the river.

Village children like me were trapped. We didn't have the money to travel far, so entertainment was home made. We Dry girls found amusement in putting on shows with our cousins, Lynne and Karen and playing doctors and nurses, Mums and Dads and kings and Queens with our neighbour's children. We all either went to church or to chapel, religion being a must in village life. The really lucky ones were also allowed to join the Girl Guides, Boy Scouts and Cubs. I was so envious of them as they had to be taken to Aslockton by car. We village children all played in the street, in the fields or in the wood and I developed into a good tree climber. Whenever possible we played rounders, cricket, football and tennis. It was only when we went to big school Bingham Toothill, that we learned that some games were played by boys and others by girls.

In the winter the bottom field, opposite the chapel, filled with rain water. When this froze over we children spent hours skating on it. In the spring our great treat was to gather snowdrops in the Hall gardens. I am sure that Mrs Burton (the owner) enjoyed this as much as we did. As a governor it was one of her duties to visit the school and this was what I always treated as a special occasion. Mrs Burton always wore a hat and looked frightfully important and impressive.

I remember the council houses being built. The land was once used by my Uncle Tom but whether he owned it or not, I am not quite sure. However, there was a beautiful building halfway down the land, which fronted onto Chapel Street. Inside this the walls were tiled, in the most spectacular fashion, it seemed to me. Anyhow, this lovely building was demolished to make way for six new council houses. We Drys moved into No. 4 and were fortunate to be able to use a long forgotten pigsty as our coal bunker.

Sam Johnson who lived at the Woodlands on his pony and trap, circa 1950

Barbara Armstong at Elton and Orston railway station, early1950s.

Coronation celebrations outside the Village Hall. The author is in the sailor suit.

Cottages in Mill lane, circa 1972, now demolished.

Donkey Derby, 1966.

Walkers, coal merchants and hauliers, Loughbon. Eric Walker (L) and Neville Foster.

The shop, circa 1960, Mr and Mrs Spencer and their daughter Muriel (left) and daughter in law, Joan..

The shop corner in the 1950s: Mrs Robson waiting for a bus to Nottingham

Chapel Street under snow.

Waiting for the Newark bus. L to R Phyllis Wakefield, Rosemary Beevers and Rose Buckingham and three unknown lads

Frank Walker outside Staythorpe House, 1930.

CHAPTER 34
ORSTON IN 1978

By Elizabeth Smeeton, aged 12, writing at that time.

There is a small shop and post office which sells most things. There is a post collection each day and a delivery every morning. There are no garages in Orston. The nearest place for petrol and motor repairs is Aslockton. The doctor has a surgery in Bottesford in the evening and morning but comes to Orston on Tuesdays and Fridays at 12.00 noon, using the village hall as his surgery. A mobile library comes round every fortnight on a Friday, otherwise the nearest one is Bingham. There are no police or fire stations. The nearest ones are at Bingham.

Orston has a church, a chapel and a school with about 90 children who come from surrounding villages. We have a village hall which is rented out for discos, parties, film shows, concerts and there is a baby clinic once a week. The village hall is also used for the youth Club, badminton and a luncheon club for old age pensioners once a week. There are also evening classes, a Womens' Institute, a Mothers' Union and Girl Guides at Whatton and Scouts at Langar. There is a public house called the 'Durham Ox' which is owned by Mr and Mrs Croft.

There is a vicarage which backs on to the side of the church. It is stone with a slate roof and has lots of chimney pots. Inside, there is a cupboard with a false back. If you remove it, there is a secret passage. It leads from the vicarage under the road across to Orston Hall. When enemies were coming, the people who lived in the vicarage would go down the secret passage and escape over the fields to safety.

Just outside Orston, on Spa Lane, there is a playing field. It is used for cricket and football matches and the school uses it for Sports day. It is said to be one of the biggest playing fields for a village in England. The pavilion has had a section built on to it. There are two mills; one is used for grain, seed, cattle food etc and, outside, an office block has been built. The other one used to do the same, but now it is used for recycling paper.

Most people go to work at Nottingham. They usually get lifts or go on the train. There is a good train service between Nottingham and Grantham but the station is ¾ mile away. Bus services are only two days a week. Some people work locally, e.g. the Mushroom Farm or the Staunton Gypsum Works at Kilvington. One man runs a lorry business. On the main street, Loughbon, there is an old blacksmith's forge. It is brick with slates on the roof; it has an old chimney which is not used. You can tell it was a blacksmith's forge because there is a horseshoe built in brick on the wall.

The soil is rich and dark. The main crops that are grown are: oilseed rape, wheat oats, barley, peas, beans, potatoes and sugar beet. Not many men in Orston work on the farms - very different from the olden days when nearly everyone did. There are five farms:

Hill Farm (Harry Blackburn) is mainly arable but they keep a few bullocks and there are no milking cows.

Yew Tree Farm (Bernard Johnson and his son John) is just arable but they do agricultural contract work.

Dovecote Farm (Brian Gunn) is mainly arable but it has a few sheep and beast and one cow which provides Gunns with their own milk. They don't sell it.

Church Farm (Les Lovegrove) is a mixed farm. It has a herd of milking cows and also arable fields.

Whiteacres (Edward Breedon) is also just arable but like Yew Tree Farm, it does agricultural contract work.

Band procession along Loughbon,1970s. Staythorpe house and old Primitive Methodist chapel in the background

The Luncheon Club in Orston Methodist schoolroom.circa 1995 L to R: Nancy Chambers, Molly White, Dorothy & Frank Clark, Jack Lambert, Bill Bampton, Monica Walker, Kath Walker and Mary Cloxton celebrating Mrs Glenn's 90th birthday.

CHAPTER 35
THE PAGEANT: FORTY YEARS OLD AND STILL GOING

The first Orston Nativity Pageant was on Christmas Eve 1965. It has been performed every year since then with the exception of 1969 which was because of the threat of foot and mouth disease.

The idea of a pageant was that of Bob Wilkinson. It was to be one of a number of projects instigated by the newly formed Orston branch of Toc H, of which he was a founder. The annual 'Donkey Derby' was another of Bob's ideas. The Toc H minute book provides a marvellous, warts and all, account of the Pageant's first four years. (Bob Wilkinson, himself, wrote them). Because of this, the minutes referring to the pageant are reproduced in full.

From its beginning, the Pageant was a great success. It was taken to and performed at Grantham and Bingham on other days leading up to Christmas. Bob Wilkinson, Tony Burton and Brian Gunn (two other instigators of the Toc H branch in Orston) wrote the script. The first performance involved as many of the village organizations as possible plus singers from the Bingham Methodist Church and the Grantham Salvation Army Band.

Originally, it was described as 'An open air nativity pageant in three acts'. Act I: 'The journey to Bethlehem' began outside the Village Hall. Then, led by the Grantham Salvation Army Band playing, it proceeded through the village to stop outside the Durham Ox Inn for Act II: 'The scene at the inn'. Act III: 'A child is born' and a promise fulfilled: shepherds and kings pay homage' was in the farmyard next to the pub, now 'The Woodlands', where carols were sung around the crib.

In 1968 the Pageant was slightly rewritten and contained five scenes: Act I, 'the city of Nazareth' - outside the Village Hall; Act II, the procession through the village, 'The journey to Bethlehem; Act III: 'The arrival at the inn'; Act IV 'The stable', on the Green outside the Church; and Act V 'The presentation of the child at the temple' which took place in the Church. There the carols could be sung. The format has not changed since then with the Church being the natural place to end the procession.

The script for the Pageant has changed very little since 1968, although the early performances did not have the wise men arriving on horses. Also, there was no narrator. Instead, the Prophet of Old was the 'anchor man'.

Once the Pageant was established, the Toc H withdrew (as was its policy) leaving it to be independent. Nowadays, it is almost self-perpetuating and run by the village as a whole.

Bob Wilkinson and his wife Jenny outside the house and business at the Homestead on High Street, circa 1967.

Bob Wilkinson – a man of vision

Although he grew up in Sutton-cum-Granby, and spent his final years there, for most of his life, Bob Wilkinson lived in Orston. Originally a butcher in Nottingham, for many years Bob had a small dairy farm at 'The Homestead' on High Street. At one stage he had a large herd of Jersey cows from which he made and sold butter.

Bob was very active in the village. The Pageant was not his only 'big idea'. The 'Donkey Derby' was very popular for many years. He also started the Orston Gymkhana for the Village Hall in the 1950s, originally held in the field at the back of Village Hall, later on in 'The Park', the field opposite the Hall.

Bob was the first to see Orston as a centre for horse riding for everyone. He converted his dairy farm into to a riding school – 'The Vale of Belvoir Trekking Centre'. Through it he was able to pioneer riding for the disabled, later to spread throughout the country. He took severely disabled and the mentally handicapped from Balderton Hospital near Newark to ride at his stables.

What really went on

Because they provide such a detailed insight into the planning, preparation and development of the early pageants, the minutes of the early Toc H meetings are produced in full.

1965
29th September
At this time the chairman Mr R.H. Wilkinson assisted by the secretary [Mr A.Burton] was preparing the script for a Christmas Pageant in three acts to be enacted on 24th December as part of the Children's Christmas Treat. Details of this script are available from the file copy.
6th October
A draft of the Christmas pageant was introduced to the meeting.
13th October
Mr Davidson expressed his willingness to take part in the Christmas Pageant. It was decided to set up a sub-committee to deal with the pageant project, the committee to comprise of the following members, Mr Bob Wilkinson, A Burton, J. Hewitt, B Gunn representing Toc H, Mrs Thornhill and Mrs J Maule representing the Anglican and Methodist Sunday Schools respectively, Mr T Graveney representing the Youth Fellowship and a Women's Institute representative.
10th November
Meeting spent discussing Old Folks meal and The Christmas Pageant and detailed alterations were made to both. A ladies catering team was formed to work under the direction of Mrs E Maule
17th Novermber
Rehearsal for pageant. Carol sheet covers arrived and had to be taken to printers.
24th November
Rehearsal for pageant. Mainly angels.
1st December
No meeting at Orston. Chairman and secretary attended Toc H. District team meeting at Bingham arranged to dispatch copies of Pageant programmes as follows:
6 copies to Beeston, 12 copies to Newark, 18 Copies to Bingham, 12 copies to North Notts, 24 to Nottingham City.
8th December
Rehearsal for22nd December
Full scale dress rehearsal of Pageant held in village hall. All well.
24th December
Pageant. A huge success attended by between 500 and 600 spectators.
1966
4th January
An informal meeting at Mr Wilkinsons house to discuss the pageant, to make constructive criticism. Mr Brian Gunn reported that we had made a nett profit of £ [blank]*. It was decided to send letters of thanks to most principal participants, and also to those persons who had made donations. Donation of 2 gns to be send to Parochial Church Council.*
12th October

First movements towards making arrangements for the Nativity Pageant. It is agreed that we should repeat this event and if possible retain it as an annual item. Sub committee set up to make pageant arrangements to comprise R H Wilkinson, B & A Gunn, J Hewitt, H Wakefield, A Burton.

21st October

Pageant subcommittee meeting.

9th November

Discussion on Pageant – casting, site etc.

14th November

Pageant subcommittee meeting.

16th November

Minister approached and will take part.

14th December

Pageant subcommittee meeting attended also by Rev Blackmore. Cooperation with Anglican clergy now assured.

21st and 23rd December

Pageant dress rehearsal

24th December

Pageant. Weather fine until just before end. Carols not well patronized. Excellent performances all round.

1967

4th January

Pageant inquest – almost verbatim! Comments as follows:

W Bampton   Prophet costume ought to be in period.

Pat Burton   Procession spacing – not obviously a procession.

Mrs E Maule Band should play with carols when children singing. No lights on Loughbon.

Mrs Hewitt   Too much singing from church.

Mr Hewitt   Not to be too professional

Brian Gunn   More people ought to be free on hand. Mrs Wilkinson to be at scene to prompt – direct etc. Crowd pattern not consistent, we should be flexible. Carol singing should be in church. Programme to be more explanatory. Alternative in case of inclement weather. Too late in starting.

Mr Wilkinson   Prophet stayed too long at Nazareth with crowd.
Band accompaniment to 'Hark Glad Sound' Poor.
Children should have to sing as soon as Innkeeper left stable.
Angels to be kept warm.
Kings ragged in voice, only backs seen at stable. Not heard at stable.
Drop band!!!
No Change to script once finalised!!
Large children in middle of stable should have been at sides.
Star not realistic.

A Burton Spot light at stable to be on firm mounting.
Cueing not good – timing out.
Innkeeper <u>must</u> be in costume
Delegate more organisers to be free
Angels seen running
Advertising inadequate
Crown surge after Mary and Joseph
Happy thought – people didn't realise mistakes

4th October

It was decided that the Pageant should be held on Christmas Eve. This subject to be reviewed in the event of the foot and mouth disease affecting the village. It was proposed that the Rev Richardson should be invited to become group Padre.

16th October
Meeting in church hall to discuss Pageant. Rev Blackmore present. Possible that Pageant may have to be held in church due to foot & mouth Disease.
13th December
Rehearsal for Pageant. Awful!! – but then it usually is first time out. Brian Gunn to act as producer. RH was prophet
19th December
Brian Gunn and Tony Burton in church, moving pews, checking lighting etc.
20th December
Full dress rehearsal. Absolute shambles!
21st December
Full dress rehearsal. A little better let's hope 'it's alright on the night'.
24th December
Pageant! Pretty good considering. All went quite smoothly anyway and no one forgot their lines. Collection an absolute farce. Matty Gladders used a plastic bucket! No noise!

1968
3rd January
Angels! Mrs Peeling! Matty! Kings singing etc! Xmas party.
25th September
Annual General Meeting – reference was made to the Pageant with a recollection of the foot & mouth disease epidemic which was rife at that time causing us to hold the pageant wholly in the church. Chairman summed up and the continuance of the Pageant was mentioned.
The Pork Pie Supper was discussed as a means of raising funds to capitalize the Pageant.
It was proposed and agreed unanimously that the Pageant should be staged!!
1969
Oct 8th
The Rev Blackmore 'entertained' us with a talk & slides on the subject of re-decoration in his previous churches. Afterwards he tried to persuade us to do the Christmas Pageant again a negative result!
The minute book ended on 30th May. Nevertheless, the Pageant recommenced in 1970 and has never since missed a year. The minute book restarted in 1986 by which time the pageant was no longer run by Toc H and there is no mention of it.

Memories of the early pageants
Barry Gibson
It is part of the Christmas story that one of the three kings was black. So in an attempt to be as realistic as possible the then vicar, Geoffrey Blackmore, arranged with the Whatton Detention Centre, where he also acted as Chaplain, to loan us a black inmate. We sat him on a horse, probably for the first time in his life, and guided him through the part of the third king. The lad thoroughly enjoyed it, as he was able to cadge a crafty cigarette or two off the other members of the cast. We dressed him up in the brightest colours possible, or otherwise we felt we might have lost him in the dark!

After a few years, however, with a change of Governor at the Detention Centre and a failure in the sense of humour at the Home Office, we had to discontinue the scheme but it was great fun while it lasted.

Brian Gunn
Let nothing in these reminiscences detract from the primacy of Bob Wilkinson in the whole concept and execution of the Pageant. The whole insane idea and the staging of the first performance were entirely due to him. Such details as the appearance of Gabriel on the Hall porch, the Sally Army band, the roughing up of the crowd by the Roman soldiery were pure Wilkinson.

He founded the Orston Toc H group and told us of his dream of this Christmas event and persuaded us to back and help him. Toc H members who helped the most were Tony Burton, now in Long Bennington, me, Jennie Wilkinson, now deceased, John and Margaret Hewitt, now in Winthorpe and Herbert Wakefield. Bob, Tony and I laboured many an hour over the script (some of my lines so awful I still wince after all these years) Tony and I were largely responsible for props and electrics. Early experiments were near disasters and there was a terrible star that ran along a clothes line. The first stable scene was in Johnson's yard, now Ford's. (After the first year this was abandoned because of the noise of crunching gravel) We installed floodlighting. I did a trial switch-on to reveal our most dignified co-worker having a pee in the middle of the yard.

As Treasurer I could see only financial disaster coming to Toc H over the foolhardy adventure but come the night there was a huge crowd assembled. Hope at last. Inside the hall, all the excitement of am-dram as we put on our costumes, mainly tea cloths and dressing gowns with a number of clip-on beards. I grew Dundreary whiskers (sideburns mingling with a moustache) to fill the gaps left by my clip-on.

Then out to meet the public. The Sally Army played. Gabriel announced. The Centurion proclaimed, the donkey was fetched and mounted, torches blazed and the crowd moved on. Along Loughbon we went. The drummer drummed, the Rev. Davidson bellowed prophecies (a glorious performance) and the crowd sang. A personal memory is the face of a bus driver forced to a halt by the wall to wall crowd. All his previous experience had made him believe the place uninhabited.
The inn scene went well, although Ben Brumfield declined any attempt at a costume. He took the couple to the lean-to stable in the yard next door. I was up on the churchyard opposite with two assistants and a pen of sheep. The angel appeared together with a heavenly host, who had had a terrible time passing among the monuments in the unlit churchyard. Hearing the news we led the crowd into Johnson's yard. The performance was carried on to a successful conclusion but much of the sound was lost to gravel noise.

Finally, the happy couple moved into church with their 'baby' to be greeted by Simeon, a good performance by the Vicar of Granby of a part that Reg Lewis was to make his own in later years. Then carol singing followed by the sound, most welcome to me, of pre-decimal currency rattling into buckets.

The weather was good, the donkey well-behaved, the public encouraging and the accounts showed a profit so the Pageant became an annual event. The next year we moved the stable scene to its present site. Other memorable years: Audrey collapsed with appendicitis at performance time once, one year it rained so hard the 500 watt bulbs we used for lighting the crib were exploding like gunshots. One year there was foot-and-mouth so we stripped out the church seats and did the whole performance indoors.

Margaret Hewitt - Angel Gabriel
I can't remember for how many years I was Angel Gabriel. As you will see from the photo I wore a white robe made by me from a sheet. Notice the jumper sleeves to keep out the cold. My wings were made of cardboard covered with foil - very amateurish! I wore white plimsolls when it was dry and ankle boots when wet. I have to smile when I think of the 'Heavenly host' of angels wearing white sheet robes and Wellingtons when it was wet.

I remember one year it was snowing. I was not too keen on climbing up the metal steps of the village hall onto the roof! Fortunately, the Rev Richardson was up there to keep an eye on me. I remember that The Stable was originally a shed (or summer house) in what is now 'The Woodlands' but when it rained the ground in front became waterlogged so it was decided to have the stable in the churchyard among straw bales. The three kings arrived on horse back led by Barry Gibson. I think there were pages to hold the horses and lead them away after the Kings had alighted.

The finale in the church was always quite moving with Mr. Lewis playing Simeon to a packed congregation and the cast arranged up by the altar to sing the final carol 'Oh Come All Ye Faithful'. Then it was into the church hall [now Launder House on Launder Street] for a nice hot drink.

Carol Wheatley (nee Beaumont) - Mary
I was first involved in 1971 as a 'village lady' along with my mum Joan Beaumont and my sister Pam. The following year - 1972 - at the age of 16 - I was Mary. I think I got the part because I sang in the church choir and at the weekends I was a stable girl for 'Willy' Wilkinson, so I had a fighting chance of staying on the rather frisky donkey that Bob had managed to find!

I remember the 1972 Pageant well. The front of the hall was lit up as I began to sing the Magnificat. Unfortunately, this was in the days before special outdoor bulbs and as the snow landed on the hot light bulbs the song was accompanied by the sound of light bulbs exploding!

Brian Flannery who played Joseph had a business making decorative resin plagues. Each year, he gave me one depicting scenes from Chaucer. He signed them 'From Joseph to Mary'!

Dr Sally Silsby (nee Jones) - Mary
In the mid 1980s, I played Mary two or three times.

'You'll have to sing the "Magnificat"'. To someone who does not pride themselves on their singing voice, these words went down like a lead balloon. Saying it didn't seem to be acceptable, so the easiest option appeared to be to sing a modern version accompanied by a friend on the flute. For me this went down very well, but not so for the more traditional amongst us. So what do you do when Mary can't sing!?

And the rain, rain, rain came down, down, down and most of the action took place in the village hall, but not before Mary was drenched. I think we made it to Bethlehem in the nick of time. But perhaps the most memorable Pageant was on a clear, cold night as Mary and Joseph, plus entourage, made their weary way towards Bethlehem. Mary fell off the donkey! (Can't sing, can't ride, what was I doing as Mary?) I was, however, rescued by a gallant Roman soldier (Michael Axtell) and perched back on the donkey and in true acting tradition the show went on.

Some of the original angels.
Gladys Andrews (nee Batchford).
The first meeting was held in the old Schoolroom at the back of the church. It was a very cold night, but the schoolroom was packed with people who must have been showing a keen interest in this village venture. My friend Rosalind Barnes was with me. I am not sure how as 12 and 13 year old girls we were 'volunteered' into this, but I seem to remember that we were keen at the time to take part. The meeting was led by Mr Bob Wilkinson.

Rosalind and I took the part as Angels – I think we were the youngest in the group. We were dressed in white sheets, with some silver tinsel on our heads. We wore some wings that had been made out of cardboard and covered with Silver Foil. Although I do not have many memories of the actual Pageant procession itself, I do remember that when the scene with the Angel Gabriel visiting the Shepherds was acted outside of the Village Hall, all of the Angels went up on to the flat area of the roof, above the Village Hall entrance. Jennifer Hibbert played the part of Mary. She had an excellent singing voice.

Rosalind McCarthy (nee Barnes)
I think we just had one dress rehearsal in the village hall. Gladys and I would have been about 12 and 13 years old, the youngest participants there. I think maybe we were involved through the Methodist Sunday School. We wore the Sunday school nativity clothes with a cardboard halo and elaborate wings. Although we were the youngest members of the cast, I don't think we were nervous because, unlike the

Sunday school eisteddfods that we had taken part in, we didn't have to remember any words or sing any solos. The Prophet of Old climbed a precarious step ladder to the roof of the Village Hall. We then all followed the procession to the Durham Ox with the crowds of onlookers. I think it was only in the later years that the event culminated in a carol service in the Church. Perhaps this is because initially it was more closely associated with the Methodist chapel? The donkey appeared on Christmas Eve loaned from a farmer in a neighbouring village.

Diane Viljoen (nee Jeffcott)

I remember the 1965 Pageant and walking to the Village Hall from my home in Mill Lane for the start. In those days, I don't think there were any street lights. I was wearing my rather primitive angel costume (I looked more like a ghost) and a motorist came up behind me, passed very slowly, stared, and with an absolutely terrified look accelerated and was gone. I am quite sure he thought he had seen a ghost!

Verna White (nee Lambert)

It was quite a brave community project and clerk Mr Bob Wilkinson was the main organiser. His wife Jennie played an angel too. Most of
the cast came from Orston including the donkey. There were some good voices in the village, from church, chapel and elsewhere. It was a simple but effective production especially because it was performed actually on Christmas Eve and during the hours of darkness. People are not always keen to give time on Christmas Eve, The cast was largely men and younger people. Most older ladies were at home performing other Christmas duties.

Because Orston was so dimly lit costumes didn't need to be detailed. This also added to the atmosphere. As an angel I wore a simple white bedsheet. I don't remember any wings! At one point we had to rush forward as the angel host crying 'Glory to God' or similar words. It was over in seconds. I was embarrassed at an earlier rehearsal in the village hall to be told off for talking. I was 24! The donkey also misbehaved and we had our Blue Peter elephant moment when Neddy produced a large dollop of manure on the polished hall floor.

On the night, it didn't rain but it was damp air. Lots of people came to Orston and became part of the crowd. As Mary, Joseph and the donkey made their way down Loughbon they were surrounded by people with towels on their heads and carrying lights. Quite atmospheric. After being turned away from the Durham Ox there was a tableau in Mr Sam Johnson's garden on the corner of Church St and Loughbon. The star was rigged up on a pulley and slowly moved across the stable roof. The three wise men say 'We three Kings of Orient are' in good voice. Jennifer Hibberts young rich voice singing 'The Magnificat' was very beautiful and certainly a highlight.

The Original Cast

The Prophet of Old	*Rev. G.P. Davidson*
Torch Bearers	*Richard Caunt*
	Peter Caunt
Joseph	*Terry Graveney*
Mary	*Jennifer Hibbert*
The Innkeeper	*Ben Brumfield*
The Shepherds	*Brian Gunn*
	Reginald Lewis
	Allen Foster
The Three Wise Men	*Tom Robson*
	Peter Wilkinson
	Brian Skinner
The Angel Gabriel	*Margaret Hewitt*
Accompanying Angels	*Pat Burton*
	Audrey Gunn
	Jennie Wilkinson
	Maureen Foster
	Dianne Jeffcott
	Susan Parkinson
	Katherine Parkinson
	Verna Lambert
	Sandra Johnson
	Vicki Kirton
	Gladys Batchford
	Rosalind Barnes
Gospel Reader	*Rev. John Price*
Simeon	*Rev. J. Pickworth-Hutchinson*

The 'Toc H' lamp was carried by Herbert Wakefield

The Cast of 2005

The Reader	*Martin Seabrook*
Gabriel	*Gina Creswell*
Mary	*Laura Harrison*
Joseph	*Patrick Newton*
Prophet	*Bob Gullis/David Perry*
Centurion	*Ian Smellie*
Soldiers	*Paul and Edward Barnes, Daniel Simpson, Ben Hawkins, David Didsbury, Ton and Arthur Langeler, Nigel and Jack Rusby, Jim Hegarty*
Innkeeper	*Anthony Parker*
Voice from the Crowd	*Will Gunn*
The Three Wise Men	
Melchior	*David Wheeler,*
Gaspar	*Peter Simpson*
Balthazar	*Tim Rogers*
Herod	*Mike Hine*
Priest's Scribe	*Derek Collett*
Simeon	*Jonathan Ford*
Trumpeters	*Nick Halstead and Harry Newton*
Drummers	*Harleigh Wilkinson and Dan Gullis*

Pages	*Lorraine and Inca Wilkinson, Thomas Newton, Natasha Oates*
Angels	*Sylvia Wakefield, Emily Pritchett, Elouise Evans, Poppy Sheppard, Jade Sheppard, Gronia White, Esme Watson, Freya Watson, Beth Wakefield, Charlotte Selby, Alice Martin, Laura, Hannah and Sophie Alloway, Chloe Booth, Natalie Greener, Alice Booth, Megan Booth,*
Evangelina Ellison.	
Shepherds	*Helen Pritchett, Thomas Booth, Max Alloway, Maria Simpson Joseph Watson, Isobel Evans, James Seabrook, John Arnold*
Villagers	*Kath Daw, Gill Smellie, Alyson Seabrook, Janet and Peter Iley, Gillian Ford, Pauline Davidson, Wendy Richardson, Cial Brennan, Mary Bridge-Collyns, Tao Tomlinson, Tim and Gill McArtney, Caroline Newton, Audrey Gunn, Pat Burton, Judy Simpson.*
Bell Ringers	*John Thacker, John Johnson, Vicky Wakefield, Berryl Parker, Mary Ibbotson, Mary Hawthorne, Herbert Wakefield.*

The Church Service will be taken by Rev. Reg Walton, supported by Rob Knight (organist) and Annie Dickinson.

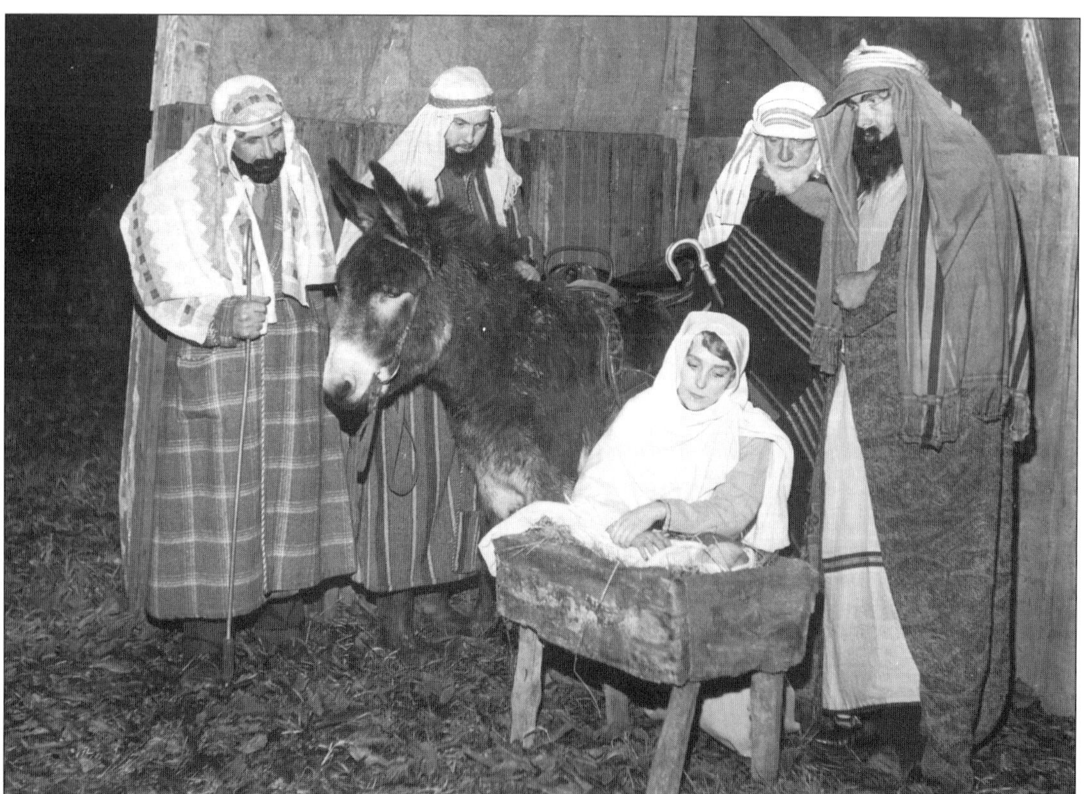

The stable scene, in 1966. L to R: Allen Foster, Brian Gunn (shepherds), Jennifer Hibbert (Mary), Reginald Lewis (shepherd), Terry Graveney (Joseph).

Scene outside the inn , 1968. Isabel Daw (nee Wilkinson) and Bill Bampton (Mary and Joseph), Ben Brumfield (prop 'Durham Ox') the innkeeper.

Margaret Hewitt as the Angel Gabriel, 1965

Stable scene in the Churchyard, circa 1985.

CHAPTER 36
ORSTON TODAY

During the Industrial Revolution of the nineteenth century the country folk took with them their customs and practices, such as beer drinking, cock-fighting and vegetable gardening, to the towns. It was a major problem for the city and town burghers to impose order on the ruffians from the countryside with their strange customs. Leisure patterns in country villages were largely based on the seasonal cycle of the farming community whilst the needs of the bosses of the new factories were simply to minimise holidays and absenteeism, thereby maximising their profits. It is ironic that the final effects of the Industrial Revolution: transportation, beginning with the railways and ending with the motor car, has brought the city workers back out to live in the countryside. Similarly, it has changed the villages, hitherto agricultural communities, as these migrants have brought with them their urban ways.

Orston probably had its first commuters soon after the building of the railway line in 1850. However, it was not until the 1920s that they were on any significant scale. My grandfather, Alfred Moor, the original librarian at Boots, was one of these. However, the number of commuters has increased enormously over the period since then.

Nottingham train at Elton & Orston station, circa 1930.

Alfred Moore outside Carlin House, circa 1940.

This trend has been accompanied by the demise of agriculture, especially agricultural employment in the village. At the time of writing no farm, in the traditional sense, is left. Johnsons are primarily agricultural contractors and Barry Gibson's estate is now farmed from Flawborough. I know of not a single agricultural worker who lives in the village.

The social change that this has brought about must be obvious to all who have lived through it. In my childhood, I lived on High Street. It was then covered in cow pats from Ted Caunt's and Les Lovegrove's farms. It was difficult to walk on the roughly kept grass verges because of the footholes made by the cows. Today, High Street is immaculately groomed and is indistinguishable from much of suburban Nottingham. Another example is the village common. All that remains of it is the small open area in front of the Church. This was used by villagers to casually leave their animals, tie up their horses whilst doing some thing in the village and and so on. It was a scruffy communal area where almost anything went. Today, it is tamed: it is mown to look 'nice' and chained off to prevent usage! (Those picturesque village duck ponds we see in certain areas have similarly different origins). The final example of the urbanization of Orston is its gardens. Nowadays, a negligible number of houses have vegetable gardens, a country custom borne out of necessity, instead flower gardens and closely cropped lawns. The emphasis is on order, quite the antithesis of the traditional cottage garden to which one may have thought their owners would aspire.

For most of its history, Orston was essentially self-contained and self-sufficient. It was only in later times (the late nineteenth century) that there was specialisation in agriculture facilitating increased prosperity through trading. Whilst that was well advanced by the 1930s, it is interesting to read and hear the reminiscences of that period. It is not a romantic notion that the village was more of a community then. The fact that the village had shops, and other shops came to the village, and most people worked in the vicinity, made excursion out of it rare and, no doubt, 'an event' for the people concerned. Today, for some of Orston's commuters, a day *in* the village, other than at the weekend, is an equally rare event!

It is tempting to conclude from this analysis that the number of social activities in the village have declined during the post-war period. Certainly, the tennis and cricket clubs have died and various generations of football clubs have come and gone. The church and chapel are probably experiencing lower congregations than at any other time in their histories. On the other hand, the village still puts on at least one event a year, whether it be a gymkhana, a flower festival or an open gardens event. Perhaps the best gauge of the magnitude of social events is the Village Hall. It is used for a variety of large and successful events and just as much as ever.

The other factor affecting this is the 'freedom of the market' which the motor car has produced. The Orstonian today does not necessarily pursue his/her leisure interests here. The city of Nottingham offers an extensive range of cultural activities and the area offers diverse sporting opportunities. Orston plays its part with a shooting club and a bourgeoning riding school attracting many from a wide area and providing local employment.

Orstonians celebrating winning the Notts Best kept Village Competition, 1983.

Most of the above was written in 1996 for the first edition of the book. I ended by saying how exciting it was to be living through, and being part of, the information technology revolution. It is amazing how things have changed. At that time the Internet was in its infancy. Emails, attachments, mobile phones and texting were unknown.

Has Orston changed much over that time? As a result of the Internet, I and many other villagers are able to communicate freely with people throughout the world who share our interests. We probably have more in common with them than with our next door neighbours! Nevertheless, there still is a community. We now have a local shop again which is thriving and we have a pub, the Durham Ox, which has been reinvigorated by the enterprise and spirit of the wife of Orston's own dot-com millionaire.

What of the future? Much has been written of the increase in working from home as a result of the use of the personal computer and electronic data transmission. In certain parts of the country, such as the Home Counties and the most deserted outreaches, this has become significant. However, in the East Midlands this is not the case. Instead, it is seen as potential commuter country for London.

The lack of new houses being built for the less well-off in country districts has often been cited as having the effect of pushing out those whose heritage and employment are there. In Orston this phenomenon may be seen with newly weds having to take cheaper housing in Bingham and Bottesford. No doubt this has contributed to Orston becoming an 'old village' in the sense that there are relatively few people under fifty. The effect that this has on the social and leisure activities of the village is obvious.

In this sense Orston is a typical village. However, prevailing factors do not exist for ever. History shows us that, whilst its population may remain about the same, economic factors continue to determine occupations and the social mix. As a compensation for those who do not like the changes, the four by fours, horses and mobile 'phone masts of modern-day Orston, are merely transitory. Unfortunately so are we.

... and in 2007

Opening of the Millennium Bridge, 2000, Barry Gibson and the Mayor of Rushcliffe

Lowering of the bridge

Orstonians, 2000.

Gymkhana on the Belholme field (opposite Chapel Garth), circa 1995.

Millennium celebrations

SUBSCRIBERS

Thanks are due to the following supporters of this book

SPONSORS

Nottinghamshire County Council
Mr C.B.Gibson
Dovecote Farm Equestrian Centre
A.W.Lymn, The Family Funeral Service
Orston Parish Council
Carlin Construction Ltd

PRIVATE SUBSCRIBERS

Mrs B. Armstrong
Mr N. Baker
Mrs O. Baker
Mr and Mrs J. Bennett
Mr and Mrs J. Billot
Mr and Mrs E. Breedon
Mr and Mrs J. Breedon
Mr and Mrs A. Burn
Mr R. Caunt
Mr and Mrs A.P. Chambers
Mrs K. Clarke
Mr and Mrs R. Clarke
Dr and Mrs R.A. Collier
The Collins Family
Mr and Mrs M Cooper
Mr and Mrs J. Cope
Mr and Mrs T. Crotch-Harvey
Mr and Mrs S. Davidson
Mrs J. Duffy
Mr T. Ellis
Mr and Mrs J.R. Ford
Mr and Mrs A.Foster
Mr and Mrs H.N. Foster
Mr and Mrs P.Gilbert
Mr J.D.Gladders
Mrs E. Goodwin
Mr and Mrs R. Gullis
Mr and Mrs B. Gunn
Mr and Mrs N. Hammond
Mr and Mrs B. Harrison
Mr and Mrs D.W. Harrison
Mr and Mrs P. Henson
Mrs C.Hill
Mr and Mrs P. Howitt
Mr and Mrs J. Hudson
Mr and Mrs P. Iley
Mrs D. Johnson
Mr B. Johnson
Mr and Mrs J. Johnson
Messrs J. and W. Johnson
Mr and Mrs T. Kennedy
Mrs P. Kent
Mrs D. Korolus
Mr and Mrs T. Langeler
Mrs J.A. Lewis
Dr and Mrs I. Livsey
Mr and Mrs K. Longden
Mr and Mrs T. McCartney
Ms J. Manchester
Dr and Mrs C. Manson
Mr and Mrs P. Marshall
Mr and Mrs T. Marshall
Mrs B. Martin
Mrs F. Mart
Mrs B. Maule
Mr and Mrs N. Mees
Mr and Mrs G. Mitchell
Mr and Mrs P. Newton
Mr and Mrs D. Parry
The Rev. K. Przywala
Mr and Mrs K.T. Radford
Dr and Mrs J. Rai
Mr and Mrs P. Reid
Mrs W. Richardson
Mrs R.A. Ruck
Professor M. Seabrook
Mr and Mrs J. Seabrook
Mr D. Simpson
Mr and Mrs A. Sheardown
Mr R. Shepperson
Mr and Mrs P. Simpson
Miss E.Smeeton
Mr and Mrs J. Smeeton
Mr and Mrs A.G. Smellie
Mr and Mrs C.P. Smellie
Mr and Mrs I.M. Smellie
Mrs P. Southwood
Mr and Mrs P. Spick
Mrs J. Steene
Mr and Mrs R. Strasburger
Professor and Mrs J.B. Tomlinson
Mr B. Wakefield
Mr and Mrs F. Wakefield
Mr and Mrs H. Wakefield
Mr L. Wakefield
Mr E. Walton
Mr J.R. Wilkinson
Mr and Mrs J. Winfield